Sources Of
American Spirituality

William Porcher DuBose

SELECTED WRITINGS

Edited by Jon Alexander, O.P.

PAULIST PRESS
New York ♦ Mahwah

Library of Congress Cataloging-in-Publication Data

Dubose, William Porcher, 1836–1918.
    [Selections. 1988]
    William Porcher Dubose : selected writings / edited by Jon
Alexander.
         p.   cm.—(Sources of American spirituality)
    Bibliography: p.
    Includes index.
    ISBN 0-8091-0402-4 : $18.95 (est.)
    1. Spiritual life—Anglican authors. I. Alexander, Jon.
II. Title. III. Series.
BV4501.2.D7352   1988
248–dc19   87-32916
                                                   CIP

Published by Paulist Press
997 Macarthur Boulevard
Mahwah, N.J. 07430

Printed and bound in the United States of America

CONTENTS

GENERAL INTRODUCTION

Faced with the challenge of the wide-scale changes that confronted the men and women of the second half of the nineteenth century, William Porcher DuBose attempted to construct a theological vision that could be true to Christian tradition and in harmony with the new thinking of the age. That thinking was indeed revolutionary, and its implications far-reaching. New ideas in the scientific realm had direct bearing on the religion of the Gilded Ages. Darwin's *Origin of the Species* shattered conventional beliefs about human life. Advances in geology, such as those made by Sir Charles Lyell in his *Principles of Geology*, called into question the biblical accounts of the creation of the world, presenting in their place theories based on the newly discovered fossil records. The new scientific method had implications for history as well. Buoyed by the belief that empirical methods, when applied to the doing of history, could produce a true record of the past as it actually was, scholars applied historical-critical methods to the study of all aspects of culture—including religion. The work of those like David Frederick Strauss and Julius Wellhausen changed century-old opinions of the Scriptures and threw into confusion traditional understandings of the faith based on pre-critical methods of exegesis. Others like Adolf von Harnack applied the new critical methods to the history of dogma, with equally disturbing results.

In the eyes of some, like the apostle of agnosticism, Robert Ingersoll, the new ideas meant an end to religion. The superstitions of the past would simply be eclipsed by the more positive knowledge of the present. Others, like naturalist Louis Agassiz or theologian

vii

Charles Hodge, stood valiantly against what they saw as the errors of the age. There were still others, however, who believed in the reconciliation of the new thought with Christian belief. There were scientists like Newman Smyth of Yale, and preachers like Lyman Abbott of Brooklyn's Plymouth Church. There were theologians like Presbyterians A. C. McGiffert and William Adams Brown, Methodists like Border Parker Bowne, and Baptists like William Newton Clark and Shailer Mathews.

They stressed the powers of the individual to do good, relegated human depravity to the unenlightened ages, and emphasized the ethical demands of the Bible in place of its miracle accounts and hymns of adoration and mystical rapture. In so doing, they often produced naively optimistic systems, the credibility of which was destroyed by the great conflagrations of the twentieth century.

William Porcher DuBose must certainly be counted as one of the most important liberal theologians of the late nineteenth century in America, certainly the most significant such figure that the Episcopal tradition produced. Like his counterparts, he struggled with the new ideas and attempted to blend them with traditional understandings. But unlike many of them, his thought retained a sense of the reality of human imperfection that set it apart from many of the more facile liberal theologies of the age. While certainly filled with the hope of a new rapprochement of the old and the new, he was always mindful of the role of human suffering. That awareness grew out of his own frequent experience of suffering, whether it was as a soldier in the defeated Confederate army, as a bereaved father and husband who buried his wife and son, or as an author whose writings sometimes brought him persecution. By focusing on how his own personal religious experiences shaped his thought, Jon Alexander shows us the depth and pathos of this little-known thinker. In those depths we discover a man who wrestled with the mystery of God and attempted through his many writings to convey the richness of that experience.

John Farina

PREFACE

I wish to express my thanks to Dr. John Farina for inviting me to prepare a volume on William Porcher DuBose for the *Sources of American Spirituality*. The opportunity to study DuBose has been intellectually and spiritually rewarding not only for me but also for many parishioners who expressed their thanks for the insights of DuBose that they heard in my homilies. I am pleased to report that DuBose speaks to the spiritual needs of contemporary parishoners, and I hope that the publication of this volume will make his insights more accessible.

I am also grateful for the opportunity to meet many generous students of DuBose's thought that this project has provided. Mrs. Elizabeth Chitty introduced me to the resources of the University of the South and supported this project with her rich knowledge of Sewanee and her generous hospitality. Miss Anne Armour graciously copied manuscripts and rare publications in the Archives of the University of the South and provided invaluable assistance to my research. Professors Donald S. Armentrout and Ralph E. Luker shared their expert knowledge of DuBose with unfailing generosity. Professors Lewis Ford, John Gesell, William R. Hutchison, W. Norman Pittinger, Victor Lowe, and Charles L. Winters provided expert answers to my questions. The Rev. Dr. Dennis Dean Kezar gave the introduction a perceptive and critical reading.

The support of my religious community sustained my work at every stage of the project. Fr. Benedict Ashley provided helpful guidance on the thought of St. Thomas, and Sr. Kathleen Hilkert helped me to see that it was impractical and ahistorical to substitute

1

more inclusive language for DuBose's consistent use of male pro-
nouns. My superiors, Fr. Harry Byrne and Fr. Donald Goergen, and
the brothers at Blessed Sacrament Priory where the project was completed were unstinting in their encouragement and support.

I wish to dedicate this volume to my Episcopal friends in
thanksgiving for their charity and Christian witness. As we have la-
bored together in the vineyard, and as we shall share in the heavenly
banquet, may we soon be joined together at the Lord's Table.

INTRODUCTION

"America should make much of DuBose," William Sanday, Oxford's Lady Margaret Professor of Divinity, wrote in a review of William Porcher DuBose's *The Gospel According to Saint Paul* published at the beginning of the twentieth century. Yet, as Sydney Ahlstrom observed in a survey of American theology published half a century after Sanday's charge, DuBose has been "almost completely unappreciated in America even by his fellow Episcopalians."[1]

Although DuBose's difficult style may explain his lack of mass appeal, the failure of American theologians to appreciate DuBose points to something more fundamental that distinguishes DuBose from the better known religious authors of his time. Unlike William Newton Clarke, Washington Gladden, William James, Newman Smyth, and other familiar religious authors who published in the age of energetic and expansive Christianity that spanned the years between Union victory in the Civil War and American victory in the First World War, DuBose was a Southerner, a member of the antebellum master class, and a man who experienced the collapse and repudiation of his world.[2]

Like the Neo-orthodox theologians who came to prominence after DuBose's death, DuBose knew the ironic dimension of history. He came to see the moral evil of slavery, but as a loser and survivor of the Civil War he knew that moral progress can be costly.[3] Yet, the seven books DuBose published between 1892 and 1912 share the optimistic and expansive spirit of his more familiar American contemporaries, as well as their acceptance of theological modernism.

3

Behind the sunny theological system that DuBose began to set before the world a generation after his service in the defeated armies of the Confederacy, lay DuBose's experience of fundamental discontinuities and the spiritual and intellectual pilgrimage through which he bridged those discontinuities. DuBose's mature thought is a remarkable act of reinterpretation and reconstruction, an example of what Paul Ricoeur has called second immediacy or second naïveté based in DuBose's personal spiritual pilgrimage and historical experience. It is a second faith reconstructed after the collapse of DuBose's first naïve and cultural faith in his first world of the Old South, and it shares characteristics with the theologies of the survivors of the twentieth century's devastations.[4]

The reinterpretive achievement of DuBose's mature thought, however, is easily missed for two reasons. First, because DuBose views the discontinuities of his spiritual and historical experience from the perspective of his reinterpretive achievement, he describes his experience as phases of a continuous, ongoing process.[5] Second, because DuBose's reinterpretive achievement shares the optimism and expansiveness of his better known contemporaries, it can be misread, therefore, as just another sunny progressive theology. For these reasons it is important that readers of this volume who seek to learn what DuBose can contribute to the spiritual and religious issues of the present time have some understanding of the contexts in which DuBose's reinterpretation developed. Indeed, it may be that DuBose's pilgrimage to reinterpretation, rather than his reinterpretation itself, will prove his greatest legacy.

In order to provide some context for reading the selections from DuBose's writings included in this volume, the remainder of this introduction will consider his life, his thought, and his influence. Specifically, in considering DuBose's life, his external life will be traced, then his inner spiritual development will be examined. Second, in considering DuBose's thought, his systematic theology will be outlined, and his system will be compared with classic Roman Catholic and Reformed theology. Finally, DuBose's significance and influence will be evaluated, and the rationale for choosing the selections included in this volume will be explained.

DUBOSE'S LIFE[6]

William Porcher DuBose was born April 11, 1836, in Winnsboro, South Carolina, near Farmington, his father's plantation, which was ten miles north of Winnsboro. The DuBoses were an extended and prominent South Carolina family that traced their American origins to Huguenots who settled in the tidewater area of South Carolina in the seventeenth century. William's father, Theodore Samuel Marion DuBose, was an able administrator and a scientific planter who would exert a powerful influence on his son's life. His mother, Jane Porcher DuBose, was also an able administrator and a lady of refined tastes who enjoyed hearing the classics read in the evening.[7]

DuBose would recall Farmington and Roseland Plantation, where the family moved when he was eight years old, as "a paradise for boys." Adjoining plantations were owned by relatives who delighted in visits from William and his older brother, McNeely. There was horseback riding, his pony Bagatelle, hospitality, and an ordered, cultured society that DuBose would recall with nostalgia.[8]

DuBose's formal education began at the Mount Zion school in Winnsboro. Here he began the study of classical languages and mathematics which at first eluded his grasp. DuBose's father decided that his son should attend a military school, the Citadel, located in Charleston, where he would be compelled to master a scientific curriculum that included mathematics. DuBose responded to the challenge of the Citadel with great success. He mastered mathematics as well as military science, rose to the head of his class, and graduated as the ranking cadet officer.

When DuBose graduated from the Citadel in 1855, he had a clear sense of his call to the ministry. To prepare for seminary studies, he attended the University of Virginia. DuBose's three years at Virginia were concentrated in study which strained his never robust health. Each department of the University was a separate school, and DuBose matriculated in the schools of Latin, Greek, French, and Moral Science. He later added diplomas in Mathematics and Physics (natural science). DuBose made a number of lifelong friends while he was a student at Virginia. He was involved in student politics, but his greatest influence, both personal and religious, was on his friends. DuBose left the University of Virginia with a master of arts degree, a comprehensive education, and a mastery of Greek which he attained under the direction of Basil L. Gildersleeve, one of America's great classicists.[9]

In the fall of 1859 DuBose began his preparation for ordination at the Episcopal diocesan seminary established a year earlier in Camden, South Carolina. Poor health forced him to leave before the end of the academic year. On a camping trip in the mountains prescribed for his recovery he met Miss Nannie Peronneau, who would become his wife two years later.[10]

DuBose's courtship of Miss Nannie would not be the only distraction during his second year of seminary studies. Abraham Lincoln was elected President of the United States in November, and South Carolina seceded in December. On April 12 the Confederate States of America bombarded the United States garrison at Fort Sumter. The Civil War had begun. As the ranking officer of his class, DuBose was asked to serve as Adjutant of the Holcomb Legion, which the commandant of the Citadel had been ordered by the Governor of South Carolina to organize.[11]

DuBose accepted this appointment and was assigned with the Holcomb Legion to guard Charleston. In 1862 the Holcomb Legion was mustered into Confederate service and transferred to Virginia. During the spring DuBose's father died. He made a brief visit home to see his mother, who died soon afterward. During the summer and fall DuBose saw action at Second Manassas (Second Bull Run) and South Mountain. DuBose was wounded twice and his horse shot from under him at Second Bull Run. During the night following the Battle of South Mountain he was captured by Union troops while reconnoitering at Boonsboro Gap.

> . . . I had come upon a sentry of two men in the midst of a bivouac, and the woods were as sunk in sleep and stillness as if there were no life in them. A man stood before me with the butt of his gun upon the ground. As he jerked up his gun I stepped quite up to him and drew the pistol which I had cocked under a light cloak. In the act of both doing this and protecting myself from him, my pistol was discharged prematurely, and he, thinking himself shot, cried aloud and precipitated himself upon me. In an instant

the mountain top was awake and alive, and I was upon the ground in the midst, in a desperate struggle for escape. The odds were against me, and I landed not many days later a prisoner in Fort Delaware.[12]

Many years later the Union soldier who captured DuBose requested his testimony for a pension application. After DuBose provided the testimony, the old soldier named Cronin came to Sewanee to visit DuBose. DuBose remembered that Cronin said, "I had come near to killing him, and he had come nearer to killing me; for when I had twice almost got away, he had at last, being twice my strength, got me down, and then, with my own pistol, was in the act of shooting, when some mysterious force had held his hand and prevented him."[13]

After two months in Fort Delaware, DuBose was exchanged and rejoined his command in North Carolina. Stopping over in Richmond on the way to North Carolina, DuBose discovered that he had been listed as dead, and he read his obituary in a "reading room." Soon afterward DuBose was "dangerously and painfully" wounded near Kinston. During his convalescence he learned he was to be sent to Vicksburg, and he obtained a short furlough to marry Nannie Peronneau.[14]

By the time DuBose arrived in Mississippi, Vicksburg had surrendered. He was sent east to Savannah and then to Charleston, where he remained until the fall of 1863. While DuBose was in Charleston, "influential friends in Church and State" arranged his appointment as chaplain to Brigadier General Joseph Kershaw's Brigade. DuBose was ordained to the diaconate in December and began his ministry in Greeneville, Tennessee, where the brigade was in winter quarters "with the most brilliant congregation, from major-generals down to privates, that I have ever had to address."[15]

During the spring of 1864 chaplain DuBose accompanied the brigade to Virginia, where they fought in the Wilderness at Spottsylvania and Cold Harbor. In late summer the brigade was sent to the Shenandoah Valley to assist General Early's unsuccessful campaign against General Sheridan. During the remaining months of the war DuBose recalled that his ministry was "mainly in the hospitals and in private ministrations."[16]

After the surrender in April DuBose returned home "to find it a picture of the most utter desolation, having lain in the center of Sherman's famous march.'' In October the DuBoses' first child, Susie, was born, and DuBose was asked to serve at St. John's Church, Winnsboro, and St. Stephen's Chapel at Ridgeway, a mission. He was ordained to the priesthood in September 1866 in Winnsboro, where he remained until the end of 1867 when the Bishop requested that he move to Abbeville. Years later, describing this period of his life, DuBose recalled: ''My family had been a wealthy one before the war, but was now utterly impoverished; the country was stript of the barest means of subsistence; our social and political condition was unendurable and hopeless.''[17]

Leaders of the Old South composed a large number of the members of Trinity Church, Abbeville, where DuBose served as rector from 1868–1871. DuBose was becoming as fully a churchman as he had once been a soldier. He cofounded a diocesan journal, *The Monthly Record,* and as a result of his growing reputation he was nearly elected coadjutor bishop in 1871. The DuBose family was also growing. May, a second daughter, and William Haskell, a first son, were born during the years in Abbeville.[18]

Although DuBose grew personally and ministerially, and his role in the establishment of *The Monthly Record* indicates the resumption of intellectual activity interrupted by the war, the first years of his ministry in Abbeville were marked by racial and political violence. Ralph Luker has noted in his study of DuBose that the Rectory of Trinity Church was robbed during the residence of the DuBose family, and that arson and Ku Klux Klan violence were commonplace throughout Abbeville County in 1868. It would seem that DuBose's sympathy was with his Church during the violence of 1868, and that he bought a pistol and took his turn at the night watch.[19]

About a month after his near election as coadjutor, DuBose received a telegram informing him that he had been elected to the chaplaincy of the University of the South at Sewanee. DuBose accepted and began his work at Sewanee late in 1871. Later DuBose would say that his decision to go to Sewanee was to determine the course of his whole life.[20]

1871 was a year of greatly increased enrollment at Sewanee, but in spite of this growth and the dedicated efforts of many, the University seemed a pale embodiment of the vision of its founders. The

University of the South had its immediate origins in the 1850's when Bishop Leonidas Polk of Louisiana called on the bishops of the ten dioceses of the lower South to establish a great university. With the support of Bishop Stephen Elliot of Georgia and Bishop James Otey of Tennessee, the organization of the University proceeded rapidly, and in 1858 the Board of Trustees took title to 9,525 acres of land on a high plateau about thirty miles northwest of Chattanooga. In 1860 when the cornerstone was laid, five hundred thousand dollars of a projected three million dollar endowment had been raised, and the Trustees had set out an impressive plan for the University to be composed of thirty-two schools, each to be headed by a professor.[21]

During the war all the construction begun on the site of the University was destroyed and the endowment was lost. Determined that a university would rise on these ruins, Charles Todd Quintard, Bishop of Tennessee, set about to raise funds. Two log cabins and a small school building had been constructed by 1866. In 1868, the year in which Bishop Quintard returned with contributions for the University from England, including a thousand volumes given by Oxford and Cambridge, a chapel was completed.[22]

The University opened as a college preparatory school in 1868 with four professors and nine students. When enrollment grew to 125 students in 1870, the organization of the University in seven schools was approved by the Trustees and the preparatory school was continued as a separate entity. A visitor to Sewanee in 1870 might have mistaken the University for a military school, because over half of the faculty were former Confederate officers and the school was organized on a military model. During these difficult years of refounding the University, it is said that Francis Shoup, Professor of Mathematics, once toasted Sewanee as the place where "People of eminent respectability lived together in cheerful poverty."[23]

DuBose's first years at Sewanee were filled with activities from architecture to academics. He built a house for his family and two other houses for his relatives who came to Sewanee to live. In 1873 DuBose organized the Order of Gownsmen, an honorary student organization that gradually permeated Sewanee with an English academic spirit. All the while DuBose was occupied in ministerial, teaching, and administrative duties.[24]

Mrs. DuBose's health began to fail in 1872, and she died the following spring. Their second son, Samuel, who was born after the

DuBoses arrived at Sewanee, died a year after his mother's death. The grief of these losses, combined with a heavy workload, undermined DuBose's health. In 1876 DuBose contracted tuberculosis. A University grateful for his services sent DuBose on an extended vacation which included a visit to the Centennial Exposition in Philadelphia.[25]

In spite of ill health and personal grief, DuBose was recognized in a short time as a powerful spiritual and intellectual force at Sewanee. He was both a principal maker of Sewanee as a University in the New South, and the principal embodiment of the Sewanee spirit. These were remarkable achievements accomplished with meager resources and many frustrations in each of DuBose's five roles of chaplain, teacher, scholar, promoter, and administrator. Some sense of the difficulties DuBose faced in creating a new spirit at Sewanee may be illustrated by a recollection and a letter from this period. During an incident of chapel rowdiness, a witness recalled that DuBose informed the students: "I have in my hand a list of the twelve men who have been leaders in this disturbance. They can control the whole situation immediately if they will. If they will not, the first name here will be stricken from the rolls of the University, and so on until the matter is settled." On another occasion when an officer of the University was reappointed over faculty objections, DuBose exploded to a correspondent: "I cannot describe my surprise and indignation . . . this is an outrage."[26]

Although DuBose influenced every aspect of life at Sewanee, it was his excellence as a teacher that would lead successive generations of students to remember him as a sage and seer. DuBose's initial duties had included ministry and the development of a theological department as well as teaching, but by 1880 the theological department was established, and in 1882 DuBose resigned his position as chaplain to devote his attention to teaching. From 1871 until his retirement in 1908, nearly every Sewanee student passed through one of DuBose's classes on Christian Evidences, Greek, Hebrew, or Scripture. DuBose's genuine and profound affection for teaching and for the students he taught stands out in his correspondence and reminiscences, and his students returned his affection. A Sewanee colleague who later became Bishop of Tennessee recalled that DuBose's "penetrating intellect and profound scholarship was so mingled with that simple sincerity of goodness, that we were so busy loving him that we forgot to be awed by his learning.'' A student who became Bishop of New York remembered that DuBose's teaching was not mere intellectual apprehension, ''but personal, spiritual conviction and experience.''[27]

Underlying DuBose's greatness as a teacher was his belief that education was an ongoing process. A progressive educator before progressive education, DuBose sought to develop reasoning in an atmosphere of openness to truth in which both teacher and students were learners. To prevent an accumulation of information from turning his classes into lectures and recitations, DuBose began each year anew without any reference to old notes. Although DuBose's instruction was based on wide reading, he taught only what he had assimilated from his reading and had made part of his own thought. DuBose was able to achieve an atmosphere of openness to discovery because he saw himself as someone seeking to learn the truth rather than an an authority who possessed it. ''I was finding and making myself,'' he later recalled, ''in and with and through and by as well as upon them.'' In dealing with exegesis and doctrine, subjects often taught like a catechism, DuBose preserved a spirit of discovery. Looking back on his teaching career, DuBose explained:

> I held that my place and part was in the mine, not in the mint, of the truth of Christianity, that free enquiry and investigation, not dogma (which would have its proper place after) was in order with us. Everything was to be tested and verified, according to our Lord's prescription, in the light and in the terms of human nature, human life, and human destiny. All that was true for us ought to be true to us. . . .[28]

The publications which DuBose began writing in the 1890's grew out of his experience as a teacher. Through the give and take of the classroom and the stimulus to study it provided, DuBose assimilated the critical biblical scholarship coming out of Germany and the evolutionary perspective that was unsettling theology in the late nineteenth century. The assimilation of these new ideas propelled DuBose's thought toward a more dynamic and pluralistic perspective.

The first of DuBose's books, *The Soteriology of the New Tes-*

tament, interpreted the incarnation of the Word as God's moving humanward and Christ's humanity as the process of human nature moving Godward toward its inherent end. On the basis of the reconciling work of God in Christ, DuBose gave full weight to the immanence of the divine, the humanity of Christ, and he indicated the inadequacy of an extreme transcendent view of God and the vicarious theory of atonement. His second book, *The Ecumenical Councils,* examined the development of Christology through the seventh century. Here DuBose found that Christ's human nature held a greater significance in the thought of the early Church than it would in subsequent theology.[29]

DuBose's next four books developed his ecumenical Christian process perspective in greater detail, and each volume grounded DuBose's perspective in a different body of New Testament literature: *The Gospel in the Gospels* in the Synoptics, *The Gospel According to Saint Paul* in the Pauline Epistles, *High Priesthood and Sacrifice* in the Epistle to Hebrews, and *The Reason of Life* in the Johannine writings.[30]

DuBose's publications brought him wide recognition and some criticism. When his name was proposed to the Sewanee Board of Trustees in 1894 for Dean of the Theological Department, Bishop Edwin Weed of Florida and Bishop Cleland Nelson of Georgia questioned DuBose's orthodoxy. DuBose was defended by Bishop Thomas Gailor of Tennessee and other bishops, and he received the appointment. DuBose also received criticism from some reviewers in the Reformed theological tradition for his rejection of the vicarious theory of atonement, but in general the response to DuBose's publications was positive, especially in England.[31]

The chief promoter of DuBose's publications was his former student and friend Silas McBee, who became editor in 1896 of *The Churchman,* an unofficial journal of the American Episcopal Church. Through visits to the McBee home on Long Island and a trip to England in the 1890's, DuBose became acquainted with a wide circle of contemporary theologians. In the early years of the twentieth century, DuBose and McBee united their efforts to promote a progressive ecumenical movement in theology. McBee founded the *Constructive Quarterly* in 1912 with an international and ecumenical editorial board to promote the twin goals of ecumenical unity and a rapprochement with science advocated by DuBose. In spite of its initial success, the *Constructive Quarterly* was weakened by the rising tide of nationalism that accompanied World War I and the theological pessimism that followed it. The fundamental obstacle to the enterprise, however, was the weight of centuries of apologetic and controversial theology and the lack of a basis for developing an irenic theology. The *Constructive Quarterly* ceased publication in 1922.[32] DuBose's final years were filled with growth and activity. Between 1913 and his death he published eleven articles in the *Constructive Quarterly,* and he was working on a long manuscript entitled "From Aristotle to Christ." His last article, "Preparedness: Some Essential Preliminaries to Christian Unity," was published after his death. DuBose died at Sewanee on August 18, 1918. In 1970 he was listed in the Liturgical Calendar of the Episcopal Church for commemoration on August 18.[33]

DUBOSE'S SPIRITUAL ODYSSEY

DuBose was seventy-five years old when he gave three "intimate talks" to a reunion of his friends and former students held in his honor at Sewanee in 1911. In these retrospective lectures, which constitute DuBose's spiritual autobiography *Turning Points in My Life,* DuBose described his spiritual development in terms of three aspects or phases which he called "Evangelical, Churchly and Catholic *(in the widest sense)."* DuBose explained that these phases were not discontinuous stages of his life, but aspects of his life that evolved into unity through the process of spiritual development and integration. The centrality of continuity in DuBose's retrospective lectures is one indication that he was viewing his life in 1911 through the lens of his mature spiritual and theological reconstruction.[34]

It is almost as difficult to go behind DuBose's retrospective lectures to describe his spiritual development exactly as it happened as it is to describe the historical Jesus from the Gospels. Although DuBose describes some of his spiritual experiences and some of the influences on his spiritual life in the retrospective lectures, DuBose's presentation is selective and the account does not go beyond his early years at Sewanee. A second source for DuBose's life is the "Reminiscences 1836–1878," which DuBose wrote for his family late in his life. The "Reminiscences" add some details not mentioned in the retrospective lectures, but like the retrospective lectures the "Reminiscences" represent the mature recollections of DuBose, and they also do not go beyond DuBose's first years at Sewanee. As a result of a fire that destroyed most of DuBose's papers, there are only a limited number of materials that can be employed to supplement DuBose's two retrospective accounts. The absence of citations in DuBose's publications makes it virtually impossible to track the authors who may have influenced his thought after the 1870's when his retrospective accounts conclude.

Given the limitations of the sources, it is not possible to reconstruct much of the social and intellectual context of DuBose's spiritual odyssey. Although the few surviving papers and the recollections of DuBose's friends add some information to DuBose's two retrospective accounts, they do not make it possible to date so significant an event as the rise of what DuBose called his Catholic phase, or to determine what influences led to this final phase of his spiritual life. Because of the importance of DuBose's Catholic phase in his spiritual odyssey, an attempt is made here to suggest when and how DuBose came to his final spiritual perspective. With this exception, DuBose's retrospective lectures, *Turning Points in My Life,* provides the framework for the present consideration of his spiritual odyssey.

DuBose began the description of his spiritual development in his retrospective lectures with the awakening of his religious consciousness in his eighteenth year. DuBose, as he notes in passing, was "born and bred in the Church," and he was exposed to the religious influences of a Christian home and community. He was baptized as an infant, taught the elements of Christianity by his family, and attended St. John's Church in Winnsboro with his family. In spite of his love of horseback riding and the active life, DuBose appears to have been an intellectual, idealistic young man with an imaginative, romantic streak that led him to be fascinated with the "Arabian Nights" in his youth and Tennyson's poetry in his mature years.[35]

Another religious influence in DuBose's early years was the spiritual awakening at St. John's Parish brought about by two of his relatives. The long standing convention that communion was only for women ended at St. John's Parish when DuBose's Uncle, Peter Porcher, called his relatives to his deathbed and lamented his and their neglect of religion. DuBose's Aunt, Betsy Porcher, established Sunday schools, and her cheerful spirituality influenced the young people of the parish. DuBose would later recall that Aunt Betsy "influenced us greatly—more than we realized, I see now."[36]

DuBose's early life was shaped by the ideals of plantation society. Many years later, reflecting on that society, DuBose, in an important statement that merits quotation, sought to balance the "compensatory good" of a world he loved and admired with its basis in slavery which he had come to recognize as a sin.

> The world is constantly outgrowing and making sinful institutions which, however they are so now, were not so to it in the age or at the stage in which they prevailed. Polygamy was no sin to Abraham. Slavery was no sin to the consciousness or conscience of the New Testament. Feudalism was no sin in its day, but would be so now. Puritanism in forms which were once admirable would now be condemned. The time will come when war will be a sin. The South received and exercised slavery in good faith and without doubt or question, and, whatever we pronounce it now, it was not sin at that time to those people. Liable to many abuses and evils, it could also be the nurse of many great and beautiful virtues. There are none of us now who do not sympathize with its extinction as a necessary step in the moral progress of the world. It was natural that we who were in it and of it should be the last to see that, and be even made to see it against our will. Knowing as others could not, and loving the good that was in it, it was not strange that we should be more and longer than others blind to its evils, and unconscious of the judgment which the world was preparing, finally and forever, to pass upon it. Now that the judgment is passed, we join in it. Slavery we say, is a sin, and a sin of which we could not possibly be guilty.[37]

Spiritually deepened perhaps by the religious revival at St. John's Parish, a thoughtful and idealistic young DuBose set off to the Citadel. DuBose saw himself both physically and academically unprepared for military school, and he viewed his father's decision to send him to the Citadel as "heroic" because it represented the most difficult course open to his father. DuBose did well until the malaise of his third year, which he called homesickness, led to a lapse in his studies and the neglect of his prayers. He described his feelings in some letters he sent home, and his father replied with a fiercely loving letter that DuBose recalled "was like a lash. It went straight to the mark—the weakness, the folly, the unmanliness of being homesick. It woke me and stirred me up."[38]

Not long after DuBose received the fiercely loving letter from his father, he received another letter from Tom Stoney, a cousin attending the University of Virginia, that described Stoney's religious awakening. Shortly after the letter from Stoney, DuBose spent a night in a Columbia, South Carolina, hotel with two other cadets, his cousin Richard Dwight and William Gaillard, following a boisterous evening at the theater. Gaillard and Dwight immediately went to sleep, and DuBose recalled:

> There was no apparent reason why I should not have been so too, or why it should just then have occurred to me that I had not of late been saying my prayers. Perfectly unconscious and unsuspicious of anything unusual, I knelt to go through the form, when of a sudden there swept over me a feeling of the emptiness and unmeaningness of the act and of my whole life and self. I leapt to my feet trembling, and then that happened which I can only describe by saying that a light shone about me and a Presence filled the room. At the same time an ineffable joy and peace took possession of me which it is impossible either to express or explain.[39]

DuBose dated the beginning of his conscious religious life, which he called his Evangelical phase, to this experience of God's presence in his eighteenth year. He found "a New World without me, and a New Self in me," and within a year he was confirmed. A year later when DuBose graduated from the Citadel, he had discerned his call to the ministry.[40]

The long-lasting effects of DuBose's religious experience are evident in his theology. The centrality of divine immanence in his thought may be traced to this experience of God's presence. DuBose seems to have experienced grace as a completion of nature—not as a radical otherness of judgment because "there was then no conscious sense of sin, nor repentance. . . . ." Indeed, DuBose observed that in finding God in his experience, he had found himself, and he illustrated his encounter with God by the analogy of falling in love—something both natural and inexplicable.[41]

DuBose described his spiritual life in the years between his religious experience that began his Evangelical phase and his entrance into the diocesan seminary in Camden as "very much in myself, and there very much in idea and sentiment." This seems too severe an assessment because DuBose's friends at the University of Virginia remembered him as a religious influence. Thomas Dudley, later Bishop of Kentucky, attributed his turn from wildness to religion to DuBose, and Samuel Preston, a rough fighter of jayhawkers, traced his confirmation to DuBose's influence. DuBose was also the prime mover in the founding of a YMCA chapter at Virginia, and active in other campus religious activities.[42]

Perhaps DuBose's characterization of his spiritual life in the years following his religious experience as in himself was not intended to indicate inactivity so much as the affective focus of his spiritual life at this time. Lacking an intellectual appropriation of his experience, DuBose found it difficult to apply its force in practical action or to communicate it in the community of faith. If this conjecture is correct, it indicates why DuBose claimed that he arrived at the diocesan seminary with pietism rather than piety.[43]

DuBose's seminary career was too short to transform him from a pietist into a scholastic, but it did serve to spur him to a deeper understanding of the Church. Soon after his arrival in the seminary, DuBose was drawn into an extended theological discussion with John H. Elliott, a senior who had studied at Princeton Theological Seminary under the master of Reformed Theology, Charles Hodge. The focus of the theological discussion was the Epistles of Saint Paul and whether they did not necessitate the five points of Calvinism. These discussions led DuBose to a close examination of Saint Paul that extended through his military service. In the end DuBose concluded that the Calvinist view was true, but was only part of the truth.[44]

Meanwhile, DuBose's second year of seminary studies was interrupted by the Civil War. The outbreak of the war confronted

DuBose with a conflict of loyalties. DuBose's father supported secession, and he wished to see his sons enlist, but DuBose was uncertain of what he should do. As he later explained: "I had put myself, as it were, in the hands of the Bishop of the Diocese, who in an even higher sense was a 'Father in God' to me at the time. . . . " At this point DuBose received a letter from his father:

> He reviewed his intercourse with his children and made the remark that so many parents lamented the want of deference to their wishes on the part of their children, but that his experience had been just the reverse. He meant to say that he controlled his children more than he wanted to, or rather that they had deferred to his wishes almost too readily. He had never wished to impair their freedom. I think the letter was intended to commend my act in following my own judgment rather than his wishes in this particular matter.[45]

When DuBose reached the decision to accept a military appointment, he found that "all agreed the time had come when I should respond to the call of my state." Soon after DuBose's decision, his father sent him a very fine set of military trappings, which DuBose took as a sign of parental approval for his decision.[46]

Several factors seem to have diminished DuBose's Evangelical phase. His seminary discussions with Elliott probably indicated that DuBose's experience of divine immanence was incompatible with the extreme divine transcendence characteristic of Reformed theology. Meanwhile, DuBose discovered the inadequacy of subjective romantic idealism through the chance reading of the "Adventures of Lieutenant Ninkum Poop," an idealistic but ineffective officer. This story convinced DuBose that idealism had to be converted into living. The experience of military service taught this lesson more concretely. In his "Reminiscences," for example, DuBose recalled his first days of imprisonment at Fort Delaware when he was weak, wounded, and infested with lice. "I have to confess," he admitted, "that the strongest religious principles I could summon to my help were inadequate to the occasion."[47]

It also seems likely that DuBose's coming of age, i.e., the responsibility of being an officer and a husband, propelled him beyond the subjective idealism and the passive, vicarious spirituality that he associated with his Evangelical phase. The letter DuBose received from his father when he was trying to decide if he should join the Holcombe Legion was a culminating and superior moment in their relationship. As DuBose's father had earlier made the "heroic" decision to send his son to the Citadel and then revealed to him "the weakness, the folly, the unmanliness of being homesick," the elder DuBose now made what may be seen as his last heroic decision—he told his son to decide for himself.[48]

As a mature theologian DuBose would interpret the trials and adversities of Christian living in a way that seems to reflect his relationship with his father. Observing that the same conditions that make for cowardice also produce heroism, DuBose would view adversity as beneficial to growth in saintliness. Of course it would be an exaggeration to attribute the centrality of the idea that adversity is a divine means of spiritual growth in DuBose's thought solely to his relationship with his father, since it is a prominent theme in the Bible and lies at the root of what is considered a characteristic form of American religious discourse—the jeremiad. Nevertheless, the central theme in DuBose's theology, that God makes "heroic" decisions for us through which we become really and actually like Christ, was foreshadowed in his relationship with his father.[49]

It was during DuBose's war years that his Churchly phase came into ascendency. Throughout the war he carried five books with him in an ammunition box: "the Greek New Testament, Tennyson's 'Poems,' Pascal's 'Thoughts,' Xenophon's 'Memorabilia,' " and the Prayer Book. DuBose worked his way through the Epistle to the Romans, reconstructing "the thought-and-life-process of that wonderful argument," on one occasion while his men dug earthworks. The outcome of DuBose's reconstruction was to see Paul as a universalizer and an apostle intent on inward life relations and process—not as a theologian preoccupied with doctrine. This conclusion cleared the way for a more organic and immanent understanding of grace which was not only consistent with DuBose's religious experience, but also pointed the way to seeing the Church as a sacramental presence.[50]

DuBose's reconstruction of Saint Paul's thought laid the basis for the rise of his Churchly phase. Although DuBose does not mention it as a superior moment, his ordination to the diaconate and his ministry as a chaplain doubtless played a role in the rise of his Churchly phase, since ordination involved him in the area of practical action that he had found wanting in his Evangelical phase. It was his premonition of Union victory, however, that brought DuBose's Churchly phase suddenly into prominence. DuBose was seventy-five when he described to a Sewanee audience what he called one of the "superior moments" of his life, his experience the night Confederate forces were defeated in the Battle of Cedar Creek:

> When we finally rested about midnight, I could not sleep; the end of the world was upon me as completely as upon the Romans when the barbarians had overrun them. Never once before had dawned upon me the possibility of final defeat for the Confederate cause. That night it came over me like a shock of death that the Confederacy was beginning to break. . . . [A]lone upon the planet, without home or country or any earthly interest or object before me, my very world at an end, I redevoted myself wholly and only to God, and to the work and life of His Kingdom, whatever and wherever that might be.[51]

Ralph Luker has noted that after the defeat of the Confederacy, all that remained to DuBose was the Church. Although there are indications that DuBose's Evangelical phase was declining before his premonition of Union victory, his Churchly phase seems to have been swept into predominance dramatically in a powerful redirection of his life that "fateful night." Like the beginning of his Evangelical phase which the seventy-five year old DuBose described as coming out of the blue without any particular preparation, so his Churchly phase swept into prominence in a moment of discontinuity when DuBose found himself lost and homeless.[52]

The experience of homelessness is a common feature in the rise of both DuBose's Evangelical and Churchly phases. DuBose characterized the malaise that preceded his experience of the presence of God as homesickness; however, the sense of homelessness that DuBose experienced that fateful night represented a more extraordinary discontinuity than the malaise of his eighteenth year. It is not unusual for a young man at military school to experience homesickness, to neglect his studies and prayers, or to be admonished by his father. It is less common to suffer military defeat, to experience the collapse of one's culture, and to realize that the way of life one had seen as moral and right had come under the judgment "which the world was preparing, finally and forever to pass upon it." DuBose had fought in the armies of the Confederacy because he believed it to be the bearer of the spirit of history. Like Saint Paul on the way to Damascus, DuBose discovered on that fateful night that he had been on the wrong side.[53]

Not only was the discontinuity preceding the ascendency of DuBose's Churchly phase more extraordinary than the discontinuity preceding the ascendency of his Evangelical phase, but the discontinuity of that fateful night was also not as easily resolved. DuBose's shift from conventional religion to his Evangelical phase overcame his sense of homesickness. And the lack of motivation and manhood his father had rebuked was overcome by DuBose's sense of a New World without and a New Self within "in both of which for the first time, visibly, sensibly, really, God was."[54]

The rise of DuBose's Churchly phase does not seem to have achieved the reconciliation attained through his experience of the presence of God. DuBose's identification with the Church may indeed have served as a substitute for his identification with the Confederacy, as Luker has suggested, but reconciliation requires more than affiliation with the only thing one has left. DuBose was still confronted with the judgment of history on his culture, on his community, and on himself. To achieve reconciliation on this level, to bring together his experience of God's presence and the world's judgment, DuBose needed something more comprehensive and dynamic than an ecclesial identity. DuBose needed a perspective that explained how the Kingdom is present in incompleteness and how its completion is realized in a process filled with adversity and error. Since DuBose would later say that slavery was a sin of which the South could not possibly be guilty, he needed a perspective that would reconcile the presence of God in his life with the incompleteness or absence of God's presence which the judgment of the world had disclosed.[55]

DuBose returned to Winnsboro with his wife at the close of the War, and in a few months he was ministering at St. John's Church and a neighboring mission. The infirmity of the Bishop delayed DuBose's ordination to the priesthood until the fall of 1866. In 1868 he became rector of St. John's Church, Abbeville. Little is known of DuBose's spiritual development during his first years of parish ministry. He recalled later that "there was little means or opportunity for a life of study or anything more than the most practical kind of thinking" at this time.[56]

At Abbeville the situation was somewhat different. It was during his years at Abbeville that DuBose learned German in order to read the theological and scriptural studies that were shaking the foundations of nineteenth century Christian thought. It is also likely that DuBose read some of the writings of the Mercersberg Theologians and the Oxford Movement, as well as some considerations of evolution while he was at Abbeville. Although most of his reading seems to have been in evangelical or ecclesial authors, there are some signs that DuBose's thinking was beginning to move in the direction of the ecumenical process perspective that would characterize his Catholic phase.[57]

There are two indications that DuBose's perspective was shifting during the Abbeville years. The first is DuBose's sincere relief in not being chosen coadjutor bishop in 1871. He wrote later that his election would have been "the great misfortune of my life." DuBose's attitude seems a strange one for a priest with a solely ecclesial identity. The second indication that DuBose's perspective was shifting is the sermon he delivered at the ordination of his uncle, Octavius Porcher, in 1870. In this ordination sermon DuBose considered the nature of the Church and priestly ministry—topics specified for consideration in an ordination sermon. Although these specified topics tend toward an ecclesial and hierarchical perspective, DuBose relativized the ecclesial and hierarchical dimensions of the Church and the priesthood by considering both from a developmental or process perspective.

In considering the Church, DuBose moved from the image of Kingdom to the image of body, and in describing the priesthood, he moved from an image of clerical separateness to an image of empathic unity. "The Church of Christ *is* the Kingdom of God," DuBose explained, "but it is much more than a Kingdom. It is no longer a Body externally controlled by the law of its Head; it is a Body internally filled with the life of its Head." Because of the presence of Christ in every member of the Church, the fullness of Christian priesthood is not found in the hierarchical separateness of an ecclesial estate, but in the identity and empathy of ministers and people. Indeed, DuBose observed, "so far as teaching and ruling the prophetical and kingly offices are concerned, angels might far better than we have been appointed Ministers of the Church of Christ." Priests, therefore, "must be *men:* suffering men, tempted men, men girt about with infirmity. To be Priests, we must be the habitual bearers of our people's burdens; yea, we must bear our people themselves, individually and collectively, upon our hearts, and be ready always, not only to sympathize with them and to intercede for them, but if necessary in the spirit of Christ to sacrifice ourselves for them."[58]

It would appear, therefore, that when DuBose arrived at Sewanee in 1871, his Churchly phase was not as prominent as it had been six years earlier. Although DuBose does not describe the rise of his Catholic phase in his retrospective lectures, it appears that his study of higher criticism exposed him to what Walter Lippman would later call "the acids of modernity," and that this exposure was an important factor in the decline of his Churchly phase. DuBose's enthusiasm for science and criticism as a purgative of external, mechanical models of scriptural inspiration and overzealous ecclesiastical piety, along with his assertion that he personally had passed through every heresy of the early Church, suggest an experience of theological and spiritual dismantling.[59]

The short paper that DuBose presented at the Fifth Church Congress in 1878 suggests that he had come to the realization that a theological reconciliation of divine immanence and transcendence which his spiritual experience led him to seek could not be attained in the context of either his Churchly or his Evangelical phases. At the beginning of his paper DuBose noted that "all the great problems which have occupied Christian thought from the beginning, may be reduced to a single problem, viz., the coexistence and union in one of the two elements of the Divine and the human." Proceeding from this insight, DuBose stated the thesis of his paper: "There is no manifestation to us of the Divine except in and through the human." After developing his thesis DuBose drew the conclusion that Christianity will gain "by the explosion of the theory of a literal mechanical infallibility of scripture," and the implication of his paper is that the same conclusion holds for the Church.[60]

The thesis of the paper DuBose presented to the Fifth Church

Congress in 1878 anticipates the resolution of the discontinuities of his spiritual experience and the theme that would become central in his mature theology. Presented here as a "fact" without the theological developmental or process rationale that would explain the why or how of the "fact" in his mature theology, DuBose simply told the Congress: "The Divine life, if it is in you and me, is not *not* Divine because it is also human, and therefore full of weakness and ignorance and imperfection."[61]

The stimulus that led DuBose to grasp the why or how of the "fact" of God's presence in human imperfection was probably his study and teaching of Aristotle. In Aristotle DuBose found the idea of teleological process, which became in his hands the key that unlocked the mystery of the presence of the Kingdom, in incompleteness, and DuBose's discovery of God's presence in his religious experience and God's absence in the judgment of the world on DuBose and his culture. Indeed, the idea of teleological process would serve to elucidate the phases of DuBose's spiritual life as a process moving toward "higher unities and reconciliations," and enable DuBose to understand the divisions of Christians as phases in the process of actualizing the unity of the Church.[62]

By the time DuBose began to publish in the eighteen nineties, his Catholic phase was predominant. By "Catholic" DuBose meant ecumenical, not only in the sense of an inclusive Christian perspective, but also in the sense of a spirituality that is reconciling, mediating, and unifying. The spirituality of DuBose's Catholic phase may be characterized by considering how his mature writings reflect the resolution of the discontinuities he experienced in his spiritual odyssey.

DuBose's mature thought reflects a resolution of the chief discontinuity of his spiritual odyssey: the experience of God's presence in DuBose himself and in the world which first came to him when he was eighteen, and the experience of God's transcendence or absence, which DuBose encountered most dramatically in the judgment of the world on the Confederacy, his culture, and himself. DuBose attained a reconciliation of these conflicting experiences, which he had come to see as the principal issue of Christian thought, by understanding the incarnation as a process of God moving humanward and humanity moving Godward.

In his personal spiritual odyssey DuBose experienced the

phases of his life as part of this process of moving Godward which began in his Baptism when DuBose was sealed in the process. In his eighteenth year, when he sensibly perceived the presence of God in himself and the world, DuBose's consciousness was involved in the process. The end of the process for DuBose was to become fully and actually the son of God that he had become sacramentally and potentially in Baptism.

By realizing his sonship as a potentiality to be actualized and made complete in the process of Christian living, DuBose reconciled the presence of God in incompleteness in his life. God was both immanent, for example, in DuBose's faith, hope, and love, and transcendent over, against, or absent from DuBose, for example, in his sin, error, and ignorance. Christian living was the process of overcoming sin, error and ignorance through adversity—the process of becoming his true self, a son of God. The end of the process was "at-one-ment" with God, and like DuBose's father, God "heroically" chose what was best for DuBose.

DuBose experienced the process of becoming a son of God as a process of self realization and fulfillment of his true nature—a sort of survival of the fittest and best of himself in the struggle with the adversity of sin, error, and ignorance. In his retrospective lectures DuBose observed that the verification of his experience of the presence of God in his eighteenth year was that "in finding Him, I found myself." DuBose did not experience the process of "at-one-ment" as salvation by magic or machine; he was not transformed by grace the way the pumpkin in Cinderella was transformed into a coach. Rather, DuBose discovered that grace was the power to become through adversity his true self and to overcome the absence of God in himself in sin, error, and ignorance.

In the manuscript "From Aristotle to Christ" that he left incomplete at his death, DuBose referred to the absence of God in the self and the inertness that resists the efforts to overcome it as the most destructive of the deadly sins against the soul. "The Soul's first cry to God," DuBose reflected, "is out of the deep unconsciousness, of practical non-being, through inertness, inaction or unactuality."[63]

The heart of DuBose's spiritual odyssey was the process of becoming his true self, a son of God, by overcoming the non-being in his life through adversity in dependence and faith in God with Christ through the Spirit. Bishop Manning remarked that DuBose "grew until he died.'' A letter DuBose wrote to his friend Silas McBee in 1914, two years before his death, indicates the accuracy of Bishop Manning's observation:

> In a sense this eightieth year of my life has been one worse than the European War between me and old age. In this I feel I can say modestly that I have conquered. It is not only old age I have to contend with, but a number of external conditions . . . and hindrances, which have broken up, paralyzed, and dissipated my energies; but all that does not touch the real root of my troubles; it has only had the beneficient effect, as most certainly the gracious purpose, of throwing me back upon a re-examination and a deeper questioning and testing of my religion. I have gone deeper into it and reached higher than ever before, and I humbly believe I can say now ''I not only believe but know.'' At any rate, I have discovered that the more persistently and perseveringly one believes to the bitterest end, the more certainly one knows and is grateful for having been spared none of the tests.[64]

The last manuscript DuBose prepared for publication in the weeks before his death was on the topic of ecumenism. With the help of his friend Silas McBee, DuBose had devoted his attention increasingly to Christian unity after 1912. When DuBose wrote ''Preparedness: Some Essential Preliminaries to Christian Unity'' in the summer of 1918, he was aware that it might well be his last statement, and it may be seen as a summation of the lessons of his spiritual odyssey. The central message of ''Preparedness'' is that the incarnation demonstrates that ''God is the infinite and Divine Democrat'' who ''rules not over but *in,* not instead of but *by,* and above all, not for Himself but *for* His people.'' It is, perhaps, an indication of the reconciliation that DuBose's spiritual pilgrimage had attained that he introduced this central message with a quotation from the chief adversary of his youth, Abraham Lincoln.

Because God's plan is not to rule people in tutelage but to bring them nearer and nearer to the realization of their completion and ''at-one-ment'' with God, DuBose finds that the principal preliminary to ecumenism is the need to reconcile religious individuality and liberty with religious community and authority. In considering this reconciliation, DuBose seems to reflect his own spiritual odyssey and the reconciliation of his Evangelical and Churchly phases in his Catholic phase. Then, in what seems like a reflection on his own struggle to unity and his keen awareness of the actual and practical obstacles to actualizing the spirit and reality of Christian unity in the self and in the world, DuBose delivered an exhortation which may stand as his epitaph:

> We need not be discouraged by the feeling that in our task of reconstruction, whether of the church or of the world (and the task is not as much *two* as it may seem), we have so much to undo before we can begin to do. The undoing and the doing are not two but one; they are only the convex and concave, the outside and inside, the back and front of one and the same process or movement. We can only, as we have seen, be truly Protestant in its best sense of individual, personal, and free, in the act and by the fact of becoming and being truly Catholic in its right sense of unity and universality—oneness with God and the world and the church (each of which is itself only as All). All these ends, which are All This End, ought again not discourage or dishearten us, because they are all so ideal, and so infinitely remote from actuality. The length and greatness of our task is the measure of our nature and our "predestinature" of our calling and our promise, our faith and our hope, our power of endurance, perseverance and perfected manhood.[65]

DUBOSE'S THOUGHT

Dr. Dennis Kezar has observed in his superb dissertation that DuBose's thought resists a linear exposition because the structure of DuBose's exposition is more spiral than linear. Topics appear, disappear, and reappear like the objects in one's field of vision on a carousel ride; however, the spiral structure of DuBose's theology is no accident. It is DuBose's way of considering issues on different

levels of his system. "Truth is not truth when it ceases to be plastic,"
DuBose once remarked, and the spiral structure of DuBose's system
gives it a certain spring-like flexibility.[66]

This summary of DuBose's thought will consider: (1) some
characteristic features of his system, (2) the overall thrust of the system, (3) DuBose's thought on cosmology, anthropology, atonement,
the Church, and the sacraments, (4) the principal sources of Du-
Bose's thought, and (5) the relationship of DuBose's system to classic Roman Catholic and Reformed theology.[67]

(I)

DuBose's developmental pattern of exposition is a reflection of
his process theology, and this pattern of development is apparent not
only within each of his books, but also is characteristic of his sched-
ule of publication as a whole. Thus, *The Soteriology of the New Testament* (1892) sets out his system, and *The Ecumenical Councils*
(1896) bases his system in the thought of the early Church. DuBose's
next four books recapitulate his system with minor modifications,
basing it respectively in the Synoptics, the Pauline Corpus, the Epistle to the Hebrews, and the Johannine Corpus. *Turning Points* (1912)
sets the system in DuBose's experience, and the *Constructive Quarterly* articles programmatically recapitulate the system from the
standpoint of ecumenism.[68]

As the preceding list of DuBose's books indicates, his theology
is based in the New Testament, but his theology is not an exegesis
of scripture. Rather, it is an exposition of what DuBose had come to
understand as the postulates or presuppositions of the New Testament. DuBose called his method "epexegesis," and on the basis of
this method DuBose develops a systematic theology that is both comprehensive and coherent. Most of the standard topics of systematic
theology are considered in DuBose's system, and they are made to
cohere through DuBose's use of three distinctions and one dynamic
principle.[69]

The dynamic principle is process. By process DuBose means
an Aristotelian teleological development with an end and a direction—not an aimless sequence of changes. It is a process like the
growth through which an acorn develops its potential to become an

actual oak tree. This principle of teleological process has two important functions in DuBose's system. First, it is the basis for defining things, such as persons or the Church, by their ends rather than what they appear to be now. Second, process is employed to explain the gap between potentiality and the fulfillment of that potentiality in actuality. For example, in Baptism a person becomes a new creature, but the actuality of that newness is realized through the process of Christian living. In other words, the baptized person is a son or daughter of God as an acorn is an oak tree.

The three distinctions employed in DuBose's theology are three levels: the natural, the moral, and the spiritual. The natural level encompasses the material world of physical bodies. The moral level encompasses the world of the intellect or reason, and it is present in creatures who have attained reason and can make decisions. The spiritual level is not so easily defined. Precisely, it is the proper end of a rational creature, the fulfillment of the human person, or the capacity for self-transcending relationships. Roughly, it is equivalent to what may be called the religious level, or in everyday language the world of the heart and soul. Each level has a good and an evil appropriate to it, and a "salvation" through which the evil is overcome. Although distinct, each of these levels is interconnected. For example, in the human person illness on the natural level has effects on the moral and spiritual levels.[70]

These levels are present in all of DuBose's mature theology. His tendency to move from level to level in considering a point is one reason for the spiral character of DuBose's theological exposition. The following scheme of DuBose's levels developed by Dr. Charles L. Winters is the simplest way of describing these connections.[71]

LEVEL	GOOD	EVIL	SALVATION
Spiritual	Holiness	Sin	Reconciliation
Moral	Righteousness	Disobedience	Redemption
Natural	Life	Death	Resurrection

(2)

The focus of DuBose's theology is human salvation or soteriology, and he considers creation and other topics only incidentally as they relate to salvation. The center of DuBose's soteriology is the Incarnation. In the largest sense the Incarnation is a process of God moving humanward and humanity moving Godward. Human nature finds its fulfillment and end in Christ's human nature (holiness, righteousness, and life everlasting), which is realized in the victory over adversity (sin, disobedience, and death) achieved by Christ's human nature in its birth, life, death, and resurrection. Individually, Christ exemplifies and actualizes the true end of human nature, "at-one-ment" with God. More significantly and generically, the victory of Christ's human nature has won "at-one-ment" as a potentiality for all humans. This potentiality is made actual for humans by the process of Christian living through which humans become like Christ's human nature by experiencing what Christ's human nature experienced and triumphing as Christ's human nature triumphed.

The process of Incarnation, for DuBose, did not end with Christ's resurrection, but continues in humanity, preeminently in the Church. The Church is in the process of actualizing its potential to be Christ in the world. The process of incarnation is both individual and communal; it is happening in individuals and groups, but it is not an automatic process. It advances to its end "at-one-ment" through human cooperation. This is true even on the natural level, because DuBose believed that the human initiative had come to count for more than the slow natural processes such as evolution.

(3)

Cosmology or teaching about the origins of the universe is not a focus of DuBose's thought, and he considers it only as it relates to soteriology. For DuBose the universe was created and is sustained through the Word of God (the Logos, the divine nature of Christ). The divine is immanent, therefore, in all existence, in nature, and in the processes of nature, but the divine is immanent in the universe as Word, not in the fullness of the Godhead. The universe is not God, and DuBose is not a pantheist. Yet, natural creation also has its proper end, which is the evolution of beings with the capacity for a personal relationship with God.

DuBose's view of human nature is shaped by his idea of human personhood. Personhood involves understanding which entails the freedom to make choices (free will), and the capacity for self-transcending personal relationships. Even on the natural level, the good of life for a human being involves more than just existing; it involves the fullness of life according to the capacity of the human being as a person. Thus, for DuBose the moral and spiritual levels are potentials of human nature. The good of the moral level for the human person is obedience to the person's true inner law, or righteousness. The good of the spiritual level is a self-transcending personal relationship with God, or holiness.

As a matter of fact, human persons fail to realize their inherent potential for good on all three levels (life, righteousness, holiness) and experience death, disobedience, and sin. DuBose understands this human experience of evil in a Thomistic, rather than in a Reformed, theological perspective. Human nature has not fallen to a mass of damnation; it is weakened but not ruined, and its capacity for the good is intact. What has happened is that human nature has turned on itself and sought to realize its potential independently of God. For DuBose this program of self-realization is not only impossible, but is also a distortion of the inherent character of human nature that leads to death on the natural level, disobedience of the human person's true inner law on the moral level, and estrangement from God or sin on the spiritual level.

Atonement, or "at-one-ment" as DuBose called it, is the way that human nature is saved from evil and set back on the process of actualizing its true inner principle and potential. Human nature generically was reconciled with God potentially in the actual reconciliation of Christ's human nature with God. DuBose calls this generic potential reconciliation predestination ("pre-destinature"), and its potential is actualized through the process of Christian living. DuBose rejects the notion of imputed atonement as something done for us or to us. "At-one-ment" is something we actualize in faith and dependence on God and through cooperation with God in Christ through the Spirit. Humans are to incarnate God as Christ incarnated God. As DuBose observed:

> There is no deliverence from evil but in the securing of its opposite or corresponding good. Thus, there is no other possible salvation from sickness but health, or from sin but holiness. . . . But Christian Salvation must mean *all sal-*

vation. It must be Salvation from all sin, the fact of it, the imputation of it, the consequences of it.[72]

The Church is the vehicle through which the Incarnation is manifested and extended through time and made available to humans for their appropriation. "The Church is as much the sacrament of His Presence, as His human Body was of the Presence, the Incarnation, of God in Himself." As a matter of fact the Church is in the process of actualizing the Body of Christ, and Christian disunity, exclusivity, and fanaticism are clear indications that the Church has a long way to go in actualizing its potential. Nevertheless, the Church is a sacrament of Christ and sacraments "are real acts of God in Christ, and they are to be received and interpreted as such, i.e., as *being* what they signify."[73]

For DuBose Baptism is a real and objective sacramental sealing in the "at-one-ment" process initiated by Christ. As DuBose explained:

> By baptism we are dead with Christ and risen with Christ, and therefore *regenerate*. The only non-regeneration of one whom God has baptized is his own ignorance, or unbelief or rejection of the fact that he is regenerate. . . . He is to *be* regenerate by believing himself regenerate; he is to realize the fact that he *is* regenerate.[74]

Eucharist or Communion is also an objective, real sacramental sealing in the actualization of the process of "at-one-ment" begun in Baptism. Once asked if he believed in the "real presence," DuBose responded, "I believe in anything real." DuBose's understanding of Eucharist is succinctly stated in his first book:

> [W]hat is given and received in the Lord's Supper is Jesus Christ, Himself, as not only our new lives, but our new selves, as the ideal and spiritual self which in every man is to take the place of his actual and carnal self. . . . Baptism may be said to correspond to what is now called our justification; and Holy Communion to our sanctification. The one is a once-for-all identification of us with Christ, and the other is the gradual and progressive identification of us with Christ.[75]

Two things should stand out from this summary of DuBose's theology: (1) DuBose saw no radical gap between the divine and the human: God is immanent as Word in creation; "at-one-ment" with God is a potential of the human person. (2) DuBose is more interested in the process of salvation than in doctrines, creeds, or ecclesial practices. As he writes in the first page of his first book, "What our salvation means, is a matter primarily determined not by creeds, not by Scripture, not by divine revelation, but by the facts of our nature and condition."[76]

(4)

DuBose's thought developed from his personal and spiritual experience. In considering the sources of DuBose's theology, his life stands out as the principal source. As to the books that influenced DuBose, there is an element of mystery. DuBose provided no documentation of his sources in his published writings, and he rarely mentions the influences on his thought. Bishop Stephen Bayne observes of DuBose's reading:

> I am inclined to think that the tradition of DuBose's "very few books" is mainly a myth. I've heard it said, indeed, that he cultivated such a myth deliberately, in order to avoid being categorized or letting himself be identified as a disciple of this or that person or school. . . . I have learned nothing of DuBose which suggests that he did not read widely and steadily.[77]

DuBose mentions some books that influenced him in his retrospective lectures. The New Testament, especially the Epistle to Romans in his early years and the Gospel of John in his mature years, held the central place in his thought. Joseph Butler's *Analogy of Religion* (1736), which DuBose probably read before the Civil War, was an influence on his rejection of Reformed transcendence, and Aristotle's *Nichomachaean Ethics* helped him clarify his thinking on the distinction within the unity of grace and nature. Both Butler and Aristotle exerted a major influence on DuBose's thought, and DuBose refers to them explicitly or implicitly throughout his writings. DuBose recognized Isaac A. Dorner's *History of the Doctrine of the Person of Jesus* (1836) as an important influence on his thought and his principal historical source for *The Ecumenical Councils*. In preparing *The Ecumenical Councils*, DuBose read widely in the Church Fathers. His reading of St. Irenaeus of Lyons seems to have left a lasting impression. DuBose's belief that "at-one-ment" is achieved in Christian living that recapitulates the victory of Christ's human nature appears to be an adaptation of Irenaeus's doctrine that Christ's human nature recapitulated human evolution.[78]

DuBose also mentions in his retrospective lectures that he carried Xenophon's *Memorabilia*, Pascal's *Thoughts* and Tennyson's *Poems* with him throughout the Civil War. Without noting the specific authors, DuBose refers to the Mercersberg Theologians and the Tractarians as a churchly influence on his thinking. Of the former it is likely that DuBose read some of the writings of John W. Nevin (1803–86) and Philip Schaff (1819–93). Among the Tractarians it seems very likely that DuBose knew John Henry Newman's *Essay on the Development of Christian Doctrine* (1845) because DuBose seems to reflect Cardinal Newman's interpretation of theological development. Finally, DuBose recalls that the writings of Johann A. W. Neander (1784–1850) and Hermann Olshausen (1796–1839) helped him sort out his Evangelical and Churchly phases.[79]

In his published writings DuBose refers to the poet Matthew Arnold (1822–1888), the church historian and theologian Adolph Harnack (1851–1930), the philosopher Immanuel Kant (1724–1804) and the Roman Catholic Modernist Baron von Hügel (1852–1925). DuBose's use of the phrase "twice-born" in *Unity in Faith* suggests that he read William James's *The Varieties of Religious Experience* (1902). It is also evident from other sources that DuBose studied Herbert Spenser's *Data of Ethics* (1879), which he later adopted as a text at Sewanee, and that he was familiar with the writings of the Roman Catholic Modernist George Tyrrell (1861–1909). DuBose's student, William N. Guthrie, in a review of Bishop Bratton's biography of DuBose, added three books that influenced DuBose to those already mentioned here: Hermann Lotze's *Last Lectures in Practical Philosophy and Religion*, which DuBose adopted as a text for his Moral Science class in the early 1890's, and Robert Browning's "Major Christian Poems." Guthrie also expressed the opinion that the "Arabian Nights," which DuBose read in his youth, exercised "a continuing unconscious" influence on his thought.[80]

It is impossible to ascertain all the books and authors that influenced DuBose, and this survey has not noted every book that DuBose is known to have read. The emphasis here has been on the primary influences and the unexpected influences such as the "Arabian Nights." It would seem correct to assume that DuBose read widely. Among DuBose's papers is a letter to Dr. Felix Adler, the founder of Ethical Culture, in which DuBose wrote: "There is no doubt in my mind as to your philosophy being the wisest [or truest] and deepest I find these days." It seems improbable that a man who used "very few books" would have known Dr. Adler's philosophy.[81]

(5)

DuBose saw his system as a synthesis of his Evangelical and Churchly phases and as a step toward unity between Reformed (evangelical) and Roman Catholic theology. A brief comparison of DuBose's system with the classic Roman Catholic system of St. Thomas Aquinas and the classic Reformed system of Charles Hodge will give some indication of the place of DuBose's thought in the spectrum of Christian theology.

DuBose first encountered Hodge's theological perspective in his seminary discussions with John H. Elliott before the war, and DuBose probably read Hodge's *Systematic Theology* when it was published in the early 1870's. As a result of the revival of Thomistic thought fostered by Pope Leo XIII in the encyclical *Aeterni Patris* (1879), it is likely that DuBose read articles on Thomistic theology published in American religious journals in the 1880's and perhaps St. Thomas's *Summa*. The objective of this comparison, however, is not to propose that Hodge or St. Thomas directly influenced DuBose's thought. Rather, the object is to provide an entry point into DuBose's system for readers who are likely to get lost in the spirals of DuBose's thought without some reference points to more familiar systems.[82]

The most obvious difference between DuBose's system and the systems of St. Thomas and Hodge is the range of the topics covered.

Because DuBose focuses on soteriology, his system does not give extensive consideration to angels, creation, heaven, hell, and other points considered by Hodge and St. Thomas. A second difference is that each of the three theologians holds a different scientific and philosophical world view that influences his interpretation of doctrine. Hodge, who inclines toward the Scottish common sense philosophy and early nineteenth century empiricism, is skeptical of the evolutionary perspective that informs DuBose's process approach. St. Thomas's world view is separated by centuries from the perspectives of DuBose and Hodge, but the centrality of Aristotle in St. Thomas's system results in several parallels with the system of DuBose in which Aristotle was also a central influence.

DuBose's view of human nature is closer to St. Thomas's view than Hodge's. For Hodge, humanity is totally fallen in nature and capable of only a self-interested civil morality. Likewise for Hodge, the human will is not free. Both DuBose and St. Thomas hold that the human will is free, and both reject the view that the fall completely ruined human nature. For St. Thomas, the fall deprived humanity of the grace by which human powers were harmonized and directed to the beatific vision by charity and thus left these powers weakened by their lack of direction and consequent internal conflict. DuBose does not go into the details but simply assumes free will and a viable, albeit a weakened, human nature. Hodge, therefore, sees a more fundamental and radical gap between the divine and the human than either St. Thomas or DuBose.[83]

DuBose, however, is the odd man out on atonement. Hodge follows the satisfaction theory with forensic, vicarious satisfaction given by Christ. Atonement is not a process for Hodge. Indeed, because of the centrality of predestination in Hodge's system, there is little scope for indeterminacy so that real growth involving a human response is limited to sanctification, which is not really essential in Hodge's system. St. Thomas also taught the vicarious value of Christ's suffering, but explained this suffering primarily as a proof of Christ's love for his Father and for humanity, enabling us to share actively in that love or cooperate with it. DuBose opposed vicarious theories of atonement because he saw "at-one-ment" as a process initiated by Christ and actualized in Christian living. From Hodge's perspective, DuBose seems to reduce justification to sanctification.[84]

DuBose is also the odd man out because of the importance of

development in his system. St. Thomas and Hodge see development on the grand scale of salvation history and to a lesser extent in the individual's spiritual life; however, the centrality of the category of substance in the systems of Hodge and St. Thomas gives a fixity to both entities and conditions that is far less apparent in DuBose's thought. Because of DuBose's emphasis on teleological process, the description of entities as substances is postponed to their final realization in his system.[85]

The way that DuBose's emphasis on process distinguishes his system from the systems of Hodge and St. Thomas stands out in the three theologians' consideration of Christ's human nature. The development of Christ's human nature and its victory over sin, disobedience, and death is the centerpiece of DuBose's theory of "at-one-ment," and the keystone of his system. Hodge denies the development of Christ's human nature in any significant way. Hodge finds the ideas that there was a real growth in the man Christ, or that Christ's human nature really struggled against sin a "departure from the faith of the Church." Although not as absolute as Hodge, St. Thomas gives a very restricted range to the development of Christ's human nature. St. Thomas holds that Christ's human nature acquired knowledge and that there was a maturation or unfolding of Christ's human nature, but for St. Thomas, Christ's human nature enjoyed the plenitude of grace from the first moment of its existence in union with his divine person. There seems, therefore, some possibility of a rapprochement between St. Thomas and DuBose on the interpretation of Christ's human nature, but the centrality of development in DuBose's view of Christ's human nature represents a fundamental divergence from Hodge's view.[86]

There is also a divergence between DuBose and Hodge on the interpretation of Scripture. Although Hodge studied in Germany and was familiar with higher criticism, he tended to reject its approach and to understand the inspiration of Scripture in a literal and fixed way. DuBose's "epexegesis" is incompatible with Hodge's canons of interpretation. St. Thomas's reading of Scripture, which is based in Patristic and Medieval hermeneutics, and therefore open to other levels of meaning beside the literal, is more compatible with DuBose's approach.[87]

In summary, DuBose's system seems fundamentally different than Hodge's and the Reformed tradition of which Hodge was the master. On the other hand, there are several similarities in the systems of St. Thomas and DuBose. The principal general difference between St. Thomas and DuBose lies in DuBose's augmentation of process or development.

During DuBose's most productive years, there was a revival of Thomism spurred by the encyclical *Aeterni Patris* (1879). Although numerous American Roman Catholic theologians published on Thomism during DuBose's lifetime, the thrust of the Neo-thomistic revival emphasized the differences between DuBose and St. Thomas rather than their similarities. Indeed, a few American Catholic theologians articulated a conception of the personality that paralleled aspects of DuBose's thought; however, the thrust of American Neothomism during DuBose's life was against a developmental reading of St. Thomas. One American who proposed that Thomism was compatible with a developmental perspective, Notre Dame Professor John Zahm, was rebuked for his efforts.[88]

A generation after DuBose's death, Roman Catholic theology began to move in the direction of a process Thomism. DuBose's thought, therefore, may be seen to anticipate some directions in contemporary Roman Catholic theology. Dr. Dennis Kezar has noted in his dissertation the striking similarity between DuBose's system and the thought of Edward Schillebeeckx. Contemporary Reformed and evangelical theology, however, continues to remain a distance from DuBose's thought.[89]

SIGNIFICANCE AND INFLUENCE

DuBose's significance as a spiritual theologian lies in his effort to reconcile the discontinuities and opposing directions of his experience and thought. In an age when many literate Americans found themselves divided in their allegiances and forced to make reductive affirmations, DuBose's achievement of a reconciling synthesis stands out as a significant accomplishment. The lack of appreciation for DuBose seems to have its basis in the comprehensiveness of DuBose's reconciling synthesis that distances his thought and spirituality from the perspectives of his contemporaries. A brief selective comparison of DuBose's spiritual development and experience with the life stories of some American religious authors prominent in

DuBose's lifetime will serve to illustrate that the difference between DuBose and his contemporaries lay in the objectivity and intensity with which DuBose experienced both God's transcendence and God's immanence.[90]

The year DuBose went to Sewanee, Henry Adams, not exactly a prominent religious author but the contemporary of DuBose who wrote the most winsome portrait of St. Thomas Aquinas in America's Gilded Age, fled Washington for Harvard. In his autobiographical *Education,* Adams describes his life as an experience of discontinuity and degradation in phases that stands in marked contrast to DuBose's retrospective lectures. Indeed, Adams portrays himself as a man swept over by history and consigned to a literate oblivion, but when Adams arrived at Harvard in 1871, he found an expanding College constructing its first great building, Memorial Hall, dedicated to the Harvard men "who died to preserve the Union," not Sewanee's "cheerful poverty" among the ruins. Like many contemporaries of DuBose who describe frustration and failure in their life stories, Adams's "failure" was more personal, subjective, and individualistic than DuBose's. Although patricians like Adams had to make way for business leadership after the Civil War, the institutions with which Adams was identified were not crushed by the war, but rather experienced continuous growth and prosperity throughout his lifetime. Indeed, Adams regretted that he was not a great statesman like his grandfather and great grandfather, but Adams's actual career as a historian was an uninterrupted success that culminated in his monumental history of the administrations of Jefferson and Madison. In fact, Adams's "seven years of laborious banishment" at Harvard was only a temporary episode that ended when he returned to Washington in 1877.[91]

The distinction between a subjective and personal crisis and a public objective one is further illustrated by a comparison of the spiritual odysseys of DuBose and William James. There are several striking similarities. Like DuBose, James knew both transcendental discontinuity, in his experience of insubstantiality, and mystical immanence, in his "Walpurgis Nacht" in the Adirondacks. DuBose's quest to reconcile transcendence and immanence corresponds with James's effort to reconcile freedom and determinism, and both James and DuBose attained a reconciliation in their mature thought. Yet, James's reconciliation in the philosophies of Pragmatism and

Pluralism focused on the individual and rarely considered an organic community like DuBose's Church. Perhaps James's individualistic emphasis reflects the fact that his experience of insubstantiality was personal and subjective. Sherman's army did not march through the place where James "became a mass of quivering fear"; his pain was personal, subjective, and private while DuBose's was public, objective, and communal.[92]

The encounter with the "acids of modernity" that contributed to the rise of DuBose's Catholic phase was a widespread occurrence in the theological world of the late nineteenth century. Modernism was a public phenomenon, and DuBose's liberal contemporaries, who described their encounters with modernism as a central theme in their stories, were not distinguished from DuBose by the privacy of their experiences, as was the case with Adams and James. What distinguishes the stories of these religious liberals from DuBose's odyssey is the absence of the experience of divine transcendence in judgment of their worlds and themselves "finally and forever."[93]

Two liberals who illustrate this difference are William Newton Clarke, who published his autobiography in the same year that DuBose published his retrospective lectures, and Newman Smyth, who lived into the 1920's and wrote his *Recollections* in the last year of his life. The atonement was a central point of concern in Clarke's intellectual development as it was for DuBose, and the theology text that Clarke wrote during his academic years resembles DuBose's mature thought in its developmental perspective, its rejection of the traditional vicarious theory of atonement, and its strong affirmation of Christ's humanity. Yet, the differences between DuBose and Clarke are more striking than the similarities. Clarke describes no experience of discontinuity in his autobiography; rather, it is a story of progress, "not an agonizing struggle." On the other hand, Clarke describes no personal experience of God's immanence similar to DuBose's experience of the presence of God. For Clarke, progress is conceived within the natural sphere, and atonement is appropriated through faith, not through a process of realization. DuBose's vision of humanity realizing its divine end individually and collectively through a process of overcoming adversity is, therefore, foreign to Clarke's perspective.[94]

Newman Smyth, like DuBose, was an officer in the Civil War, but Smyth served on the Union side. Smyth, like DuBose, was also deeply influenced by German theological scholarship, but where DuBose was forced to study the new scholarship in the spare moments he could steal from ministry in parishes depleted by the war, Smyth studied in Germany. Nevertheless, there are several parallels in the thought of Smyth and DuBose. Smyth's theology was developmental, and he came to embrace an organic developmental view of Christian creeds similar to DuBose's Christian ecumenical process perspective. Smyth wrote his *Recollections* after the First World War and after the apparent failure of his efforts to develop Congregational-Episcopal unity. There is a touch of soberness in the pervasive cheerfulness and progressive faith of Smyth's *Recollections* that implies his sense that moments of graced opportunity had been lost in his generation. Smyth, however, describes neither the experience of discontinuity in his life nor the sense that he or his world had been judged by history "finally and forever." In contrast to DuBose who returned defeated from the Civil War to a home state devastated by Sherman's soldiers, Smyth recalled that "flags carried by men and women and children without number waved us homeward at the crossroads all along—and last and best of all—home!" Smyth's spiritual odyssey, therefore, did not propel him to seek a comprehensive reconciling reconstruction because he experienced his life as a linear course, determined at important points "by some unseen power," but not involving phases and definitive defeat.[95]

Without attempting any final answer, this comparison of DuBose and his contemporaries suggests why DuBose was, as Sydney Ahlstrom noted, "almost completely unappreciated in America." DuBose's quest to reconcile the transcendence-immanence discontinuity seemed to his liberal contemporaries to address a problem they did not see because they did not experience transcendence as intensely as DuBose, or see it with the same significance that he did. After the First World War, when discontinuity and transcendence loomed large in religious thought, DuBose's experience of divine immanence and his acceptance of divine immanence as a fact seemed to America's Neo-orthodox thinkers to see something that wasn't there.

Indeed, the closest parallels of DuBose's theology are found in British, not American, authors. The remarkable similarity of DuBose and the British theologians of the Lux Mundi movement, such as Robert C. Moberly, who sought to reconcile scientific thought and traditional Christian theology, may explain why DuBose's books received more favorable attention in Britain than in America, and why DuBose's thought anticipates the direction taken by recent Roman Catholic theology rather than the Neo-orthodox approach that came to prominence in America in the generation after DuBose.[96]

As a theologian, therefore, DuBose's influence has been much more limited than his achievement would lead one to expect. Although DuBose was probably America's first process theologian, no DuBosian school of theology arose to pursue his insights, and DuBose is not mentioned in Professor Welch's magisterial survey of Protestant thought in the nineteenth century. Professor W. Norman Pittenger of Christ College, Cambridge, is perhaps alone among contemporary theologians in expressing an indebtedness to DuBose.[97]

THE SELECTION OF THE EXCERPTS

The selections in this volume were chosen to illustrate DuBose's spirituality and to spare readers as much as possible from the repetitions involved in DuBose's spiral style of exposition. Readers interested in DuBose as a systematic theologian will find the excellent *DuBose Reader,* compiled by Professor Donald S. Armentrout, the best place to pursue this topic.[98]

The first selection comprises chapters one, three, and four of DuBose's retrospective lectures, *Turning Points in My Life.* This is DuBose's spiritual autobiography reprinted for the first time. The second selection comprises nine chapters from *The Gospel According to St. Paul.* This selection may be seen as DuBose's reconsideration of the roots of evangelical Christianity and his own Evangelical phase from his mature theological perspective. The third selection comprises the introduction and nine chapters from *The Gospel in the Gospels.* This selection may be seen as DuBose's reconsideration of the roots of ecclesiastical Christianity and his own Churchly phase from his mature perspective. The fourth selection comprises nine chapters from *The Reason of Life.* This selection may be seen as DuBose's consideration of the New Testament roots of Catholic Christianity and his own Catholic phase.

Insofar as DuBose's spiral style permits, the arrangement of the selections presents DuBose's Evangelical, Churchly, and Catholic phases or aspects from two interconnected perspectives—the experiential and the theological. In the first selection from *Turning Points*, DuBose describes the Evangelical, Churchly, and Catholic phases or aspects of his spiritual odyssey. In the second, third, and fourth selections, DuBose reexamines the basis of each of these phases or aspects respectively in the New Testament. It is hoped that this arrangement of the selections will convey some sense of how DuBose passed beyond the aspects or phases and the discontinuities of his life into what he called "higher unities and reconciliations."

Notes

1. Reprinted in William Sanday, *The Life of Christ in Recent Research* (New York: Oxford University Press, 1908), p. 281; Sydney E. Ahlstrom, "Theology in America," in *The Shaping of American Religion*, ed. James Ward Smith and A. Leland Jamison, 4 vols. (Princeton: Princeton University Press, 1961), 1:299.

2. This is not to say that Clarke, Gladden, James and Smyth did not experience changes and redirection in their lives—a point considered in the section of this introduction where DuBose is compared with his contemporaries.

3. William P. DuBose, "Wade Hampton," *Sewanee Review* 10 (1902): 364–65; Ralph E. Luker's interpretation of this obituary notice differs from mine: "Liberal Theology and Social Conservatism: A Southern Tradition, 1840–1920," *Church History* 50 (1981): 198.

4. Paul Ricoeur, *The Symbolism of Evil*, tr. Emerson Buchanan (New York: Harper and Row, Publishers, 1967), p. 352; see, for example, Richard L. Rubenstein, *After Auschwitz* (Indianapolis: Bobbs-Merrill, 1961).

5. William P. DuBose, *Turning Points in My Life* (New York: Longmans, Green, and Co., 1912), pp. 54–55.

6. This introduction draws principally from three secondary sources: Theodore DuBose Bratton, *An Apostle of Reality: The Life of the Reverend William Porcher DuBose* (New York: Longmans, Green, and Co., 1936), which is based on the manuscript "Reminiscences 1836–1878," compiled by DuBose's son, William Haskell DuBose, in the DuBose Papers (University of the South Archives, Sewanee); Dennis Dean Kezar, "Many Sons to the Father's Glory: A Study of Salvation Theory in the Works of William Porcher DuBose" (Ph.D. Dissertation, Oxford University, 1974); Ralph E. Luker, *A Southern Tradition in Theology and Social Criticism: The Religious Liberalism and Social Conservatism of James Warley Miles, William*

Porcher DuBose and Edgar Gardner Murphy (New York: The Edwin Mellen Press, 1984).

7. George Boggan Myers, "The Sage and Seer of Sewanee," in William Porcher DuBose, *Unity in the Faith*, ed. W. Norman Pittenger (Greenwich, Connecticut: Seabury Press, 1957), pp. 2–3. Professor Myers notes that DuBose's father was a graduate of Yale, but this fact could not be confirmed by the published catalogue of Yale University graduates or by the records in the Yale University Alumni Office.

8. Bratton, *Apostle of Reality*, p. 11.

9. Myers, "Sage and Seer," p. 5; Kezar, "Many Sons," pp. 30–31; Bratton, *Apostle of Reality*, pp. 32–41.

10. Bratton, *Apostle of Reality*, pp. 45–47.

11. Because DuBose's chapter on his war experiences in *Turning Points* is chiefly historical, I have omitted it from the following selections and included the material touching on his spiritual life in this introduction.

12. Donald S. Armentrout, "William Porcher DuBose: An Introduction to the Man," in *The DuBose Reader: Selections from the Writings of William Porcher DuBose*, comp. Donald S. Armentrout (Sewanee: The University of the South, 1984), p. xvi; DuBose, *Turning Points*, pp. 36–37.

13. DuBose, *Turning Points*, p. 38.

14. *Ibid.*, p. 38; The Right Reverend Stephen Bayne, "In the mine, not in the mint," paper presented at the DuBose Symposium held in Charleston, South Carolina, December, 1970, p. 11.

15. DuBose, *Turning Points*, p. 39.

16. *Ibid.*, p. 39.

17. *Ibid.*, pp. 39, 51.

18. Ralph E. Luker, "The Crucible of Civil War and Reconstruction in the Experience of William Porcher DuBose," *South Carolina Historical Magazine* 83 (1982): 66, 69.

19. *Ibid.*, pp. 66–67, 71.

20. Moultrie Guerry, "William Porcher DuBose," in Moultrie Guerry, Arthur Ben Chitty, Jr. and Elizabeth N. Chitty, *Men Who Made Sewanee* (Sewanee: The University Press, 1981), pp. 82–83.

21. Arthur Ben Chitty, Jr., *Reconstruction at Sewanee: The Founding of the University of the South and Its First Administration 1857–1872* (Sewanee: The University Press, 1954), pp. 45–74.

22. *Ibid.*, pp. 83–108.

23. *Ibid.*, pp. 115–142; Guerry, "DuBose," p. 69.

24. *Ibid.*, pp. 82–86.

25. *Ibid.*, p. 83; Luker, *A Southern Tradition*, p. 202.

26. Guerry, "DuBose," p. 85; William P. DuBose to A. T. McNeal,

March 30, 1883, DuBose Papers, Archives, University of the South, Sewanee. Chapel rowdiness was common in American colleges at this time. The point is not that Sewanee was rowdy, but that as disciplinarian, DuBose had to deal with rowdiness.

27. Thomas F. Gailor, *Some Memories* (Kingsport, Tennessee: Southern Publishers, 1937), p. 93; William T. Manning, review of T. D. Bratton, *Apostle of Reality, The Living Church* 95 (October 24, 1936): 457.

28. DuBose, *Turning Points,* pp. 7–8.

29. *The Soteriology of the New Testament* (New York: Macmillan Company, 1892); *The Ecumenical Councils* (New York: The Christian Company, 1896, volume three of *Ten Epochs of Church History,* ed. John Fulton). DuBose's books were reprinted by various publishers, and as of 1987 all are out of print except *The Ecumenical Councils,* reprinted by Gordon Publishers.

30. *The Gospel in the Gospels* (New York: Longmans, Green, and Co., 1906); *The Gospel According to Saint Paul* (New York: Longmans, Green, and Co., 1909); *High Priesthood and Sacrifice: An Exposition of the Epistle to Hebrews* (New York: Longmans, Green, and Co., 1908); *The Reason of Life* (New York: Longmans, Green, and Co., 1911).

31. Gailor, *Some Memories,* pp. 96–97; Kezar, "Many Sons," pp. 415–417, provides a list of reviews of DuBose's books; Luker, *A Southern Tradition,* pp. 227–234, 256–271, 380–390 describes responses to DuBose's publications.

32. Luker, *A Southern Tradition,* pp. 399–420; Kezar, "Many Sons," devotes his concluding chapter (pp. 356–391) to a consideration of themes in recent theology anticipated by DuBose.

33. The eleven articles are reprinted in *Unity in the Faith,* ed. W. Norman Pittinger (Greenwich, Connecticut: Seabury Press, 1957); "From Aristotle to Christ," ed. A. C. Cannon, Jr., typescript copy, Archives, the University of the South, Sewanee; "Preparedness: Some Essential Preliminaries to Christian Unity," *The Churchman* 145 (February 13, 1932): 10–12, (February 20, 1932): 13–15; Bratton, *Apostle of Reality,* p. 214; *The Church Year: Prayer Book Studies* 19 (New York: The Church Hymnal Corporation, 1970): 68.

34. *Turning Points,* p. 16 (These three lectures are the first of the following selections). In current English usage, "phase" may mean something passed through in linear motion (e.g., the adolescent phase), as well as something recurrent (e.g., a phase of the moon). By tying "phase" to "aspect," DuBose seems to incline toward the recurrent sense. Thus, his phases were not stages he passed through in either a dialectical or a developmental sense. Therefore, in spite of the stylistic infelicity I will describe DuBose's phases in terms of augmentation and diminution.

35. Bratton, *Apostle of Reality,* p. 14, reports that when a school bully attacked him, DuBose paused to reflect if he really wanted to fight; William N. Guthrie, "The Doctor as I Knew Him," *The Churchman* 150 (December 15, 1936): 16; *Turning Points,* p. 40.

36. Bratton, *Apostle of Reality,* pp. 21–23.

37. "Wade Hampton," *Sewanee Review* 10 (1902): 364–65.

38. Kezar, "Many Sons," pp. 21, 25; DuBose, *Turning Points,* pp. 18–27 (included in the following selections).

39. *Turning Points,* pp. 18–19, 23–24. A slightly different description of this experience is given in the "Reminiscences 1836–1878," and this version is printed in part in Luker, *A Southern Tradition,* pp. 87–88.

40. Kezar, "Many Sons," p. 28.

41. *Turning Points,* p. 21; Kezar, "Many Sons," p. 29.

42. Luker, *A Southern Tradition,* p. 101.

43. *Turning Points,* pp. 27–28, 53.

44. Luker, *A Southern Tradition,* p. 102; *Turning Points,* pp. 30–31, 53. The five points of the Synod of Dort are: unconditional election, irresistibility of grace, the final perseverance of the saints, limited atonement, the total depravity of human nature. In the history of Christian thought the Dortian view is usually incompatible with the degree of divine immanence DuBose experienced at eighteen. For a Dortian grace does not complete nature; it ravishes some of it.

45. DuBose, "Reminiscences 1836–1878," comp. William Haskell DuBose, typescript copy, Archives of the University of the South, p. 70; Luker, "The Crucible of Civil War," pp. 53–54.

46. "In the mine, not in the mint," p. 5.

47. *Turning Points,* pp. 28–30; "Reminiscences 1836–1878," pp. 102–103.

48. See above, n. 38, and n. 25.

49. See, for example, *Unity in the Faith,* p. 145; Kezar, "Many Sons," p. 22; Sacvan Bercovitch, *The American Jeremiad* (Madison: University of Wisconsin Press, 1978); DuBose, *Turning Points,* p. 11.

50. *Turning Points,* p. 40 (DuBose lists only four books. I assume the Prayer Book from p. 42), p. 43. Pascal's "Thoughts" is the incomplete magnum opus of a Jansenist (something like a Roman Catholic Calvinist) working his way toward a more universalistic, organic faith. Xenophon's *Memorabilia* is about Socrates and probably influenced DuBose's teaching. For the Church as sacrament see *Unity in the Faith,* pp. 67, 99.

51. *Turning Points,* pp. 48–50. At this point in his retrospective lectures, DuBose seems to have overlooked his wife, Nannie.

52. Luker, *A Southern Tradition,* p. 168; *Turning Points,* pp. 18–19, 49–50; Myers, "Sage and Seer," p. 19.

53. DuBose, "Wade Hampton," pp. 364–65 (a longer quotation of this passage may be found at the beginning of this part of this introduction). In *Turning Points* DuBose describes no discontinuity preceding his experience of God's presence, and the discontinuity described in this introduction is my interpretation. DuBose does not specify a date for the rise of his Catholic phase.

54. *Turning Points*, p. 21; Luker, *A Southern Tradition*, pp. 96–97.

55. DuBose, "Wade Hampton," p. 365. See *A Southern Tradition*, p. 281 for Luker's interpretation of the Wade Hampton obituary notice. My phrase, "the only thing he had left," is a paraphrase of Myers, "Sage and Seer," p. 19: "In class one day he told us that after the War, he had lost his fortune and his civilization. The Church was all that he had left."

56. *Turning Points*, p. 51.

57. *Ibid.*, p. 52. DuBose writes that his reading was in evangelical authors, but the Mercersberg theologians opposed several aspects of American evangelicalism. See J. H. Nichols, *Romanticism in America* (Chicago: University of Chicago Press, 1961). Articles on evolution appeared in American religious journals in the 1870's. See James R. Moore, *The Post-Darwinian Controversy: A Study of the Protestant Struggle to Come to Terms with Darwin in Great Britain and America 1870–1900* (Cambridge: Cambridge University Press, 1979).

58. Bayne, "In the mine," p. 12; Bratton, *Apostle of Reality*, pp. 76–77; DuBose, "The Christian Ministry: A Sermon Preached at the Ordination of Rev. O. T. Porcher" (Charleston: Walker, Evans and Cogswell, 1870), pp. 8, 14. On the first page DuBose notes that the topic for an ordination sermon is prescribed. For a different interpretation of this sermon see Luker, *A Southern Tradition*, pp. 168–170.

59. *Turning Points*, p. 57; Kezar, "Many Sons," p. 41 cites the opinion of Rev. Richard C. Nevins that DuBose "may have had a mild case of English Modernism." Walter Lippman, *A Preface to Morals* (New York: The Macmillan Co., 1929).

60. DuBose, "The Interpretation of the Bible" in "Relation to the Present Condition of Learning and Science," in Fifth Annual Church Congress (New York: M. H. Mallory and Co., 1878), pp. 25–26.

61. *Ibid.*, p. 27.

62. Bratton, *Apostle of Reality*, p. 105; Kezar, "Many Sons," pp. 76–77; *Turning Points*, p. 31.

63. DuBose, "From Aristotle to Christ," comp. A. C. Cannon, "Our Father," p. 24 (at end of vol. II), Archives, University of the South, Sewanee.

64. Kezar, "Many Sons," pp. 51–52.

65. *The Churchman* 145 (February 20, 1932): 14. The quotation is

from the Gettysburg Address and is in the first section of the article in the preceding issue (February 13, 1932): 11, col. 2.

66. Kezar, "Many Sons," p. 58. Dr. Kezar's dissertation is the most comprehensive analysis of DuBose's thought. See also: Luker, *A Southern Tradition*, pp. 216–234, 253–273 (the latter section includes a summary of the reviews of DuBose's books); John S. Marshall, *The Word Was Made Flesh: The Theology of William Porcher DuBose* (Sewanee: University of the South Press, 1949); J. O. F. Murray, *DuBose as a Prophet of Unity* (London: SPCK, 1924).

67. This summary is intended as an aid to readers in understanding the following selections. It is not a complete consideration of DuBose's thought, and it does not consider objections to his system.

68. DuBose's spiral style is similar in some respects to John Dewey's Instrumentalist style. There is also a parallel in the doctrinal vagueness of their youthful religious experiences. See Max Eastman, "John Dewey," *The Atlantic Monthly* 168 (1941): 637. The English language describes a stable world view with ease, but using English to describe a world altering and being altered continually is like trying to nail jelly to the wall. The development within DuBose's system is examined in: Theodore Martin Williams, "Humanity and Logos: An Essay in the Theology of William Porcher DuBose" (Ph.D. Dissertation, Emory University, 1974, University Microfilm no. 74–18, 396). The four phases Williams finds in DuBose's mature thought should not be confused with the three phases described by DuBose.

69. DuBose, *The Reason of Life*, p. 30.

70. DuBose, *Soteriology*, pp. 2–4.

71. Charles L. Winters, review of *The DuBose Reader*, ed. Donald Armentrout, *St. Luke's Journal of Theology* 28 (December, 1985): 61–62.

72. DuBose, *Soteriology*, pp. 23–24.

73. *Ibid.*, p. 377.

74. *Ibid.*, p. 107. As an Episcopalian, DuBose does not give an extended consideration to the other five sacraments of the Roman Catholic Church.

75. Myers, "Sage and Seer," p. 18; DuBose, *Soteriology*, p. 389.

76. DuBose, *Soteriology*, p. 1.

77. Bayne, "In the mine," p. 16. The reference is to Murray, *DuBose as a Prophet of Unity*, pp. 31–32.

78. DuBose, *Turning Points*, pp. 42–43, 84, 57; Kezar, "Many Sons," p. 77.

79. DuBose, *Turning Points*, pp. 40, 61.

80. William P. DuBose, "The Late Course of Religious Thought," in *Matthew Arnold and the Spirit of the Age*, ed. Greenough White (New

York: G. P. Putnam's Sons, 1898), pp. 44–50; DuBose, review of *What is Christianity* by Adolph Harnack, *The Churchman* 83 (October 10, 1901): 538–39; DuBose, *Unity in the Faith*, pp. 136, 67, 63; Guthrie, "The Doctor as I Knew Him," p. 16; DuBose, Manuscript Notebook on Herbert Spencer's *Data of Ethics*, DuBose Papers, Archives, University of the South, Sewanee; The University of the South Calendar 1883–84, under "Moral Science;" Mercer Green Johnson to William P. DuBose, April 7, 1908, DuBose Papers, Archives, the University of the South, Sewanee.

81. William P. DuBose to Felix Adler, August 21, 1917, DuBose Papers, Archives, the University of the South, Sewanee. DuBose probably became acquainted with Dr. Adler through DuBose's student Edgar Gardner Murphy; see Luker, *A Southern Tradition*, pp. 338–341. For Adler see Benny Kraut, *From Reformed Judaism to Ethical Culture: The Religious Evolution of Felix Adler* (Cincinnati: Hebrew Union College Press, 1979).

82. Saint Thomas was selected rather than the American Roman Catholic theologian, Francis P. Kenrick, because Kenrick's *Theologica Dogmatica* (1834–40) is not available in English or in most libraries. Using Kenrick for comparison would have produced different results, in my opinion, because the *Theologica Dogmatica,* while patterned on St. Thomas is Suarezian, less Aristotelian, and less teleological than St. Thomas.

83. Charles Hodge, *Systematic Theology,* 3 vols. (Grand Rapids: William B. Eerdmans Publishing Co., 1981/1871), 2:129, 255, 278–309. Citation of the *Summa Theologica* will be by part, question, and article so that any edition may be used. The best English translation is the Blackfriars Edition, 65 vols. (New York: McGraw-Hill Book Co., 1964). *Summa Theologica* I-II, q. 6, a. 1; I, q. 98, a. 2. The effect of the fall for St. Thomas has been compared to removing the conductor from an orchestra. Each musician can play but they can't make music together. For Hodge the conductor is absent, the musicians on strike, and the instruments broken.

84. Hodge, *Systematic Theology,* 2:480, 495–96, 3:117–120; Aquinas, *Summa* III, q. 24, a. 3. St. Thomas's view of predestination differs from Hodge's in that for Thomas predestination does not affect the natural faculties (*Summa* I, q. 23).

85. However, St. Thomas is more processive than Hodge. For an excellent recent study of St. Thomas's spirituality see Walter H. Principe, "Thomas Aquinas's Spirituality," The Etienne Gilson Series, no. 7 (Toronto: Pontifical Institute of Medieval Studies, 1984), pp. 10–26.

86. Hodge, *Systematic Theology,* 2:430–31, 437. Hodge died in 1878 before DuBose's system was published, but Hodge's disciple, Benjamin B. Warfield, was critical of DuBose's approach in his review of *The Gospel in the Gospels, Princeton Theological Review* 5 (October, 1907): 690–697. St. Thomas, *Summa* III, q. 9, a. 4; III, q. 7, a. 12.

87. Warfield, "Review of *The Gospel in the Gospels*," noted that DuBose did not give the full Gospel; Beryl Smalley, *The Study of the Bible in the Middle Ages* (Oxford: Clarendon Press, 1941).

88. Joseph Perrier, *The Revival of Scholastic Philosophy* . . . (New York: Columbia University Press, 1909) lists the authors to 1907; Edward Pace, "The Soul in the System of St. Thomas," *Catholic University Bulletin* 4 (1898): 50–61; Ralph E. Weber, *Notre Dame's John Zahm* (Notre Dame: Notre Dame University Press, 1961), p. 107.

89. Kezar, "Many Sons," pp. 365, 379–388. See for example Donald G. Bloesch, *Essentials of Evangelical Theology*, 2 vols. (New York: Harper and Row, 1982).

90. In his magisterial study "Cultural Strain and Protestant Liberalism," *American Historical Review* 76 (1971): 386–411, William R. Hutchison notes that one criterion for inclusion in that study was "explicit commitment for or against that movement in Protestantism known initially as the New Theology and later as Protestant Liberalism" (p. 410). Professor Hutchison informs me that DuBose was not included in his study because "he had a foot in liberalism and a foot in more conservative traditions." This is just the way DuBose appears in my opinion. I wish to acknowledge the generosity of Professor Hutchison in responding to my inquiry about his classification of DuBose for his study.

91. "Thomas Aquinas" is the last chapter in Adams's *Mont Saint-Michel and Chartres* (Boston: Houghton Mifflin Co., 1926/1904), pp. 347–383; *The Education of Henry Adams*, ed. Ernest Samuels (Boston: Houghton Mifflin Co., 1976/1918), p. 294ff. On Memorial Hall see Samuel Eliot Morison, *Three Centuries of Harvard 1636–1936* (Cambridge: Harvard University Press, 1936), p. 332; *Education*, p. 317.

92. William James, *The Varieties of Religious Experience: A Study in Human Nature* (New York: Longmans, Green, and Co., 1902), pp. 160–61; William James to Mrs. James, July 9, 1898, in *The Letters of William James*, ed. Henry James, 2 vols. (Boston: The Atlantic Monthly Press, 1920), 2:75–76. The experience of having one's world repudiated by conquest and swept aside by force is not a majority experience in the United States. It was the experience of the aristocracy of the Old South, immigrant emigrés, and to a greater extent, the experience of Native Americans, Mexican citizens in the areas annexed in 1848, and Africans captured and brought to America in bondage.

93. DuBose, "Wade Hampton," p. 365. Many liberals saw the world called to judgment and in need of reform, but this was not a final judgment. See William R. Hutchison, *The Modernist Impulse in American Protestantism* (New York: Oxford University Press, 1982/1976), pp. 185–225.

94. William Newton Clarke, *Sixty Years With the Bible: A Record of*

Experience (New York: Charles Scribner's Sons, 1912); Newman Smyth *Recollections and Reflections* (New York: Charles Scribner's Sons, 1926); Clarke, *Sixty Years,* pp. 110–120; Clarke, *An Outline of Christian Theology,* 17th ed. (Edinburgh: T. and T. Clark, 1908), pp. 131–132, 349–360, 305–308; *Sixty Years,* pp. 183, 120. DuBose affirmed justification by faith, but for DuBose part of justification is the process of actualization. To my reading, Clarke's view is closer to Luther's "simultaneously justified and sinner." That actualization is not central to the Lutheran view as it is for DuBose can be seen by particularizing the language "simultaneously justified and sinner" to simultaneously chaste and promiscuous.

95. Smyth, *Recollections,* pp. 57–75, 89–96; Smyth, *Passing Protestantism and Coming Catholicism* (New York: Charles Scribner's Sons, 1908), pp. 171–172; *Recollections,* pp. 75, 198.

96. Kezar, "Many Sons," pp. 379–389.

97. Claude Welch, *Protestant Thought in the Nineteenth Century,* 2 vols. (New Haven: Yale University Press, 1972–1985). Lucian Price mentions in *The Dialogues of Alfred North Whitehead* (Boston: Little and Brown, 1954), pp. 9, 151, that Whitehead read theology in the 1890's when DuBose's books were receiving favorable reviews in the British press. Whitehead's publications after he moved to the United States in 1924 are widely considered a major impetus to process theology in America. Unfortunately, it does not seem possible to determine if Whitehead read DuBose. See Lewis S. Ford, *The Emergence of Whitehead's Metaphysics* (Albany: SUNY Press, 1984), and Victor Lowe, *Alfred North Whitehead The Man and His Work: 1861–1910* (Baltimore: The Johns Hopkins University Press, 1985). Both Professors Ford and Lowe generously responded to my inquiries that they know of no record of the theological books Whitehead read. Professor Ford noted that "Whatever theology W read seems to have affected him adversely."

98. *A DuBose Reader: Selections from the Writings of William Porcher DuBose,* ed. and intro. Donald S. Armentrout (Sewanee: The University of the South, 1984).

I.

TURNING POINTS IN MY LIFE (1912)*

The University of the South held a reunion in DuBose's honor in 1911. DuBose delivered three autobiographical lectures which constitute a retrospective reflection on his spiritual odyssey to this gathering of former students and friends. Turning Points in My Life, the last book DuBose published in his lifetime, had its genesis at this reunion. In preparing his autobiographical lectures for publication, DuBose made some additions to the lectures and added a fourth lecture on his experiences in the Civil War. He included the sermon he delivered at the reunion and two occasional papers to round out the volume. Each of the original three autobiographical lectures became a chapter in Turning Points, and the new material on DuBose's Civil War experiences was placed in chronological order as chapter two between the original first and second lectures. Because most of DuBose's description of his war experiences is not directly relevant to his spiritual odyssey, it was decided to incorporate those portions of chapter two of Turning Points that concern DuBose's spiritual development in the introduction to this volume, and to reprint chapters one, three, and four of Turning Points, or the original three lectures describing DuBose's Evangelical, Churchly, and Catholic phases, in their entirety.

I. EARLY SPIRITUAL LIFE

I am here today, in my old home and in my so long accustomed seat, not as a host but as a guest. I come at the instance and by the

---

* The original text that follows is from *Turning Points in My Life* (New York: Longmans, Green, and Co, 1912), pp. 13–32, 53–93.

invitation of those who were my sometime pupils and followers—
some of whom have become in the most real sense my leaders and
teachers. I have most carefully pondered all the terms in which the
request to me to be here has been variously expressed, with this desire: that what I may have to supply or contribute to the purpose of
our reunion may be as nearly as possible conformed to the demand.
I have been asked, first, to sit here, in this old seat, for several con-
secutive days, and talk just as I used to talk to you just as you used
to be. That is, perhaps, in many ways the most impossible form in
which the request has come to me. But in the one way in which it
was felt and meant, I am going to try my best to comply with it.

It has been said again, or hoped, that I should, at this our last
session together, sum up and put as it were into a nutshell the special
truth, the definite lesson of life, which I was for thirty-six years en-
deavoring, with your help, to learn and to teach. Yet again, it was
suggested, not at all inappropriately considering my threescore years
and fifteen, that I was to give my last counsels for the time, and the
times to come.

You may imagine that a call such as this has awakened long,
long thoughts in me, both of the past and of the future. It has made
me live my life over and ask: What has it been for me and for others?
I have nothing to give you but what I myself have got. We can never
really give to others anything but what is ours and ourselves. And
now as we meet in this relation for the last time, I ask myself: What
has life given me—what has it given me that I have taken and that I
have—that I may give you, if you will take it? Reflections such as
these have led me to take as the subject of the three lectures this
week: The Lesson of my Life—or, perhaps better, Lessons from my
Life. What I mean is: the lesson or lessons that life has taught me,
and that may perchance be of help and use to you. I am very far from
thinking that my life is the properest life, or the properest thing, to
present to you; but it is the only life and the only thing that is mine
to give: such as I have, give I unto you.

I have another motive in the selection of this subject. This is a
personal reunion, a fellowship of souls, and not a comparison of
views or clash of opinions. As to these latter we are of all sorts, but
we come together to illustrate the unity of life that lies down underneath the infinite diversities of thought or view or human expression.
This is a social gathering, and let nothing be lacking to it of the light

or the graceful or the playful that properly adorns the surface of all pure human social intercourse. But first of all let us secure that unity of the spirit which will make our fellowship together a fellowship too with the Father and with the Son. The Life was manifested, and we have seen it and know it, and all our fellowship is with it and in it.

I have always spoken from myself, but I have never spoken of myself. It is not easy for me to do so now, and I do it only in the privacy of this old class, always changing yet always here with me through all the years that I was here. I speak then in the intimacy and the confidence of those whom I know and trust, and who know me. In the course of nearly sixty years of actual and conscious spiritual experience and observation, I have touched and felt Christianity on pretty much all the sides which during that time it has presented to us. I could not recall or portray myself except in all those several aspects or phases, and in such a composite, or I should say unity, of them all as I am now conscious of in myself. In describing my life then, I shall do it in three lectures: (1) as Evangelical, (2) as Churchly, and (3) as Catholic (*in the widest sense*), these being distinctly phases, and not stages.

It has been said that life is really lived, and is itself, only in its supreme moments: only the gods can sustain it continuously at its height. I don't know that any of us can claim to have attained to supreme moments. At any rate we have had superior, or relatively supreme ones; and of some such I will speak, but only of such as were not only what they were at the time, but have been with me since, and are in me still. I think that you will agree, when I have described its moments, that my conscious, voluntary religious life, beginning say at eighteen, was distinctively of the type that we have called evangelical.

I was born and bred in the Church, and brought up religiously in what St. Paul calls the nurture and admonition of the Lord. No life, natural or spiritual, is of ourselves, and it is impossible to tell just when and how it begins. Its causes, influences, and processes are in operation before our consciousness of it awakens. I cannot say when religion in me began; but I am now concerned only with the rise and progress in myself of conscious and voluntary religion. Whatever be my own theory of Christian nurture, and of the imperceptible and continuous genesis and growth of spiritual life under it, as a matter of fact my own, at least conscious, life began with a crisis—with what had all the appearance of a sudden and instantaneous conversion. It has been with me a life-long matter of scientific as well as religious interest to analyze and understand that experience. More and more, as I grow older, I live over again through every minutest detail of it and apply anew to myself what I know to be the eternal and essential truth and meaning of it. In this day of the attempted scientific verification of spiritual as well as other phenomena, I should not hesitate among just ourselves to submit to you all the facts in this case, as they are still indelibly fixed in my memory— if only we had time. As it is, I will narrate only the essential points. Three cadets, returning from a long march and series of encampments, and a brief stoppage at their common home, spent on their way back to their garrison a night in a certain city, and returned at midnight hilarious and weary from what was called a ''roaring farce'' at the little theatre, to occupy one bed at the crowded hotel. In a moment the others were in bed and asleep. There was no apparent reason why I should not have been so too, or why it should just then have occurred to me that I had not of late been saying my prayers. Perfectly unconscious and unsuspicious of anything unusual, I knelt to go through the form, when of a sudden there swept over me a feeling of the emptiness and unmeaningness of the act and of my whole life and self. I leapt to my feet trembling, and then that happened which I can only describe by saying that a light shone about me and a Presence filled the room. At the same time an ineffable joy and peace took possession of me which it is impossible either to express or explain. I continued I know not how long, perfectly conscious of, simply but intensely feeling, the Presence, and fearful, by any movement, of breaking the spell. I went to sleep at last praying that it was no passing illusion, but that I should awake to find it an abiding reality. It proved so, and now let me say what of verification my life has given to the objective reality of that appearance or manifestation.

God has His ways of coming to us, of entering into our world and into our life and making them new: heaven is with us when our eyes are open to see it. There is only one earthly and very far-off analogy which God Himself uses and we may therefore venture modestly to use. There comes to a man the love of a woman, which is different in kind from any other human love. It comes for a reason and with a meaning, for the endless ends of a relation which is the highest and holiest that can exist between mortals, and that is the earthly source and spring of all other human relations and of all human life. What we call "falling in love" comes to us just as naturally and just as mysteriously and inexplicably as that other only more spiritual experience of which the Lord says: "The wind bloweth where it listeth, and thou hearest the sound thereof, but canst not tell whence it cometh or whither it goeth: so is every one that is born of the Spirit." The human love comes simply because of the fact that the man is made for the woman and the woman for the man, and neither is complete or satisfied without the other. The divine love in which God makes Himself one with us comes simply for the reason, and because of the fact, so perfectly expressed in the ever new old words: "My God Thou hast made me for Thyself, and my soul will find no rest, until it rest in Thee."

My proof, I may say my verification, of the fact of God's coming to me, apart from all mystery of the way, may be expressed in this simple truth of experience, that in finding Him I found myself: a man's own self, when he has once truly come to himself, is his best and only experimental proof of God. The act of the Prodigal's "coming to himself" was also that of his arising and returning to his Father.

As this was the beginning of my awakened and actualized spiritual life, and must be supposed to have contained in it the potencies and promise of all that was to be, I have sought to recall just what, at the time, there was in it. And the first thing that strikes me was its lack of explicitness: so little was there in it of the definite and defined features of Christianity, that it would scarcely seem to have been as yet distinctively Christian. Of course I knew my catechism and was familiar and in sympathy with the letter of Christianity, but I am tracing my religion now solely as it became the living and operative fact and factor of my actual spiritual being. There was then no conscious sense of sin, nor repentance, nor realization of the meaning of the Cross, or of the Resurrection, or of the Church or the Sacraments, nor indeed of the Incarnation or of Christ Himself. What then was there?—There was simply a New World without me, and a New Self in me—in both which for the first time, visibly, sensibly, really, God was. In just that, was there already implicitly and potentially included the principle and truth of Regeneration, Resurrection, and

Eternal Life, of the putting and passing away of old things and the
coming to pass of new, of the as yet hidden meaning of the Cross,
of the heavy cost to both God and man of the only possible or real
human redemption? To instance in a single item: I for a long time
thought it strange that in my conversion, if that was it, there was with
me so little conscious thought or conviction of sin. But then, also, I
recalled that there had been a previous state of self-dissatisfaction,
which however had been all swallowed up and lost in the consciousness of being lifted out of it into a new life of love and life and holiness. Had there not been implicit repentance and faith, although I
did not yet know in them all the death upon the Cross of the one, or
all the life from out the grave of the other? I recalled also that when,
after the spiritual crisis, I returned to my natural habits and duties,
the form which the intervening change in me assumed was mainly
that of a sensitized and transfigured—not only consciousness, but—
conscience. I had a sense of walking in the light, and of at least desiring and intending to have no darkness in me at all. I can perfectly
recall the ways and even the little instances in which this disposition
manifested itself. The task of materializing or actualizing that as yet
only ideal, of embodying the sentiment of it into habit and character
and life, I was indeed far enough from realizing. But were not the
principle and the potency of the whole already present and operative
in me?

The moral so far I would draw in passing is this: the spiritual
irrationality and impossibility of extorting from converts or begin-
ners, or indeed of Christians all, any true or real confession of the
sum total or detailed contents of Christianity. The articles of the
Creed may properly be required to be repeated for entrance into the
Church, but only so as they are outwardly confessed and accepted as
being the historic, organic, and developed faith of the Church, and
assuredly not as all digested, assimilated, and converted into the actual life of the incipient member. In other words, there is a great deal
which we may outwardly confess as *the faith,* which we rightly hold
on the reasonable external authority of corporate and historical
Christianity, which nevertheless to be compelled to profess, as in its
totality our personal subjective actual and attained faith, would simply involve us in either self-deception or hypocrisy. On the other
hand, I shall endeavor by my own example to justify the humble acceptance of the Church's faith in the beginning, and then the life-

time process, as one can, of gradually digesting, assimilating, and converting that faith into one's own, and finding in it the full food and content of one's life. But to exact of every Christian at every moment full conversion to every item or every particular of even the essentials of a complete Christianity is no more a Christian procedure than it was that of Jesus Christ Himself.

I do not wish to lose sight of the fact that, in even so inchoate a conversion and faith as that I am describing, there was, however implicit, the reality of a distinctly Christian life. The God into living relation with Whom it brought the soul was none other than just the God and Father of our Lord Jesus Christ. God has been always in the world, and there has always been in the world a less or more true conception and knowledge of God, but the only full and real God of the soul is the God of Christianity. The soul of man is our only ultimate judge of what is true of or in God, and that for the reason that the human soul and God are correspondent and correlative entities and energies. That is God, in correspondence with Whom the soul is its complete and perfect self; and that is the soul, in which God most truly and completely realizes and reproduces Himself. At the very beginning and ever since, my one all-sufficient evidence of God and of religion has been this: that in Him and in it, and nowhere else, am I my own truest and best self; the better and more closely I know Him, the truer, better, and higher I am, and the reverse: when I least believe is always when I am at my lowest and my worst. If we are to judge truth by the principle of "values," then that which puts the most reason and meaning, the most fulness and blessedness, the most worth and consistence and permanence into human life, is in itself the truest. My conversion made me a worthier and higher self, and my life a more valuable and a happier life: and the more that is the case, the more I know it to be true.

Not only is there the distinctively Christian's God in such an experience, but the most developed Christian doctrine of the status and relation between the soul and God is likewise implicitly presupposed and involved in it: we are reconciled, justified, at-one-d, and made one with God—not by any act or work or merit of our mere selves, but only by placing ourselves within and identifying ourselves with the love, the grace, the fellowship with us, of God Himself. The little child, no matter how weak, how bad, whatever it be, finds not only love and peace and rest, but hope and fresh strength and new beginnings of life in the bosom of its mother. And to come to God "just as we are," not waiting to be good, and find in Him, in His eternal love, His infinite grace, His perfect fellowship, all we want for holiness, for righteousness, and for eternal life, is only a simple way of putting all the vexed doctrine or dogma of justification by faith.

Once more, this may seem, so far, that merely personal religion which is in terms the opposite of what religion means: "God and the soul, the soul and its God!" And I must confess that for long that was all that was in it for me. I wanted to keep it all to myself, to hide it as much as possible from all others. Yet at the very time I was to all others, as well as to myself, better and more than I had ever been before. In fact I was, so far as I can measure, never after so communicative to others of the good I was receiving and estimating for myself as in that time in which I was least presuming—nor, I fear, caring—to help or save others. In every one of three acknowledgments from fellow-students, which I can never forget, of what I had been to them in their college lives,—when I had to plead guiltless of any intention or even conscious will to help them, the answer was that it was just that, that if I had ever interfered even in thought to do them good, I should have failed to do it. There is this of truth in that, that we help or hinder others most in and by what we are, and not by what we say or do. Know God and yourself, be true to God and yourself, and you will be to others all that you are to God and yourself. For when you truly come to look for God and yourself, you will never find them in yourself for long, but only in others.

I am telling the story of my evangelical, not yet of my high-church or my broad-church self. During my university life I did little more than hold fast that whereunto I had attained. I was busy, under physical difficulties and discouragements, with my mental work; spiritually I was, as it were, marking time,—that is, keeping up the motions without much forward movement. And it is not my desire to record anything else than actual steps forward, permanent and integral additions to my spiritual self and life. When I passed from university to seminary and took up directly the study of religion and of Christianity, I did so not without what I am a little disposed to call pietism,—but will not, because I think it was not altogether unworthy of the better term piety. But still my religion was very much in myself, and there very much in idea and sentiment. I think that with me naturally idea is more than sentiment, I am rather disposed to be ideal than sentimental. But at that time certain things, most of all music, moved me very deeply and always religiously. Under the spell of such coöperant emotion my mind was very active with its ideals and speculations.

I remember just at that period a singularly trifling incident which nevertheless in its effect has been present with me as an actual force for fifty years. What a very little spark may kindle the most destructive conflagration, or sometimes the most illuminating and beneficent flame! In this case so ridiculous a suggestion could not have awakened so lasting a train of thought and consequence if the occasion and material had not been ripe and ready for it. In an idle moment I chanced to pick up an old magazine in which were narrated the military experiences and exploits of a certain Lieutenant Poop. His Christian name was Ninkum—Mr. Ninkum Poop. First, in most descriptive and expressive terms, were elaborated and described the heroically high and noble ideals and sentiments with which the newly fledged lieutenant devoted himself to the sacred service of his country, the great British Empire,—what aspirations, what hopes and expectations and high-wrought purposes, what dreams and visions of self-sacrifice, and then of honor and greatness and glory! Lieutenant Ninkum Poop arrives at the seat of war, where all his ideas are to be put into action and all his sentiments to be converted into conduct and character and achievement. He goes through it all, his thoughts and expressions to the end swelling with the magnanimity of the great-souled, his actions on the contrary evincing only the pusillanimity of the little-souled, the coward and the poltroon.

I would not tell this simply as the undignified illustration of a principle; I give it as an historical life-moment and life-movement in my spiritual history. That arrow went home and still rankles in my breast. I cannot tell how often I have found and called myself a Ninkum Poop; how often, in very other terms, I have preached the fact it illustrates to myself and others:—that life is not life as long as it is only in the mind, or even in the heart; that it is only life when it has been converted into life. Christianity has only begun when it begins to live what it believes and what it feels: "If ye know these things, blessed are you if ye do them." Have we the Christianity that does what it says, that practises what it preaches? What we want is not to have a new Christianity, but to have a new way of having

Christianity: a new way which is the old one, the way of Him who was, and still is, the Way. He is not alone in Himself the truth and the life, but no less the way to us of really knowing the truth and living the life.

There was nothing to me for some time in seminary life beyond pleasant association and useful routine work. The first thing that touched and really set going the forward movement of life and thought in me came in the form of provocation from a fellow-student. There was in our diocese at that time a centre and school of Calvinistic low-churchmanship, over against another party of moderate anti-Calvinistic high-churchmanship. An intelligent and aggressive theological student of the former school had gone to Princeton to find there under the Hodges and Alexanders of that day meat strong enough for his spiritual pabulum, and had then been brought home by the Bishop to spend his senior year at our seminary, where we were entering as juniors. Being fresh from the university and more immediately at home in Greek than the rest of us, I was drawn by our senior friend into the question whether the language and argument of St. Paul did not necessitate all the essential principles, the five points, of Calvinism. It is impossible to overstate the difficulties and perplexities into which I was thus led for several years to come, and the results in all my future thinking and teaching. It soon passed with me beyond the mere issue or question of Calvinism, to which, as you know, I have never reverted; although, as a living question in that day, it did sorely try me until, having absorbed what of truth and of discipline I found in it, I had passed beyond into higher unities and reconciliations. But at the time I encountered and had to overcome this temptation: We are often enough tempted to believe what antecedent prejudice or inclination makes us wish to believe. Sometimes a strained honesty compels us to accept what we do not wish to believe, as a heroic sacrifice of inclination or prejudice. I asked myself, Am I prepared to make the necessary sacrifice in order to follow the truth wherever it may lead me? And I came near identifying that query with this one, Am I strong enough and selfless enough to accept Calvinism? Whereas it should have been this, Am I open and prepared to accept Calvinism if it is indeed, and I fairly find it to be, the truth?

But the permanent profit of that experience was that it made me such a life-long student and companion of St. Paul's faith and life, as has really determined my whole subsequent character and career. How that disposition and bent was intensified and fixed in me by the long interruption and peculiar circumstance of the war, which followed immediately upon this phase of my spiritual experience, I must reserve for another chapter.

2. CHURCHLY INFLUENCES

It will be agreed, I think, that my life as so far described was evangelical in its general type and character. It turned upon a well-defined experience of conversion; it was fed and grew upon the Bible; it was essentially a life of subjective, reflective, personal religion. Whatever may be said of evangelicalism, it was in possession of our spiritual world of that time; and with whatever may be its limitations we owe much if not most of our good to it. But however evangelical I was, and am, and would ever more and more be, I was never, either by prejudice or in principle, in sympathy with evangelicalism—that is to say, with the *ism,* with the name or the thing, as badge or confession of a school or a party. I love its affirmation and emphasis of great truths, but not its dissents, denials, and contradictions of other truths, or sides of truth, contradictory perhaps of itself, but not of its own truth, or of the wider, higher, greater All of truth.

Brought at the beginning under the influence of the most beautiful, refined, and attractive phase of the newer Oxford Movement, I entered upon life with all prepossession in its favor, with all the poetry, romance, and loyalty of my nature enlisted on its side. Before any knowledge, or with little realization, of what the Church is, I was with all my heart and soul a churchman and disposed in favor of everything that is churchly. Call this prejudice, if you please, but one is not improperly or injuriously prejudiced in favor of his home, his own, his native land, the truth or beauty or beneficence into which he has been born. How much of what we are have we received as an heritage and do we rightly and necessarily reverence and value as such! When I was awaked to the more actual assumption of my spiritual selfhood, the older evangelical type took possession, and I cannot say that there was much of the Church visible or sensible in the change that I was conscious of. Nevertheless, there was no discrepancy or contradiction, and my conversion carried with it only an access and heightening of at least the sentiment and inspiration of the new churchmanship: I was not any the less for it a high-churchman. And I am now to trace the help and contribution to my life of this high and loyal sentiment for the Church. Let it be remembered that if the Church was not to me at that time the broad and all-inclusive thing that it is, neither was it the narrow and exclusive thing that it might have seemed to be. In fact I knew little of either the inclusiveness or the exclusiveness: the Church was to me simply the divine institution that claimed and attracted all the fealty and devotion of my heart, mind, soul, and life. The more divine it could be made to appear, the more willing and satisfied was my loyalty.

We all find contradictions in ourselves hard to reconcile and unify. My heart is very disposed to faith, to recognition of truth, to trust, and consent, and agreement. But my mind is naturally analytic and sceptical. I have all my life been coming to what of truth I hold, and there is truth to which I have all my life been coming, to which I have not yet come. All the truth of the Church is not yet mine: there are points of it that I know to be true, because I have been all the time approximating to them; but I am still waiting, and shall probably die waiting, for them to become true to me. Truth is not an individual thing; no one of us has all of it—even all of it that is known. Truth is a corporate possession, and the knowledge of it is a corporate process. It enters slowly and painfully into the common sense, the common experience, the common use and life of men. There is a corporate, catholic, Christianity, actually extant on this earth, which no one or no set of us holds all of, or perfectly even what we do hold. Christianity, even so far as actualized in the world, is more and greater than any one or any body of us, and the full actualization of Christianity will come only with the fruition of the world's destiny, in the end of the ages. When a man learns that, he will be modest either about his own truth or about impugning other people's truth.

Without at all defining its meaning or measuring its universality or its authority, I realized from the first that there is a Church, and that there is a faith of the Church, to which my loyalty never wavered, even when I was freely and deliberately setting myself, in the light of it, to determine and establish my own individual and personal faith. I have long since discovered that the actual historical process by which the faith of the Church was originally formulated is the natural and logical process by which the eternal, divine and human, truth of Jesus Christ necessarily defines, defends, and verifies itself in our human experience. My own mind like that of the Church, and under the guidance of the Church, passed successively and in the same order through all the heresies. I was never historian enough to justify my undertaking, as I did twenty odd years ago, to tell the story of the Great Councils, the period of the settlement of the Catholic faith. I was tempted to do so by my interest and my studies in the "Development of the Doctrine of the Person of Christ." The history in my book was second-hand, but the description of the process of evolution of the doctrine was my own. Dorner's great work is an analysis of all living and serious thought on the subject from the beginning down to his own time. The mass of it was too great for my digestion, but I felt more and more the unity, continuity, and inevitable outcome of all truth in the theme, and was under the necessity of ordering my own thought and bringing out my own faith, so far as it had reached. I am convinced in my own mind, beyond all question, that the evolution of interpretation and expression of the truth of Jesus Christ to the end of the Sixth General Council was in the straight line to the inevitable end. I am standing now for absolutely nothing in the Councils but the simple outcome of expression of faith in the one truth of the union and unity of the divine and the human in the one Person of Jesus Christ. After that Council thought ceased, and faith receded to its stage even before Chalcedon. Much of what had been gained for the completeness of the humanity of our Lord was lost, and Christianity became too much a one-sided worship of deity made visible for adoration under the eikon or semblance of humanity. To me the necessary deity of our Lord is there to a thousandfold more purpose and effect in the actual, realized, and deified humanity in which we recognize all ourselves and accomplish all our destiny.

Truth is not truth when it ceases to be plastic, and faith is faith only in the making. We cannot simply receive it, for then it is not yet ours; and we can never finish making it, for it ends only in all truth and all knowledge of the truth.

I can accept the Church's, or the Catholic, Creed; and could with good conscience accept it, even though it were not yet all my own creed, or though I could not see my way to ever making all the incidents or details of it my own. Shall Christ not be mine, and I His, because I cannot see all the steps of my way to Him?—or all the steps of His way to me? On the other hand, to exact of a man, at any stage, an *ex animo* acceptance of every point of the Creed, the incidental as the essential, is to demand that which is for any man an impossibility. A complete personal possession of faith, like a perfect personal conversion of life, is an impossibility at any time and certainly at the beginning of the spiritual life. We may confess the faith as the Church's faith and profess the life as the Church's life, but to start out with saying that either of them is all personally ours is either ignorance or hypocrisy. On the one hand, therefore, I would say that for one to suppose that, because the general or catholic creed of the Church is not in every point and particular, in every interpretation or understanding of it, his own personal and actual creed, he has therefore at once to teach or preach against it, or else so to avow and proclaim his dissent as to read himself or be read out of the Church, is illogical and unreasonable. And on the other hand, I should say that for the Church to require and demand that, *ipso facto* and *instanter,* her fully developed and complete creed should be *ex animo* and in every jot and tittle the personal and actual creed of every member, or of any member, is equally irrational and impossible. There ought to be, at the least, as much of divine patience and tenderness on the part of the Church toward the incomplete and even the wilful believer, as there ought to be of modest deference and obedience on the part of the individual believer to the reasonable and rightful authority of the Church.

For my part I have never balked at the raw beginning nor on the uncertain way of faith; I have both pressed on and waited until I could get something of a general view of the end and purport of it all. The creeds mean the truth, the whole truth, and nothing but the truth—the truth of God and of man, and of the eternal, predestined, realized relation between them. Since I have seen that, nothing else has disturbed or bothered me. Either what is crooked in the Church's way of putting it shall be made straight in time—and I do not say that it is not the business of any one of us that can to help make it straight; only let us go about it in the right spirit and way, and in the meantime be modest and patient about it, and take and make use of what we have got—or else, if the fault or defect is in us, the right use of the part we have got will be the best way to the fuller revelation to us of the whole of truth.

My own churchmanship, as it happened, did not come to me through Oxford or Anglican sources. I have mentioned how my mind got turned into German channels; there too I discovered and equally followed different bents or leadings. There was, on the one hand, the pure and high spirituality, the personal subjectivism of a Neander; and, on the other, the more objective and churchly, or corporate, but not less spiritual, tendency of an Olshausen. Both of these entered simultaneously into my life, and I felt no discrepancy between them. While the Oxford revival was in progress there was a corresponding "churchly" movement going on in Germany. It extended to this country within the German Reformed, or Calvinistic, Church, became more emphasized and defined under one or two famous leaders, and gave place and name to what was called the *Mercersberg Theology*. This attracted me as dealing with the Church less as an external fact and authority, and more as a necessary principle and a true philosophy.

The churchly principle begins with Christianity, not as a human faith, but as a divine fact, an actual and present life of God upon earth and among men. Faith is indeed an actual necessity for us, but it is necessary only as our appropriation and experience of a prior fact; and the fact must be kept always prior to the faith, the divine conveyance to the human reception. If the extreme and danger of churchliness is a one-sided objectivism, that of evangelicalism is a one-sided subjectivism. Man has not created God in his own image; and as little is Jesus Christ a human creation or production, a human ideal or imagination of what God with us and in us would or should be. Incarnation is just as much a divine act and fact antecedent to our faith in it as creation is a divine act and fact anterior to our sensible experience of it.

Incarnation, again, is not the mere revelation or manifestation of a Life in Jesus Christ; it is the gift and communication of life in Jesus Christ. Its end and operation is not realized and exhausted in the individual human person of Jesus Christ; it is in operation and to be realized in that Mystical Body which is Humanity realized and glorified in and through Him. Consequently the Church is in a true sense Jesus Christ Himself, and relation to it is relation to Him and to the divine Life which He is. The Church is the Life incorporate and corporate in Jesus Christ. The Sacraments of life, or of The Life, are acts not of man but of God, the acts of His incorporation of us into Christ. They are not expressions of our faith but of the divine acts of grace and adoption in Christ which are the objects of our faith and in which our faith stands. When Luther says that Christianity is the simple realization of our baptism, what he means is, not that we are magnifying a mere form or rite, but that we recognize in that rite of divine appointment a word and act of God to our souls. God's words are never mere signs: they are what they mean. To realize our baptism is to see in it, and appropriate to ourselves, and make real in our lives, the thing and the whole thing signified by it. The way not to be formalists is not to reject form—certainly not divinely ordained form—but to see in it only the spirit which it expresses and conveys. The Sacraments, if they are anything, are divine means of grace; and the grace meant by them and wrought through them is the presence and spirit and life of Christ born in us and made ours in baptism and fed, strengthened, and refreshed in us in that sacred and stated feast in which we have communion and fellowship, actual participation of common life with God and with one another in Christ, through His Spirit which is given us. Is it formalism to see and receive all this in the Sacrament?—or is it not rather so to take the Sacrament because it is divinely commanded, but to see in it nothing but a form?

There is a catholic faith in Christianity; but prior to the faith, and the ground and object and content of the faith, there is a catholic life, and that life is the present, living, working Life of God of which the Church is the divine embodiment, the vital organ and organism, and the Sacraments the organic means and channels. When Dean Stanley said that we outgrow Sacraments, and that they are becoming obsolete, the one side of me recognizes in that a certain, perhaps, truth for spirits such as his; but I am glad that the other, the corporate or churchly side of me, has kept me loyal and faithful long enough to know that in the Sacraments I am living at the very perennial springs and fountains themselves of the Life which is Christ.

Upon the revival of life and reality in the Church and the sacraments there followed necessarily a rehabilitation of divine worship. We must not confound the true revival of ritual with the excesses and follies of a shallow ritualism any more than any other truth or reality with its attendant *ism*—evangelical life with the narrowness of evangelicalism, or the regeneration of the Church with the extremes of Tractarianism. The lawlessnesses and abuses of ritualism are but the foam and scum upon the surface of a very real and true undercurrent and movement of genuine Church life. When I came to Sewanee, I came ignorant and inexperienced in all the fermentation that was then coming to its height in these matters. My one sympathy with the movement that I felt coming might be expressed in these words: The need of more reality in life and in religion, a more actual and real presence of God in His world, of Christ in His Church, of Spirit and power in what were too much become to us mere obligatory forms. I remember writing to a friend on my way to Sewanee, in reply to some questioning about the "Real Presence," that I wanted all the Real Presence, all the "objective" Real Presence, I could get in every act of my religion.

Again, we must not confound the fact or reality of the Real Presence, in the Church, in the sacraments, or anywhere else, with the logomachies or the superstitions as to the modes or the effects of the presence. What I have wished, and wish, to see at Sewanee, as a religious and educational centre, is a high, dignified, and truly typical worship, fully expressive of the reality with which we are dealing and of what we are doing; neither manifesting by our carelessness and indifference our contempt of or superiority to forms, nor, on the other hand, supposing that we have to be oriental or Latin in our exhibitions of reverence. If there were a ritual exactly and distinctively expressive of the truest and most real reverence of our race, it would be a simple and severe one. We are least demonstrative when we think the most seriously and feel the most deeply, and least of all in matters the most sacred. At the same time, the highest good manners in the world are those that show themselves in the presence of divine realities.

As there is a catholic faith and a catholic life and worship, in all which there is an underlying and pervading unity which is their essence and content and of which they are but the expression, so there must be in the Church, if it is one also in effective operation, a catholic order. That the order of the Church, as well as its faith and even its life, is so often and so much broken and divided, and so little at one with itself, proves nothing against this truth. Christianity, the Unity of humanity with and in God, is an ideal which is not *ipso facto* an actuality; but it is an ideal which it is our whole Christian business in this world, as much as we can and as fast as we can, to bring to actuality. What is an ideal but an end and a goal, and what is the

Christian ideal of a Unity which will be in and of itself all of Holiness and Righteousness and Eternal Life, but an end and a goal which we have the divinest warrant and evidence for believing shall be our inheritance and destiny, just so fast and so soon as we, in faith and obedience, will enter into and possess it? The Church is an organism which must of necessity organize itself for the ends of its proper function and business. Its commission is one and its mission is one, and it must itself be one in order to carry the one or discharge the other; the more so too since its commission and mission is to reconcile, at-one, or unify, the world with God, and with itself in God: "God was in Christ reconciling the world with Himself, and hath committed unto us the ministry of reconciliation."

If there is to be in the Church of Christ, as one, any unity, not alone of faith and life, but of order or organization or operation, of influence and effect upon the world, there must be in it some principle and law of order. What that is, or is to be, when the Church is in any organic sense or degree one again, although it must always have been a truth and duty of the past too, is just now the question of the future. The answer to it will have to be submitted to a longer and larger tribunal than is now extant. The several answers that may be already on hand, or even any new ones that are worthy of consideration, in the great solution that lies before us ought to be both urged and considered only in love and amity, not in competition and strife. The one end to be sought, and the one spirit in which it can be found, is unity—whatever, or however great, may be the differences and the difficulties. The time has come—and something of the disposition and the will—for the exercise and the experiment of a universal and supreme act of reason, love, and self-sacrifice in behalf of Christ and of His work of human salvation.

Is it possible that there can be one body of Christians that shall remain deaf to the plea, indifferent to the ideal and the aspiration, that, in fact as in theory and profession, all Christians shall become one in Christ? There is no condition which, if it only remain actual long enough, we cannot become accustomed to and come, not only to acquiesce in, but to defend and maintain as normal and necessary. There is no question that the world around us has taken separation and alienation, even strife and schism, as the natural and inevitable state of things among Christians. There is a somewhat general softening of spirit and relaxing of acrimony now in process, but still even the theory of the one Church of Christ, and anything like a practical unity among Christians, is far from being recognized in our popular religion as a desideratum, much less as an essential principle and a practical necessity of Christianity. Nevertheless, if they are so, however afar off we may see the promise, we must be turning our face toward it and moving our steps in the direction of it. It may be as yet a matter for only the thinkers and the leaders, above all for the seers, the Abrahams of faith and hope; but these are the movers of the world, and if they do not move in the matter the world will not be moved.

We have undertaken, in our measure, to be standard-bearers of mediation, reconciliation, and unity. It is only by example, as representing the spirit, and ourselves walking in the way of these, that we can exercise any such mission. The attitude which we should take for ourselves, if we would impress it upon others, I would state somewhat as follows: Our claim to be a catholic Church must mean only this, and nothing more, that we desire and intend and believe ourselves to be within all the essential and necessary principles of the catholic faith, life, and worship, and order of the one Church of Christ. We are churchmen as members of this, and not as Episcopalians, Anglicans, or whatever else, in particular, we may also be. As members of The Church, in this its only sense, we are members of all who are members of It—that is to say, not only, visibly, of all baptized persons, but invisibly of all who by the grace of God are in Christ, by which I mean all who are in the saving operation of His Word and Spirit. We have, as churchmen, no right to claim, as in any sense exclusively our own or exclusively the property of any part of the Church, that which is catholic and therefore the right of all—whether or no all are in actual possession or practical use of it. On the other hand we cannot ourselves forego the possession or use of any part of what we believe to be essential to, or even a necessary means or condition of, actual or ultimate unity. On this account, for example, I may not feel myself at liberty under ordinary circumstances to avail myself of the Sacraments of other Christians and yet, still less, to exclude them from, or not welcome them to, participation in my own. What we need in order to know ourselves catholic, or within the Church of Christ, is to be able to answer on the right side such questions as these: Are we, so far as in us lies, in love and sympathy and unity with Christ and Christianity whereever these may be? If not in actual or outward communion with, are *we* responsible for and guilty of alienation and separation from, any part of the living and loving and working Body of Jesus Christ in this world? How deeply and sincerely are we wishing and praying and laboring to be at one, and to be one, with God and Christ and all their living and saving presence and operation in our universal humanity?

The time is gone to be dwelling upon or debating past responsibilities, faults, or failures. All we can do now to any profit is to repent and regret them, and go straight on to see how we can best repair them. The present business of every fragment of Christianity is to set itself in preparation and readiness to be at one with every other. But we shall never prevail against any *ism* or replace it with anything better, until we learn to meet and overcome it with a true and a real catholicity.

All human life, individual or collective, begins under authority and ends in freedom. Human government began monocratic and ends, or is to end, democratic. There was a time when the king ruled, rightly because necessarily, by a divine right—the divine right of an external authority when there was as yet nothing internal on the part of the ruled to direct and control in its stead. But because monarchism, even despotism, was at one stage necessary, it does not follow that individual, personal, popular responsibility and freedom will not be in order at another stage or in the end. It ought not to be doubted that Roman spiritual monarchy and absolutism was a necessity and a world-wide benefit in its time. But equally ought it to be remembered and realized that the law and authority and control of all human faith and life cannot remain in one human head or self. However the sacred oil or chrism was poured upon the head of Aaron, it was not to remain there only, but was to flow down to his beard and finally to the very lowest hem of his garment. The thought, experience, verification, determination of faith, as of all human life, is corporate. It works downward and outward, and there as everywhere else the goal, and the ultimate criterion, is not in the mind and will of one, but in the intelligent consent of all. This is no easy goal to reach, or even to foresee; all we can do is to be looking and moving slowly and wisely in the direction of it. All passage from monocracy to democracy is more or less through conflict and confusion; nevertheless there is nothing to do but to press onward toward it.

3. CATHOLIC PRINCIPLES

When I speak of my life as catholic, I use the adjective as expressive of freedom or liberty of thought and conviction in religious matters. My aim is to determine what is the true freedom or liberty in such matters. It is not freedom from any authority whatever, for if there be any real authority, freedom will consist in and be measured by the ability to recognize, regard, and obey it. Freedom is not freedom from law, but freedom to obey one's law; the law of a thing is only the expression of the normal being and activity of the thing, its completion and perfection. The law of a person is the mode of his true self-determination or liberty. Whatever expresses that for us possesses a real authority over us. To illustrate in anticipation, on to the very end: If Jesus Christ is indeed the revelation to us both of God and of ourselves—of the ultimate unity of God and ourselves, and so of the Life which is our end and destiny—then Jesus Christ possesses a supreme and final authority over us as Lord of our life, obedience to which is upon penalty, not of any external or arbitrary sanction or consequence, but of our own sacrifice of life and liberty and true selfhood. So, too, the process and progress of our freedom is conditioned upon our determining the true sources and bases of authority and conforming ourselves to them.

We say, "All things change, and we change with or in them." It would be even more true, perhaps, to say, "We change, and all things change in or with us." Our world is very different from that of one or two or three thousand years ago; but the change has been primarily and mainly in us not in it. Men change, not nature; or nature changes, chiefly if not exclusively, through men's discovery, control, and use of it. Evolution now is that of the human, the personal, the spiritual. Nature is so wonderfully other and more than it used to be, because we are so other and more in our relations with it. In itself it does not really change;—and in ourselves we do not really and truly change, except to higher and more of ourselves. In the right sense our creeds—our holds upon eternity and infinity, upon life and destiny—are our most intimate and permanent part, and are as unchangeable as ourselves. And yet, too, our creeds change with us, change in the respects in which we necessarily change if we are to go further and be more.

Our creeds then do change and are always changing—because we change and are always changing in our conception and comprehension of them, in our appreciation, appropriation, and realization of them. I hold that the Creed ought to be other chiefly in the sense of being more and truer to us than it was even to those who first framed it, and in this way: In humanity and in everything human, and so no less in our hold upon God and upon things divine, in our Creed, there is a natural and a spiritual element, there is something which changes with our change and is therefore subject to constant change; and again there is something which belongs to and ministers to the abiding and the unchangeable, the eternal, in us and never changes except to become more, and more true, to us. There is no use for the temporal in religion except to be the figure and symbol of the eternal, and the longer and fuller and firmer our grasp upon the eternal, the less our dependence upon, the greater our independence of the merely natural or temporal. I look upon the creed from its spiritual and eternal End, from which there can be no possible question or doubt of it, because it simply is the truth, and the truth seen cannot be mistaken. I have ceased to look upon it in the merely natural setting of its temporal and sensible, because human, origin and process. There is a necessary mystery and veil over anything like a revelation, an inspiration, an incarnation, or any other form or degree of the union or uniting of the divine and the human—when looked at from only the human or the natural side. It can never be explained, investigated, verified, or even perceived from that side only: except one be born again, he cannot see it. It requires other eyes, other observation and experience, other tests and criteria than those of natural science or criticism. One who genuinely and really applies and thoroughly applies to the things of the spirit enumerated in the Creed the only possible and proper scepticism and criticism, investigation, evidence, and verification, will learn and be content to leave the mere natural fringes and joinings of such truth under the veil and in the mystery that belongs to them. If the natural language applied to the fact of the Incarnation is an enigma to you, pass by the word and take the thing: test, prove, verify that, and the mystery will not trouble you.

I believe that I am naturally sensitive to mental movements and changes. I think that my mind has become a thoroughly modern mind; I feel and know that, for example, the speech and language of

mediaevalism, of the pre-scientific and pre-historic age, is already
one "not understanded of the people." We still use older words and
phrases, we still say "The sun rises"—but they stand for different
conceptions of the thing, and the thing is what we are after and not
the mere historic ways of seeing or saying it. It is useless to fight
against actual movements and changes; our wisdom is to see in them
the truth, the whole truth, and then, if possible, nothing but the truth,
and let the rest pass by, as it surely will. The best way to dispose of
the error is to establish the truth; emphasize, prove, demonstrate, and
manifest that, and time and inanition will take care of the other.
There was an incalculable wealth of truth and devotion, as of unqualified good, in the scientific revival of the last century; as there
was no little of perversion, pretension, and wide-spread harm upon
the mere top. I believe that I always felt that scepticism and criticism
were inevitable instruments of truth and righteousness and life, and
that nothing in this world was proved, tested, or verified that had not
passed through them to the uttermost end and limit. What is scepticism in principle but enquiry, investigation, examination? and what
is criticism but separating, distinguishing, judging, determining between the true and the false, the good and the bad? We must not judge
these divine instruments by their superficial perversions and abuses,
but by their necessary and salutary uses. Our Lord says, "For *krisis*
am I come into this world." He Himself was spared no question or
test, and He is the supreme Critic and Judge of our lives: "The Word
of God is quick and powerful and sharper than any two-edged sword,
and is critical of all thoughts and intents of the heart." "His fan is
in His hand and He will thoroughly purge His floor." The truth or
right that cannot stand all test is not genuine, and that which has not
stood all test is not only unproven, but in us it is unpurified truth or
righteousness.

I was myself, as doubtless many others were, subject to a very
specious and dangerous temptation. There was no little insinuation
and actual charge against Christianity that it was not willing to go
with science all the way to the end of truth, wherever it might lead.
There was the assumption here that scientific investigation or historical criticism could lead all the way to the very end of truth, and
many, through fear of unveracity and dishonesty, of unwillingness
to accept the truth to the very end, were misled by it. The mere natural cannot and is not intended to compass that which is beyond it,

cannot pierce the mystery of even such palpable earthly facts as human freedom and personality, much less that of such heavenly things as divine revelations, inspirations, and incarnations. Yet, if there be any God at all, or God to any human purpose, there must be such things—whether they be palpable to the faculties of mere evolutional nature or not.

My own experience was this: many a time I was impressed and attracted by the honesty and thoroughness of natural truth, unequalled, as I feared, in my observation or experience, by our spiritual truth, which seemed ever afraid to be brought to full or final proof. I might at any time have been led away by this; and then, under the stimulus and satisfaction of the sacrifice, drawn more and more into the noble pursuit and love of natural truth, and more and more out of that of spiritual things; I might have lived and died in the conviction that I had done the hard, the real, and the true thing; and doubtless God would have forgiven me the wrong, if indeed I was sincere in believing I was doing the right. I thank God He did not let me take that course. I reflected that there was another course which I was under obligation not to despise and dismiss without at least as full and fair trial as the other. Our Lord teaches us of a truth of God, a will of God, a work of God, which He says consists in believing in Him Whom God has sent. And He tells us that he who will do the will shall know the truth and work the work of God. The only and whole test and proving of the truth is in the doing. This is not unreasonable; it is a question of what life is, and there is no way of verifying and knowing life but by living it. He who will do the will of God, which our Lord says is to believe in the Son of God, will have the witness in himself. And this is the witness, That God hath given unto us eternal life, and this life is in His Son: he that hath the Son hath the life. If we will give to the testing and proving, the verifying, of that truth the thorough-going honesty and devotion that science gives to natural knowledge, there will be no doubt of it in us, and there will be no doubt of it in the world. For the world does not doubt what is actual and real; its doubt of Christianity is disbelief in us Christians. My experience was that if I suffered myself to be drawn away from spiritual things into only natural things, I found myself coming to think that truth and reality and honesty lay only there; but that if, on the other hand, without at all having to give up the natural, I was equally honest and in earnest in applying God's test to God's truth of faith and life in Jesus Christ, I soon became a thousand-fold more certain that all reality lay there—even the reality, the meaning and end, of natural science itself. That which makes you the most in yourself in making you most to all else, you cannot but accept as truth for you and the truth of you.

The contribution of modern thought or the modern mind to Christianity has been chiefly the doing away the chasm which had been widening between the natural and the spiritual. We find God now not only in the non-natural, but wholly in the natural. This is not to deny the supernatural, but to see in it the essential, the higher and ultimate natural. "There is a natural, and there is a spiritual; howbeit, that is not first which is spiritual, but that which is natural, and afterward that which is spiritual." It is more natural and rational that we should grow up spiritually from ourselves into Christ than that we should have developed naturally from the brute into the man. The more fully we know Christianity, the better we know not only the spiritual but the natural also—the natural as explicable and justifiable only as ground and setting of the spiritual.

It was through Bishop Butler that I came first to meditate deeply upon the relation of the natural and the spiritual—and to feel not merely the analogy between, but the identity within them. Later it was Aristotle's "Ethics" that trained me to see, along with the difference and distance between, no less the unity within the life and principles of nature and those of grace—as only stages of the same evolution.

I may illustrate certain respects in which the modern mind, while it enables us to hold truths of religion even more clearly, compels us to see and understand them differently. Take, for example, the truth of the divine Providence: the old idea of "special providences" was distinctly that even in natural events God acted outside and independently of a course of nature, or of an invariable natural sequence. We can no longer, or shall not much longer be able to hold the truth of providence in that form. And yet I confess that I hold the truth of a universal and particular providence more firmly and I believe more really than I ever did before. I believe in a personal providence in nature, because I believe that nature is God, is how God is and acts in those things that we call natural because they are the operation of fixed and invariable laws. If those laws and operations were not fixed and invariable, we could not live and be rational and be free in this world. Therefore God in natural things acts naturally and never contradicts or is inconsistent with Himself. In so far then as His providence is in and through natural things, there is no deviation by any hair's breadth from the course or what we call the causation of nature. And yet, within the course of nature, if any Christian man will, as St. Paul says, love God and enter into the meaning and operation of His eternal and divine purpose, I know that he will find that literally all things are working together, that God is working all things together, for his individual and particular good: "If God be for us, what can be against us?" "They have not known my ways," is God's charge against His people. God's ways are not easy, He did not spare His own Son, and He does not spare any that are His sons; but some of us live long enough to know that His ways are better than our ways, and that He never fails to help those whom He brings up in His steadfast fear and love. I cannot see where God ever promises to change natural things or natural sequences for us. I do see where He promises that in them all and through them all we shall be more than conquerors. To St. Paul's prayer to take away, the answer was, My grace shall be sufficient for you. Our Lord did not wait for that answer: He preferred for Himself God's will and way as eternally and essentially best. "Not as I will, but as Thou wilt." I may not see how God in a uniform course of nature can provide what is best for each soul in each case any more than I can understand that I myself am free in such a sequence of nature. But what actually is, is—whether it be possible or no. There are more things than we think that we accept simply upon that ground.

The question of Prayer is not separate from that of Providence, in so far as prayer is connected with natural or temporal benefits. The principle of prayer is rooted in the fact of need, want, poverty. Our Lord makes poverty the first condition of spiritual blessedness, because in it begins all that dependence upon God the end of which is oneness with Him. Out of that poverty come all godly sorrow, all noble meekness and humility, all hunger and thirst for rightness and fulness of life, all faith in God, all hope in self, all true self-realization and soul satisfaction. Nature is meant to be deficient and self to be insufficient: the natural is complete only in the spiritual, and every self only in God. Therefore prayer is the breath and life of the soul: we want God as we want the air we breathe and the food we eat. Prayer is properly for all we want, from the daily bread of the body to that which nourisheth to life eternal. We pray for natural and temporal things as well as spiritual and eternal. But there ought to be a difference: when we pray for natural goods, we ought to pray for them "as God wills"—that is to say, as they are given, naturally; and when we pray for spiritual things, we ought to pray for them spiritually.

What I mean by praying for natural things naturally is this: we ought to recognize that they come to us in the way and course and order of nature. But nature is not a dead thing, a senseless mechanism or blind fortuity: is not God in nature, and is not nature God? Let us pray to God for all we want in the way it comes,—but let us learn more and more just what we want, and just how it comes: let us learn His ways. There are two ways of God, or two modes of the one way: First, He will not change nature for us, but He will, if we love Him and enter into His purpose, make everything in nature, the good and the evil, good to us, work together for our good. I do not mean that He will do this merely by fitting or adjusting us to things as they are, but that He will make the things, whatever they are, actual instruments and ministers of our good—as He made Judas and Herod and Pontius Pilate, and Satan and death and hell all minister to the human glorification, because spiritual perfection, of Jesus Christ. Sin is the deepest, the only essential evil, and He makes our sin itself the instrument of our good, as that which drives us out of nature and self into Him and holiness. And second, I do not say that God will not change nature, do away with natural evils and provide natural goods, but only that He will not do it for us, in the sense of instead of us: He will not do it magically or miraculously, or by what we mean by "special providences." There is absolutely no limit to what He will do through us and by us in these ways if only we will be workers with Him for good. God does not want to put away our sin by magic, He wants us to put it away by holiness; and so He does not work upon us by miracle, but works in us by grace: which means that He calls and moves and enables us to put away our sin by repentance and to put on holiness and life by faith. And so in natural as well as spiritual matters, God does not want merely a clean, healthy, wholesome earth; He wants us to make the earth clean, healthy, and wholesome by living so in it. He is not going to convert the wilderness into a garden for us; what He wants is not the work but the working and the workers, the love that bears all, believes all, endures and survives all, accomplishes all, and so at last becomes and is all. And so what do we come at last to pray for, and how? By *at last* I mean when we have passed beyond praying for things as we think we want them and come to take them as God knows we want them. I am a thorough-going Trinitarian in prayer: I find God personally only in the person of Jesus Christ, and Christ only by His presence to me and with me and in me by the Holy Ghost. I pray to God only for God, to Christ only for Christ, to the Holy Ghost only for the Holy Ghost, and for everything else natural and spiritual only as through them and by them God will give me Himself. Have we not been assured that "All things are ours"? And I see nowhere or how otherwise they are so than by the love of the Father, through the grace of the Son, and in the unity and fellowship of the Spirit; let the distinction or the identity of these be defined or left undefined as they may, they both exist somehow for me.

As the modern mind in me has corrected and enlightened, without weakening my faith in providence and prayer, so has it acted in other ways. We have our Christianity through the Scriptures and through the living witness and tradition of the Church. These are human records and evidence; they are part and parcel of human history and cannot escape the natural tests of historical scepticism and criticism. Nor can we escape, if (alas!) we would, the actual and real results of such inevitable handling—our Lord in the flesh was handled yet more roughly and survived it. There is no question that the case has been made out for the very humanness and fallibility of the Scriptures as of the Church. Is their divine origin and authority gone with it? I confess that the Scriptures are more divine to me now than they ever were before, that I was never more a believer in their inspiration. If there has ever been anything in all my life verified by actual experience, it has been the divinity of the New Testament, after all that criticism has done with it. Just as I have been brought to see and feel the utter humanity of our Lord down to its very depths, and have been only thus the more convinced of His deity: it is the utterness of His humanity that is the proof of His divinity. "The work that Thou gavest me to accomplish, that work which I have accomplished, beareth witness of me."

So with the Church and its witness: surely, if anything has ever manifested itself in fact and in history, it is the humanness and the fallibility of the Church. Men may well exclaim, where is the

Church?—and what is Christianity? Yet I take my stand upon the fact of the Church and upon the truth of Christianity. I believe that our Lord will be with us to the end of the world, and that the gates of hell shall not prevail against Him. There is a Spirit of truth, of whom our Lord says, "The world cannot receive Him, for it seeth Him not neither knoweth Him: ye know Him; for He abideth with you and shall be in you. Yet a little while, and the world seeth me no more; but ye see me: because I live, ye shall live also. In that day ye shall know that I am in my Father, and ye in Me, and I in you." Is there no real experience expressed in these words, nor any real evidence given or verification reached through it? The wisdom of a merely natural scepticism or investigation is to recognize its natural limitation, to be satisfied with its own proper agnosticism as pertaining to the facts of the spirit. The "comparing, or combining, spiritual things with spiritual," of which St. Paul speaks, is best accomplished by meeting spiritual truths with spiritual minds, proving and verifying them by spiritual tests and experiences. "The natural man receiveth not the things of the Spirit of God: he cannot know them, because they are spiritually examined and judged."

I have striven to keep a free and an open mind, and it seems to me that the freest mind is that which is open alike to the claims of the natural and of the spiritual in us, not to either as against the other. I should rather try to hold both, though in unsuccessful combination and adjustment, than to be, through a narrow and one-sided devotion, ever so expert in the one at the sacrifice of possible untried and unknown worth and value in the other. But again, I am not only as I was before the nineteenth century opened and liberated my mind. I see all that is divine and permanent in Christianity, in my Christian Creed, in a clearer light, in better perspective and truer proportions, than I ever did before. What if on the natural edges and joinings of it, as I have said, all is not perfectly even yet clear and smooth—I have learned to hold my mind in suspense upon matters which we have eternity in which to know, and to know which eternity will not be too long.

II.

THE GOSPEL ACCORDING TO ST. PAUL (1907)*

During DuBose's first year of seminary studies he was challenged by a senior who believed that St. Paul's perspective corresponded with the Calvinistic position of Reformed theology. This challenge led DuBose to an extended study of St. Paul which finally convinced him that St. Paul was intent on inward life-relations and processes, not on dogma. The Gospel According to St. Paul represents DuBose's mature reconsideration of what had been in his early years the scriptural foundation of his Evangelical phase. The following selection, therefore, may be seen as DuBose's theological reconstruction of his Evangelical phase, which is described in the first chapter of the preceding selection.

INTRODUCTION

In advocating and pressing any particular point of view, one is inevitably liable to press it unduly and at the expense of other points of view. In the quest of truth this danger ought not to be too much of a deterrent to either freedom of thought or boldness of expression. The ultimate aim of each one of us should be not to save ourselves from error but to advance the truth. We may safely rely upon it that

---

* The original text that follows is from *The Gospel According to St. Paul* (New York: Longmans, Green, and Co., 1907), pp. 3–16, 57–82, 171–202, 233–292.

our truth will in the end be accepted and our error corrected. If I had been too much afraid of going wrong I should have made no progress in growing right;—who of us that has really thought or spoken may not say that of himself? For my own part, I have not merely traditionally believed but become personally convinced that there is a truth of the Scriptures and that there is a mind of the Church; and that each of these will take care of itself as against the infinite errors and vagaries of individual thinkers and writers. I have in my mind not only an implicit faith but a rational science or philosophy of these things, which at least satisfies myself and gives me security and rest from the fear of even my own shortcomings or too-far-goings. I do not hesitate to say then, on the one hand, that I hold what I hold subject to the revision and correction of the deeper truth of the Scriptures and the larger wisdom of the Church; and, on the other hand, that, leaving to these their function of final acceptance or rejection, I conceive it to be my duty to the truth, and my best service to them, to think the thoughts and express the conclusions, as best I may, which I have found to be to myself their own best interpretation.

The particular method which, after a lifetime of study and reflection, I have found to be the best for entering into the meaning of the Gospel of Jesus Christ, or into the meaning of Jesus Christ as Himself the immediate Word or Gospel of God, may be brought out by a parallelism or analogy between the independent and very different treatments of St. Paul and St. John. The starting-point, and standpoint all through, of St. John's interpretation of our Lord is best expressed in the words, The Life was manifested. The Life had been manifested first to the outward eye and then to the inward vision of a few; and it was the mission of these few so to declare and present it to all others that they too might know and enter into and share it. St. John, both in his Gospel and in his Epistles, acts upon the true Aristotelian principle that in every investigation of reality the fact or the actual (τὸ ὁτι) is the proper starting-point (ἀρχή). The fact which is the starting-point in this case is the simple objective truth that Jesus Christ is the Life. That is fact in itself, independently of any external dogmatic affirmation or logical demonstration of it. And it is, if fact in itself, then fact verifiable in itself; for truth, if allowed to do so, always can and always will prove itself. And this is truest of what is to us the ultimate truth, the truth of Life and of truth, is justified of her children. There *is* the Life—human life in all the fulness of its meaning and divine reality. There is the Truth—the Life expressed and manifested, something not only ideal or potential but actual, not only vision or shadow or symbol but eternal substance. There is the Way: Life, human life at least, God's life in us, cannot come just so, out of hand, by immediate *fiat* or creation from without. It can come only in conjunction, in reaction, in conflict and strife with human environment as it is and with all human conditions as they are. Jesus Christ is not only the truth or reality of life; He is the way of it to us, and He is so only as Himself our own true way of life.

Life can be lived by ourselves, and our Lord's life was lived, only in and through the mastery of the one true way of human life, by practical solution of the meaning, the reason, and the use of all actual human conditions. In this world none of us can escape its conditions, or be saved otherwise than by discharging its inevitable tasks. Only through conquest of the world, the flesh, and the devil may we attain unto life eternal. But we have His parting assurance, In the world ye shall have tribulation; but be of good cheer, I have overcome the world. The overcoming was His way and ours: He drank the cup and was baptized with the baptism which we must drink and be baptized withal, if we would be where and what He is. In leading us all to glory, it behooved God to make the author of our salvation perfect through the sufferings which are the conditions and the means of our own perfection and salvation. The point to be emphasized is, that our salvation, in all the conditions, means, and way of it, was first enacted or wrought out in the personal human experiences and life of our Lord. He is in fact to us the Way: no man can come to God, and so to himself and to life, save through Him.

Thus St. John saw Jesus Christ as The Life; the truth or reality or actuality of it, as distinguished not only from its falsities, but from its mere dreams or shadows; the way of it, as including and involving all its conditions and causes, all its necessary means and processes. Precisely analogously, though not with the contemplative, poetic vision of St. John, but rather with his own more active and practical insight, St. Paul sees Jesus Christ as not so much our Life as our Righteousness. He regards salvation less in the accomplished fact than in the accomplishing act or process; in the making rather than in the made product. St. Paul does indeed see in our Lord Himself a process completed, but in the joy of the completion he never forgets or loses sight of the process; in all the glory of what our Lord is as man, the important thing to remember is the one lifelong human act of faith and obedience through which He became the man He is. Life, and therefore salvation, is indeed an act, a lifelong act or activity, a process of self-actualizing or becoming ourselves. Life can be lived, or self realized, only as they are so rightly, in accordance with their own meaning and reason and law. That is what the whole Bible means when it so emphatically and persistently proclaims that rightness or righteousness alone is life, that he who obeys the law shall live by it, and he who violates it shall die by it. It is a universal and necessary fact in itself that life, blessedness, or salvation is to be found in nothing else than in right being and right doing.

The first truth with St. Paul, then, is that righteousness is salvation; and the second is that Jesus Christ is righteousness. This determines for us the standpoint from which, I think, we may best interpret the Gospel according to St. Paul. Our task is first to interpret righteousness in itself, as realized and manifested to us in the person of our Lord. It is then, secondly, to learn how that righteousness is to be made ours. The method in a word is this: through the constant appropriating or taking it to ourselves in faith, it is gradually and in the end made or becomes our own in fact. This introduces the fact or principle of the marvellous assimilative and transforming power of faith. Man believes unto salvation—that is to say, unto righteousness and life. Faith in the righteousness and life of Christ assimilates and transforms us into the likeness of Christ's righteousness and life: reflecting as a mirror the glory of the Lord, we are transformed into the same image from glory to glory, even as from the Lord the Spirit.

To understand this new-creative power of faith, we must comprehend something of the complex and comprehensive nature of faith. In the light of the mystery or miracle by which all nature is made ours through the senses, we ought not to halt at that higher mystery whereby God makes Himself our own through faith. After all there is as much of higher naturalness in the latter as there is of lower in the former. Faith is the highest and most distinctive function and activity of the spirit of man. It involves the highest energy not alone of his intelligence but of his affections, his will, his entire selfhood or personality. If we realize even in the lower spheres a truth in such sayings as that: what we think, we are; what we love, we are; what we believe or mean or intend, we are;—how much truer should it be that what our most real self and selfhood concentrates itself upon, attaches and gives itself up to through every spiritual faculty and passion of its nature, that, if we not already are, we most assuredly shall be. This, I repeat, gives a sort of naturalness, if not indeed the highest and truest naturalness, to the truth that we believe unto righteousness or unto life; that faith saves; and that there is no other way of spiritual salvation or of personal self-realization than through faith.

There are those who object to our making salvation, the life of the spirit, the life of religion in general, too natural a process. We cannot kick against the pricks; the world has begun to make the discovery, and it will not go backward in it, that the natural is God's way. The natural is the rational and the divine. There is no real break between the natural and the supernatural; the one is only the higher or further other. We shall come to see that Adam and Christ are the same Man; that earth and heaven are one continuous life, easy here or there to be made a hell of; that nature and God are one world, too easily divorced and set at enmity, incapable of too close reconciliation or at-onement. Under the prevalence of the modern scientific principle of evolution we have discovered that the great primal truth of God creating is neither denied nor obscured, but is as much as ever not only a possibility but a postulate of thought in what, nevertheless, appears and can appear to Science only as a world self-evolving. Still more shall we need to learn in Jesus Christ and His Church that the greater truth of God redeeming and saving is neither diminished nor obscured by the fact that it is a truth made visible to us only in the phenomenon of a humanity self-redeemed and self-saved. No man hath seen God at any time; if God be in a man, He will be visible in him only in what the man himself is. God was in Christ *sub specie hominis,* not *Dei.* He was here to fulfil and manifest Himself in us and us in Him; not Himself otherwise than in us, or in any other revelation of Himself than as our holiness, righteousness, and life. That was effected for us objectively, or as an object or end to our faith, in the person of the Incarnate Word; it is effected subjectively by a power working in us through faith, the power of the Incarnate Spirit. That the personal Spirit of God and the personal character and life of God should be ours through faith is as truly natural an operation and result as that nature's breath and life should be ours through our bodily organs.

Forasmuch then as God was in Christ for the specific purpose and to the specific end of being to us and in us the whole truth of ourselves, of manifesting and imparting to us Himself as our holiness, our righteousness, and our eternal life, it follows that it should be our part to see in Jesus Christ just that as what God wills to reveal, and to accept in Him just that as what God wills to bestow. I say so much in explanation and justification of what will seem to some an undue insistence upon the humanity of our Lord. There will be statements no doubt so one-sided in themselves as, if they stood alone, to endanger or to obscure other no less essential sides of the truth. But I hope it will be seen and felt that they do not stand alone. One such statement I would make clear in the beginning: I lay down the principle that in interpreting the human life and work of Jesus Christ I construe Him to myself in terms of humanity. I make no difference there between Him and us save in the one particular, which is the one Scriptural exception, of His sole perfect sinlessness or holiness, His sole complete and perfect victory over the world, His accomplished task of uniting humanity with God and so redeeming it from sin and death. That is enough for me as demonstration of our Lord's deity also, enough not alone to enable but to compel the confession that Jesus Christ was as truly more than man as He was also truly man. I bow before not only the work of Jesus Christ as truly God's but the Worker in Jesus Christ as truly God. God's eternal Wisdom and Word which are eternally God's Self were truly incarnate in His person, and wrought with His hands the creed of creeds. I go further and repeat the conviction that, so far as our knowledge and experience can go, nowhere else in all God's universe, in all His infinite and manifold activities, is God so God as in the person and work of Jesus Christ. For in Jesus Christ God is all love, and love of all things is most God.

I might be allowed to use the opportunity to say an additional word upon the subject of discussions such as we are here touching upon. These are times—but, let us remember, not more so than were the earliest and most living ages of Christianity—of thought and speculation, original and independent thought and speculation, upon the truth as it is in Jesus Christ. They are not times of unthinking and unquestioning acceptance of foregone and foreclosed inquiry and investigation. The fact may be condemned and lamented, but no amount of shutting our own or others' eyes and ears to it will make it any the less a fact. The whole truth of Scripture and the whole mind of the Church might surely, one might say, be accepted as being conjointly the ultimate expression to us of what Christianity is, what constitutes the essential or necessary truth of it. This, however, as a matter of fact, does not end the matter. What is the whole truth of the Scripture, and what is the whole mind of the Church? Some will say, these are things which have been determined for us, and the very reopening them is fatal to the fact or the possibility of any such thing as a catholic truth or unity. Are these questions indeed closed? They may be for those who say they are. But what of the great living, thinking Christian world to which, as a matter of fact, they are not closed? They are tremendously not closed, and tremendously in question. And they are not going to be closed by any possible amount of mere saying or asserting that they ought to be. A few bewildered and weary souls, to escape doubt and in despair of any self-determining power of truth or life in itself, will from time to time seek, and perhaps find, refuge and rest in the quiet places where they are no longer in question and under the assurance that they are infallibly settled. But there is in fact no such rest for a really living and a really thinking world. The whole truth of the Scripture and the whole mind of the Church are not dead but live things. The fact of their being alive and forever obliged to keep themselves alive with a life that is within themselves will not preclude the possibility of their gaining for themselves assent, consent, and agreement; of their attaining even, as every other kind of truth does, a catholic unity and permanence of form and expression, a *quod semper, quod ubique, et quod ab omnibus*. The fact of truth's being always alive and always in question for its life does not militate against its credit for truth or its tenure of life. And there is every advantage in truth's being under the necessity of being always our truth, and not merely that of other thinkers and of another age.

The initial difficulty before us lies in the want of assurance that there is such a thing possible, such a thing to be sought and found, and to be held in union and unity with all our might, as a truth of the Scripture and a mind of the Church. We need to have and to spread such a conviction; and the best and only way to extend the conviction is that we who share it shall as much as possible act in union and harmony with one another in the common cause of its extension. There is no real unity in which there is not diversity, and in the highest unity there is the utmost diversity. We shall not all agree in the methods or in the infinite details; we shall not all be altogether right; we shall all be wrong in many ways. But for all that, if we are thoroughly agreed that there is a truth of the Scripture to be known and a mind of the Church to be understood and shared, we shall not fail to accomplish great things towards a necessary and a possible result, the divine result of Christian unity. In that spirit, we shall gratefully acknowledge one another's contributions of truth, whatever they may be; and we shall not content ourselves with anathematizing one another's shortcomings or errors, but rather labour in love for mutual understanding and mutual correction and amendment. If we are to work successfully to the common end, we must learn so to work together as that our very faults and falsities shall, through the sympathetic and cooperating correction and amendment of one another, be made to work together for the common good. In this spirit, I offer all I shall have to say to the furtherance of the common cause of Christian unity, subject to correction by the higher truth of the Scriptures and the larger wisdom of the Church.

The position here taken is, to my mind, independent of any present or future conclusions of scepticism or criticism with regard either to the Scriptures or the Church. I fully recognize not only the function but the necessity of both scepticism and criticism, in their true meaning and use; and I presume neither to limit nor to define these. But the fact will always remain that we receive our Christianity through the Scriptures and the Church, and that these are the tribunal of final resort for determining what Christianity is. Human reason and human experience have a great part too to play in the matter, but that is both later and different. It was not theirs to give us Christianity, but it is theirs to pass upon the question whether Christianity as given is not what it claims to be, the whole truth of ourselves, because the whole truth of God in ourselves. Through them we set-to our own seals that God in Christ is true. But by reason and experience I mean not those of each but those of all, which really means of those who know. The judges of spiritual things are spiritual men.

I. THE WRATH OF GOD AGAINST SIN

Perhaps we should have said that the most complete and proper presupposition of the Gospel was the fact, and the universal fact, of sin. And yet, I do not believe that the coming, or the primary end and function, of the Gospel was conditioned upon the fact of sin. The Gospel of the Incarnation means the completion as well as the redemption or restoration of humanity. I for one, speculatively and not dogmatically, cannot see how there could have been a personal evolution or completion, a production and development of holiness, righteousness, and spiritual life, without what we call the fall, without an experimental coming to the knowledge of good and evil, of sin and holiness, of life and death. I cannot see how there could have been generated in us the sense of holiness except in reaction against a sense of sin, or a fact of holiness except in conflict with and victory over an actuality of sin. But if humanity could have attained spiritual completion without sin, and therefore without redemption or restoration, I hold that the Gospel of Jesus Christ would have been as necessary for that as in fact it was for that and the other also. Man is essentially incomplete without God, and the relation to God which he needs for his completion is not an immanental unity and oneness with God by nature, but a transcendental personal union and fellowship with God by grace and faith,—that is, by the mutual spiritual intercommunion and intercommunication of love and service, which is the life of God, and of all in the universe who share the personal or spiritual life of God. Jesus Christ is human completion in that He is, not the natural unity, whatever it be, of God and man, which is true of all men, but the personal union and fellowship of God and men, which is perfectly true only in Him as at once God and man, and is true in us just in the measure of our knowledge and participation of it in Him.

Sin, however, is in the world, and is universal, and there is no deliverance from it and its consequences except in a divine salvation. And the Gospel of Jesus Christ is not only the divine proclamation but the divine manifestation and fact of that salvation. Whatever may be thought of St. Paul's, either traditional or speculative, account of the origin or natural history of sin, we need only to remember that all that is material to his truth of the Gospel is—not his theories but his facts. Those facts are, that sin exists; that sin is universal, a race as well as an individual fact, inseparable from *the flesh* in itself; that nevertheless sin is not the true nature or law of humanity; that it is its death and not its life, which is holiness; that humanity can be or become itself only through a redemption or salvation from sin and the death which is its consequence; that the natural condition of humanity on its spiritual side is a sense, which grows with the growth of the spiritual consciousness, of want or need, which is in itself a prophecy and promise of the divine supply which we call grace, by which we mean the personal knowledge and fellowship of God Himself. These as far as they go are the materials on the human side of which the Apostle constructs his conception of the Gospel. To complete the picture, in anticipation, we might add that the materials on the other side are, the eternal love-nature and love-purpose of God; the predestination in nature itself, as well as in the mind of God, of the whole creation in man its highest part to that personal participation in the divine spirit, nature, and life, which constitutes him son of God; the realization and revelation of that relation in the individual person of Jesus Christ; the provision for such a real and vital fellowship with Christ and participation with Him in the divine power of His life as to make us actually in Him partakers of the divine nature, and sons of God.

I have given the above preliminary outline of the whole Gospel according to St. Paul only, for the present, to show the place of sin in it. All evil, as Kant says in substance, is primarily spiritual and moral. Extract the sting of sin, as St. Paul teaches, and death itself is converted from a supreme evil into mere transition or birth into the supreme good. Deliverance from the evil of sin is to convert all other curse of the world into blessing. But the only possible exemption or redemption for a personal spirit from sin is through its own conquest of sin. The conquest cannot be made for it, but only by it; because in its own conquest alone is its holiness, its righteousness, its life. The victory of any other can be for it, only as it is capable of being made, and will be made, its own self-undertaken and self-accomplished victory. The power of God to save us actually saves us only as it is made our power to save ourselves.

To revert to St. Paul's account of sin, The wrath of God, he says, is revealed from heaven against all ungodliness and unrighteousness of men. In what way is that wrath revealed? There is no better illustration than here of St. Paul's mental habit of seeing God's attitudes or acts only in the facts of nature or of human experience, that is to say, in the working of things. If, as Bishop Butler says, all experience of life shows what part God takes in it, on what side He is, viz.: on the side of righteousness and *against* unrighteousness; if the agnosticism even of Matthew Arnold can see clearly enough that the power not ourselves in the affairs of men makes for righteousness only and wholly, it was not too much for the more spiritual vision of St. Paul to discern that to say that the Righteous Lord loveth righteousness can mean no more nor less than that He hates unrighteousness. And indeed no terms can express too strongly the wrath of God actually revealed in nature and in human affairs against the ungodliness and unrighteousness of men as it exists in the world. St. Paul expresses himself neither otherwise than as the actual facts revealed nor more strongly than the actual facts justified. Those facts were no doubt at their darkest when the true Light dawned in the person of our Lord, and St. Paul saw and described them in all their contrast with it. Nevertheless the facts of the world are practically the same always, and the contrasts are sufficient still to mutually exhibit each other.

The material points in the Apostle's treatment of sin we may briefly consider. The first is a very essential one in his view of the Gospel. It might be expressed as his sense of the relation between ungodliness and unrighteousness. It is identical with the question still with us of the mutual dependence or independence of morality and religion. No one denies the possibility or actuality of a, relatively, high morality in a nonreligious individual person. That is not at all the question. When a social morality exists, whatever or however essential may be the causes or conditions of its existence, it may nevertheless exist in a high degree in those who mentally deny or contradict those conditions. The true question is, what would be the morality or moral condition, the righteousness, of the world if there were no such thing as godliness, if man were not really a spiritual and religious being, and were not often, in his better types, actually more religious than is consistent with his own theory, or than he knows or thinks himself to be. At any rate it was St. Paul's conviction that man is a spiritual and religious being, in the sense of being constituted and having a capacity and a need for spirituality and religion. His highest and true righteousness is not a mere experimental matter of right relations with things and persons other than himself, rather is it a vastly deeper personal harmony with the spirit and law and, what these include and imply, the Personality and personal meaning and purpose of the universe. Of course that conviction is at the very root of the Apostle's central truth—that righteousness is not a mere law, nor even a mere abstract, impersonal, spirit, but the Personal Spirit of the living God in us and become our spirit too, God Himself our as well as His own righteousness. I have often thought that in the Prayer Book there is significance and point in the very mode of printing the emphatic words in the Epistle for the Sunday before Advent, as though it were an inscription upon the very portal of the Church, or the Church Year: This is His name whereby He shall be called, THE LORD OUR RIGHTEOUSNESS.

It is not merely that St. Paul connects the two words together, godliness and righteousness, as though they belonged so—spirit and body of one and the same thing—but he explicitly states and explains the fact of their genetic connection. Moral corruption is the consequence of which spiritual perversion is the cause. *Wherefore,* he says, God gave them up in the lusts of their hearts unto uncleanness. And he repeats, *For this cause* God gave them up unto vile passions. For what cause? For this: Even as, or because, they saw not fit to have God in their mind, God gave them up to an unfit or reprobate mind. Like every other part of his nature, the spiritual or God-related nature of man is liable not only to non-use but to mis-use. And on the principle that the corruption of the best is always the worst, the perversion of the spiritual or religious affections and passions has been responsible for a very large part of the evil and confusion of the world. Superstition and idolatry, fanaticism and spiritual pride and intolerance, have always been recognized by religion itself as quite as possible and actual in the world, and often even more positively pernicious and injurious and hateful, as a mere negative unbelief or disbelief of the facts of the spirit. Much of the immorality which St. Paul so graphically describes was actually associated with so-called religious worship. So that the Apostle assigns as the cause of the universal condition of moral corruption in the world the universal prevalence not so much of no religion as of false religion. We must remember, however, that the natural and proper remedy for false religion, for the untold damage that has been done in the name of religion, the immeasurable harm and hindrance that so-called religion has been in the progress of human affairs, is not to be found in an impossible abolition of religion, but in the bringing it, as it devolves upon us to bring everything else in our lives, to its true meaning and function. The bodily passions, the selfish impulses, of our nature have wrought and still work evil enough surely in the world, but who dreams of abolishing them—and not rather of reducing and subordinating them to the reason and end of their existence in us? In the knowledge of God stands, and will forever stand, our eternal lives. Only in knowing Him can we know ourselves, and only in the right knowledge of Him, which is not a mere conceptual or representative but an experimental and real knowledge, can we have that right knowledge and possession and direction of ourselves which is the first condition of rightness or righteousness in our lives.

It is important, too, to observe in detail *how* the wrath as well as the approval and favor of God manifests itself in the actual working of things. What religion recognizes as the divine sanctions are all attached as natural consequences. The blessing or the curse of the thing is always sooner or later, but inevitably and invariably, in the thing itself; and it lies in the nature of the thing to breed or multiply itself and so to be forever accumulating, organizing, and consolidating, and so fixing and determining, within itself its own inherent blessedness or accursedness. Nor can there be any possible exception or objection to this natural working of things. For how is it possible that the divine holiness, righteousness, and life should be in itself and in all its consequences a perfection and blessedness to us, and that the opposite and contradiction of all these should not be a corresponding imperfection and curse? What can God's love and approval of holiness revealed in its inherent blessedness be but His hatred and condemnation of sin revealed from heaven in the awful logic of its visible consequences in the world?

We are studying the Gospel in its meaning for ourselves, and it is unnecessary for our purpose here to go into the details of the profound and overwhelming exposure by which, himself a Jew, St. Paul turns the tables against the Jews, and proves that for all their horror of the corruption of the Gentile world they themselves, in their self-righteousness, were no better. The Jews had had, as the peculiar people of God, greater advantages and opportunities—advantages that were very substantial and real, and that had been to the true spiritual children of Abraham, the Israelites indeed, divine preparations and helps. But what use had they made of their opportunity? They had rested in the objective possession of their privileges, without turning them to the subjective use or account for which they were given. They were Jews outwardly and not inwardly; and their circumcision was outward in the flesh, in the letter, and not that of the heart, in the spirit; whose praise is not of men, but of God.

The outcome of the Apostle's profound reflections upon a whole world lying thus in sin; upon the utter failure of God's own people as a whole to realize the divine promises or bring about the divine fulfilments; upon the universal and disastrous collapse of the Gentiles, under natural as of the Jews under the revealed law, in the effort to manifest the righteousness which was their own as well as God's and nature's law;—I say that the conclusion of St. Paul's thought upon this depressing picture is one which we might well take to heart still, and with which reassure ourselves and revive our drooping faith and hope. Is the righteousness of God dead in the world? No indeed! Let every man be a liar, and God is still true. What if few, or even none, have faith? Shall the faithlessness of man defeat the faithfulness of God? Shall the absence of human faith disprove or dissolve the divine objects of faith? No, God's promises and gifts are there still, and will be there forever, to be accepted or rejected for salvation or condemnation, for life or death. But more than that, the Apostle's words imply, if they do not directly state, not only that the good faith or faithfulness of God shall not be defeated by the faithlessness of man, but that faith in God shall not be brought to nought, and that the divine righteousness and life shall prevail over the unbelief and indifference of men.

2. THE NEW RIGHTEOUSNESS

The conclusion of the previous chapter brought us up to the point in St. Paul's argument where the reason and meaning of the Gospel most clearly appear. The truth and need of righteousness, the recognition of the claims of righteousness, the existence of a law of righteousness, whether speaking in the hearts and consciences of men or thundered from heaven upon Sinai, all these somehow do not avail to make righteous or to produce an actual righteousness in the world. For, as a matter of fact, righteousness does not exist. Where it professes to exist, it is at best only a conceit of righteousness, a self-righteousness, which is the most fatal and hopeless form of un-righteousness. Where the real meaning and truth of righteousness has been best conceived, and regard for the external divine law of it has produced its best fruit in life and character, what has that fruit been? Not by any means a consciousness of the possession or the conviction of a possible self-attainment of righteousness, but on the contrary, just in proportion to the high valuation and real love of the law, the consciousness of not only shortcoming but transgression, and the sense not only of sin but of impotence. Had not the Lord Himself when on earth felt that the one hopeless symptom or condition of a man was the conceit of his own righteousness? Was He not driven to the conclusion that it were better for a man to be the worst sinner and know it—than to be a so-called righteous man and unconscious of the sin that was in him? There is an absolute identity in the point of view of Jesus and of St. Paul on this point. The science or knowledge of the principles and rules of morality is not morality. The only real righteousness is the spirit and the life of Him whose law righteousness is. And the more profoundly we know and feel what His righteousness is, the more we know and feel that we need Him as the spirit and power and life of it. This, then, is St. Paul's absolutely exact induction or generalization from the spiritual facts of the world as he saw it, and as it is still: There is none righteous, no not one. By the law is only the knowledge, the sense, of sin. That only can the law do for us; and yet in doing only that, how much more has it in reality accomplished! For the very sense of sin which the law gives is itself the promise and condition of the Gospel. God takes away from us our righteousness only to give us His own, Himself. The law does not exist merely to exhibit its own weakness and unprofitableness, and in consequence to be discredited and annulled. It exists rather to create a need, a capacity, a hunger and thirst for holiness, righteousness, life—so deep, so high, so great, that only God Himself can fill and satisfy it. Truly, as St. Paul says, The Law was and is a schoolmaster to bring us to Christ.

From works of law shall no flesh be justified in God's sight; for through law comes knowledge of sin. It is not said here that through law there comes not actual righteousness, but that through law no man is before God recognized as being righteous. No man who knows what righteousness is will come into God's presence with a claim of his own to it. And if he does, so far from the claim being recognized, it will be regarded as the one disqualification for the reality to which it pretends. The Gospel of Jesus Christ was for sinners of every type save the impossible one of self-righteousness. This sense of being received, accepted, regarded, treated, as righteous is carried on from the mere negative statement under consideration to a positive form of it which gives a new and important step in St. Paul's Gospel. Not only will the most righteous man who comes before God with the claim of his own righteousness not be allowed as such, but the chief of sinners who comes to God with a true sense of his own unrighteousness and a sincere faith in God's righteousness made his own in Jesus Christ *will be* received, accepted, regarded, and treated, as being righteous. It is this being *treated as,* not on the ground of being righteous, but on the ground of a certain relation of faith to Christ's righteousness, upon which is laid the chief emphasis in St. Paul's system. It is impossible to attach too much importance to this turn of thought, and we shall be largely occupied with it as we go on. But in order to do justice to it we must understand it, and in order to do that we must question it.

The Pharisee who went up into the temple to pray and reminded God of his own righteousness was not thereby justified; while the publican who afar off was conscious only of his own sin in the sight of God was, we are told, justified. That cannot mean either that he was recognized as actually being sinless, or that he was by act of God at the time made sinless or righteous. The term "justify" is not in the parable of the Gospel used in the developed, almost technical, sense of the epistle before us, but it is exactly on the line of it, and it illustrates the progress and the propriety of its later use. If the publican, rightly and truly knowing himself to be a sinner, or a transgressor of the law of righteousness, could be justified—which meant could be regarded or accepted as righteous—it must of course be, not on the ground of his actually being so in life and character, but on the ground of his, at the time, occupying the right posture or attitude, the only right attitude possible for him, towards righteousness and at the same time towards his own conscious unrighteousness. What was that attitude? There is only one which it could possibly be, and every sinner who in his sin is in any sense or degree justified before God, can be so only on the ground of that one attitude. It is the attitude which negatively towards our own unrighteousness we call *repentance,* and positively towards the righteousness of God we call *faith*. If a man did not have some sense of the righteousness which he violates, he could have no sense of the unrighteousness which is his violation of it. The condition of possible or future righteousness is the right attitude or intention of mind and feeling towards actual present unrighteousness. It is possible in any sense to justify or accept as right only that personal attitude towards the matter which at the time is the nearest right possible for the person. In the initial moment of contrition the only possible and the necessarily first right posture of the sinner is that consciousness of himself which could not be the beginning of hatred of his sin if it were not to the same extent the beginning of a love of holiness. Where this exists in truth and sincerity, even though it be but the beginning of what is an infinite process, it is possible and right to accept and treat already as right that which as yet is only a first turning to and direction towards the right. St. John expresses more fully this divine propriety of justifying and accepting the simple sense of sin as the beginning of holiness, when he says: If we say that we have no sin, we deceive ourselves and the truth is not in us; if we confess our sin, God is faithful and just to forgive us our sin and to cleanse us from all unrighteousness.

We see already in our Lord's parable of the treatment of the publican the precise and entire principle which in St. Paul we find developed into the doctrine of justification by faith. At its fullest and completest that doctrine means this: that the veriest sinner who begins to see and feel his sin in himself, by repentance, and his holiness or righteousness in Christ, by faith, is as truly on the way and as near to the end of righteousness as is then possible for him, and it is divinely right that his faith should be received and treated as being righteousness, because it is not only the actual beginning of righteousness in him but is the righteousness proper for him at that stage. Righteousness in us cannot begin otherwise than as an incipient sense of sin and that *prolepsis* or pre-vision and apprehension of holiness which we call faith. Faith is therefore with a divine truth and propriety reckoned or imputed to us as being righteousness, for it is a necessary moment or stage in our righteousness.

The above view is supplemented and completed by the fact that God has first promised and now given us in Jesus Christ the holiness or righteousness which is the end and meaning of all repentance and faith. So sure are His promises and so certain His gifts, that there is no excuse for faith's not accepting them as already in possession; and that which faith already appropriates as its own, God's grace goes beyond our faith in imputing to us as already our own. Such, in so brief a preliminary sketch, is the new righteousness of the Gospel of Jesus Christ. It differs from the old in that, while the righteousness of the law consists in our own obedience, and is thus a self-right-eousness, and under the law righteousness on our part is the condi-tion of our acceptance with God; the righteousness of faith, on the other hand, begins with only our sense of sin and experience of weakness or insufficiency, God's loving and free acceptance of which in us is the condition and starting-point and earnest of a right-eousness of our own: which righteousness, then, is further and fully assured to us by the actual revelation of it to us in Jesus Christ, in whom we see all the presence and power of God in us, and in con-sequence all the power in ourselves in God, necessary to its actual attainment and possession.

It is true, then, that St. Paul's justification by faith is not pri-marily and immediately a righteousing or making us righteous, but an acceptance of our own sense of unrighteousness and our faith in God's righteousness as being our own; but nevertheless there is a vital and necessary connection between the two things which has to be taken into the fullest account. The Apostle says that by works of law shall no flesh be justified before God. Why is it that no man shall be accepted or accounted as righteous through the operation of the law? Is it not solely because the law, merely as such, that is, merely through the man's knowledge or obedience of the law, is incapable of making the man righteous or of operating or producing right-eousness? Is not the point after all the fact that the end of the whole matter, which is man's salvation, which again is the effectuating or actualizing of his potential righteousness and personal life, is not to be accomplished through any command on God's part or any obli-gation on his own to be righteous, but only through the grace and power of God in him to make him, by enabling him to make himself, righteous? As the law is not the end but only a means, and a means which, effectual as far as it goes in bringing us towards the end, is ineffectual to bring us to the end,—so the Gospel itself, too, however effectual to the end, is only a means, and as such must be interpreted not in itself but by its end. And what is the end of the Gospel? It is not that men in order to be righteous in the end shall be provisionally accepted and treated as such in the beginning; but exactly the reverse, that they shall be so lovingly and graciously taken into God's righteousness and treated as righteous in the beginning that they shall become, or be made so, in the end. It is the end always that determines the meaning and nature of the thing, and the Gospel is the power of God unto an actual righteousness of men; and only by the way, or in a secondary sense, a gracious treating of sinful men as not sinful, and of a faith which is not yet righteousness as being already such.

The point I am insisting upon may be more plainly put in the following way: It is true that the meaning of the words in the passage before us is that no man is accepted or accounted as righteous through operation of the law; and then that a man is accepted as righteous, or accounted righteous, upon faith in Christ, and apart from any claim of righteousness of his own. But why is he not accepted as righteous through the law, and why is he accepted as such through faith? The answer to the first is, that he is not justified or accepted as righteous through the law, not only because as a matter of fact he is not so righteous, but because he cannot be; the law has not for him any promise or power of righteousness. Its insistence or enforcement so far from imparting holiness only plunges him more and more deeply into sin. Is not the answer to the second question then this: that a man is accepted as righteous through faith in Christ, because Christ *is* his righteousness, and because faith in Christ has in it the potency and the promise of his own actual righteousnes in and through Jesus Christ? The law cannot justify a man or pronounce him righteous, because it cannot make him so. The Gospel or faith in Jesus Christ as our righteousness can justify us, because it is based not only upon the only condition in ourselves of becoming righteous—viz.: knowledge of our own unrighteousness and faith in God's righteousness—but upon the only power without ourselves to make us righteous—viz.: the love and grace and fellowship of God; and all that manifestly expressed and communicated to us in the person of Jesus Christ.

The importance, and even necessity, of insisting upon this last point is that Christianity is constantly in danger of becoming a mere blind trust in the general and indiscriminate goodness of God, apart from or even in spite of what we are or do ourselves. We look for our salvation in God or in Jesus Christ and not in ourselves, as though there were any salvation possible for us apart from or other than what we ourselves are and do. We find a weak and selfish satisfaction and comfort in what God is to us, without knowledge or thought that the only real satisfaction or comfort that we can ever know will be through what God is in us and we are in Him. Of all the good things that it is more blessed to give than to receive, that we can continue to receive only through giving, the chiefest is the supreme good of God Himself. The Spirit of God, the holiness, righteousness, or life of God can do us no good save as they are our own, and they are our own only in our own possession and exercise of them. It is an infinite initial blessing, a present Gospel, to us that God does not wait for us to be good, that He takes us to Himself from the moment of the birth in us of the will to be good, and by treating us as though we were makes us good. But let us beware of stopping with the Gospel of being accepted and not going on to the real Gospel of being good. For there is no other real good for man than that of being good, of his own goodness. Any other is only a blessing on the way, a refreshment and a help to the consummate end and blessedness of being what God is. And let us remember, too, what the goodness is that is our only real good. It is the spirit, nature, and life of God, it is love, service, and sacrifice. We have heard it said, I am content to be a sinner saved by grace. In the first place, in its truest and highest sense, to be a sinner saved is to be one who having been a sinner is so no longer; to be content to be saved in and not from sin, to be saved and still a sinner, is no true contentment. To be content to have been a sinner and to be saved by grace, or by God, only, is the highest contentment of which we are capable. It is St. Augustine's bride content to be adorned only with the gifts of her divine spouse. But, in a lower sense, we may with truth and right, in the impossibility of an immediate or instantaneous attainment of the divine perfection, and even with the consciousness of a still inhering defilement of sin, be content to abide sinners still, waiting, without the undue impatience which would be want of faith and an insisting upon sight, for the glory that is to be revealed in us, the glorious liberty and perfection of the sons of God. For one in that stage and attitude of faith and waiting, it is indeed a present though not the whole or highest blessedness of the Gospel that we are already, with God and in faith, all that we shall be in God and in fact. Indeed, in St. Paul's immediate crisis of thought and contention, this stage and phase of the matter is so uppermost for the time that he almost seems to treat it as the whole Gospel. He never really does this, though his ardent and one-sided partisans have abundantly done so ever since. St. Paul has ever in his own mind the whole undismembered conception of salvation in Christ, but he is passionately in earnest in establishing the present gracious status of believers as already and completely in possession in faith, though not yet in fact, of all that God has made ours in Christ. And as the word which the Apostle has deliberately chosen to express the matter of God's gift to us in Christ is righteousness, it is the point of his contention to insist, as the very crux and substance of faith, that we—not shall be, or are becoming, but—*are* righteous before God. We may come to Him as perfectly accepted and justified as Jesus Christ Himself, and be treated by Him as though we were as complete in Him as is our dead, risen, ascended, and glorified Lord in heaven. Such is the unreserved fulness of divine grace, and the unlimited and unhesitating power and confidence of human faith!

But the very and simple fact that our present justifying and justification are called—not as in English by different words but in Greek by identical ones—righteousing and righteousness, is sufficient evidence that God's calling or treating us as or accounting us righteous means His thereby already potential and in the end actual making us so.

3. THE CHRISTIAN IN CHRIST

Our relation to the act of Christ as our redemption has been practically resolved into our relation to the person of Christ as our actual redeemer. It is He in us, and not merely an act of His once performed for us, that is our real salvation. It is true that in consequence of that act and through our faith in it we are in a status or state of grace which is the condition of salvation; but the condition of salvation is not yet salvation. It is only as the act of Christ becomes not only imputatively our act through faith, but also really our act through participation, that we are actually saved. That Christ died for us is everything to us if it means our dying with Him; it is less than nothing at all to us if His death and ours, He and we, are not, or are not to be, so conjoined. To stop between the What Christ did for us and the What Christ is in us is a fatal halt. The co-crucifixion, co-resurrection, and co-eternal-life, is just the gist of the matter of our salvation. Now how are we to apprehend this conjunction of Christ and ourselves, and—what is the focal point of the relation— how are we so to conjoin His death and resurrection with our own as that He shall be to us, not only a salvation provided for us as the object of our faith, but a salvation effected in us as the attainment and end of our faith? In order that we may the better realize the meaning of our part not only in Christ Himself but in His distinctive act of death and resurrection, it will be necessary to reflect a little further upon St. Paul's interpretation of our Lord's death and resurrection in themselves first.

The death that He Himself died, what was it? It was, the Apostle replies, a death to sin. Now what would be on our own part, and what was actually on Christ's part, the death to sin? It could not be a mere physical fact; it must be a moral, spiritual, personal act. I will endeavour to analyze and construe that act in terms used by St. Paul himself and by St. Peter after him. St. Peter, we will remember, speaks of Christ's having brought us to God through His own death in the flesh and life in the spirit. Now the more we think of it the more we know that we were not brought to God by the mere fact of Christ's having been put to death in the body and having lived again after the body, or in a resurrection body. But St. Peter himself makes it plain for us by going on to say: Christ then having suffered (or died) in the flesh, do you arm yourself with the same mind. To go no further, it is the mind of our Lord and not merely the bodily expression of its acts or sufferings or achievements that is the main point and the essential thing. Moreover, and what is of more consequence still, the mind of Christ in the matter is that which ought to be our own, it is the universal right mind of humanity under the conditions in which He is its divine representative. What that right mind is the Apostle goes on further to specify: For he who hath suffered—or, that suffering carried to its limit, hath died—in the flesh hath ceased from sin. Christ has reached that limit of suffering in the flesh or for sin, and humanity in His person has ceased from sin. The thing to be further explicated is the meaning and character of that suffering, and consequently of that death. Jesus Christ was one with us in our nature, our conditions, our temptations, with the sole difference from us of having been sinless in them all; which He could be only through a human victory over sin in them. The sinlessness or holiness of Jesus could no more than ours be a painless experience. Given human nature, human condition, and human temptation, and the possibilities, the solicitations, the deceptions of sin, the toil, the difficulties, the pains of holiness are not to be met and overcome without suffering. The Scriptures do not only directly state that our Lord's immunity from sin was a painful victory over sin, that He was perfected by means of the things He suffered and through successful suffering of the things,—they no less distinctly testify that there was that in Him which He needed to deny, to mortify, to crucify; He had to resist unto blood striving against sin; He had to call as we with strong crying and tears upon Him that was able to save from death, and was heard for His godly faith and fear; He needed to be obedient unto the bitter limit of death, and that the most painful and shameful death of the cross. More explicitly than in all these details of His human subjection to the human conditions of holiness and life, we have here in the passage now before us the comprehensive statement that Christ's death was the crucifixion of that old man of sin whose death in Him and in us is alike the condition and the very act and fact of all human salvation and life. It will appear impossible to object to the existence of these necessities in our Lord Himself as in all us whose common humanity He shared, when we remember not alone that He did thus share our humanity, but no less that this subjection to outward and inward conditions and circumstances and possibilities of sin are as necessary to the existence of human holiness and righteousness as they are the conditions and causes of human sinfulness and unrighteousness. Just as truly as the universal existence as well as possibility of sin, the strength of its allurement and the power of its hold upon us, is the explanation and account of our human sinfulness, just so truly is it the fact that our Lord's own human subjection to all these circumstances of sin and His triumph in them and over them is the only conceivable and the only possible explanation or account of human holiness. If our holiness must be alone our own victory over our conditions as to sin, as our sin is a yielding to and being subjected by those conditions, then Christ's act, in order to become our act, must have been just the reverse and the reversal of what our own had been: it was a not yielding to or being subjected by our conditions as to sin, a victory in and over those conditions.

Going then only so far as St. Peter's words, we might say that Christ so suffered in our flesh of sin—the flesh in which we all are sinful—and so suffered for or because of sin in the flesh, as to have overcome and destroyed sin and been Himself sinless in the flesh. The flesh which is called sinful not only because it is the place of the possibility of sin, but because of its actual subjection to sin in all us the rest, was actually without sin in Him because in it He broke that subjection and abolished that sin. He did this, moreover, precisely as we must do it, not by the will of the flesh or by the will of man— not even by the will of His own matchless manhood—but by that grace which is the power of God working in us through faith to the overcoming of sin in the production of holiness. But St. Paul's choice of a word carries us further than St. Peter's. According to the latter, to have died in the flesh, as he means it, is to have ceased from sin. We only conjecture when we undertake to say how much further his meaning goes than simply that of physical death. I have carried it the whole length of a spiritual death to sin in the flesh. St. Paul's language is less open to uncertainty. He says that he who has died is justified from sin. The death which is not merely a cessation from sin but a justification from sin must with much more explicit or ex- pressed necessity be a distinctively spiritual and moral death. The ground and meaning of that necessity it will be profitable to analyze and endeavour to understand.

It is impossible that we should be justified except for something in ourselves which can be in us a ground of our justification, or at least can justify our justification. The freest justification that even St. Paul can preach is not an absolutely gratuitous one, for it is a justification of us upon the ground of our faith—which means, taking it negatively as well as positively, upon the ground of our repentance and faith. When I say that God cannot do a thing I mean simply that He cannot contradict Himself; He cannot, for example, do what is absurd or immoral. One who is insensible of either sin or holiness is incapable of justification; one who through the law knows what they are but neither hates the one nor loves the other is in the nature of the thing morally unjustifiable, and therefore cannot by God be just- ified. He who however sinful comes to anything whatever of a sense and hatred of his sin and the beginning of a love and want of holiness can be justified, because he has arrived at the point of becoming, not worthy or deserving, but susceptible of it. Now whether it be the initial justification with which God invests even our beginning of re- pentance and faith, or invests us prior to these even upon condition of them later; or whether it be the great final justification when God shall recognize all Christ in us and ourselves all in Christ,—one thing from beginning to end is the inseparable condition and ground of our justification, and that is our own personal attitude or posture towards sin and holiness. From the beginning it must mean and in the end it must be that which in its totality and completion cannot be expressed otherwise than as a death to sin and a new life in and to God. There is the sin and the sinner in every one of us to be resisted unto extinction, to be denied, mortified, crucified. There is, potential if not actual, in every one of us a spirit, a nature, a life of holiness, a personal sonship to God, which needs to be quickened, confirmed, and brought to perfection. There is no justification whatsoever, either possible or promised, which is any more separable than sanctification itself from the express condition of that repentance and faith which mean from the beginning the death to sin and the life to God. The definition of any thing whatever is that which defines it not in its process or progress alone *but* in its end or completeness. The death and resurrection of Jesus Christ is the very definition of justification, because it is not only the human condition of all justification brought to perfection—that is, repentance and faith carried to their limit—but it is the divine investiture of that condition manifested in a realized righteousness and life. He that has realized his own death and resurrection in Jesus Christ, in the true meaning of it for himself, though it be as yet only in faith, is justified in his faith, is as though already dead to sin and alive to God. He that shall realize his own death and resurrection in Jesus, in the fuller and truer sense of having brought it to the actual reality of an accomplished and finished death to sin and life to God, will know the greater truth and joy of a higher justification; but the merit and the glory of the righteousness in fact will be as much Christ's and not his own as those of the righteousness in faith. In either sense, however, whether in faith only or in fact also, he who has died with Christ, who has died Christ's death, has in the meaning and measure of that act not only ceased naturally from sin but been justified morally and at the bar of eternal justice from his sin.

St. Paul had fully realized the danger, then and always, inseparable from the conception of an objective salvation. If our salvation is complete in Christ, and we are already upon right terms with God upon faith in that, then there is a natural disposition in us to rest in that as though it were all. If we are saved we are saved, and we have only to go on believing that we are saved, and continuing otherwise as we are. The general answer to all such mental fallacies is the insistence upon an obliteration of anything more than a mere logical distinction between a grace of God which is objective to and for us and one which is subjective in and with us. There is no Christ for us really separate or separable from Christ in us. Baptism into His death and resurrection for us is nothing except as it is also and equally baptism into our own dying and rising with Him. We must not conceive of the possibility of any real difference in the things, however it may be possible or even necessary to separate them in thought. The root principle of it all is the fact that nothing can be really ours, spiritually or personally, that is not *ourselves* not only *potentiâ* but *actu*. Our virtue, righteousness, life, salvation, blessedness, cannot be things without us; they are determined and constituted solely by ourselves and our personal activities. Not my righteousness but Christ's must mean inseparably and identically Christ's and mine. Not I but Christ in me, is really—I only in Christ; for Christ is not another instead of myself, but is only my true, divine, selfhood and self. It is impossible to understand St. Paul without entering into his conception of Christ as our universal spiritual humanity, ourselves in God, as Adam is ourselves in nature. The first man is of the earth, earthy; the second man is of heaven. As we have borne the image of the earthy, we shall also bear the image of the heavenly. For that which is born of the flesh is flesh, and that which is born of the spirit is spirit. As we are one with Adam, and what he is, by fact of nature; so by God's grace, which means through God and His activity in us, are we one with Christ, and what He is, by act of spirit.

The essential matter is of course our relation to Christ in His death and resurrection, but we shall certainly understand this better by considering what Baptism has to do with it. And it may be worth our observation, in passing, that St. Paul makes as little distinction between baptism and the reality it stands for as He does between our righteousness as Christ's and as our own. When Luther made Christianity to consist in the realizing our baptism, it has occurred to me that his meaning might be, that if we could really take our baptism as *being* actually both for us and in us all that it *means*, we should know and possess for and in ourselves all that Christ is as our righteousness and our salvation. Baptism doth represent unto us our profession, which is—to be made like unto our Saviour Christ; that as He died and rose again for us, so should we who are baptized die from sin and rise again unto righteousness. Baptism does indeed represent unto us our profession, but it does much more than represent, according to St. Paul. It is God's own anointing and endowing us with the grace of that profession; it is our birth from Himself with the Spirit and into the life of that profession; it is consequently a burial with Christ not only into His death but into a fellowship with His dying, and a resurrection with Christ not only into the fact of His life but into the power of His living.

It is surely the least that we can say of the two sacraments of His life ordained by Christ Himself, that they were instituted to be conveyances to us of Himself. This they are to us, to begin with, as expressions to us of what He is to us and what we are in Him; representations to us of our Christian profession. They are the contents of our faith, moulds as it were, into which our faith is to be cast and to be given shape. They are God's specific and distinctive Word to us of Himself in us and ourselves in Him in Christ. But let us remember what a Word of God is. It not only means, but in itself and to faith is, what it means. If the sacraments are direct Words of God, what they mean they are, and what they are in themselves they ought to be to our faith and to ourselves. It is only the proper response of faith to God's direct Word to say, that baptism not only means but is what it means; that in it we are not only declared but made members of Christ and children of God. It is only a similar language of faith to say, that the Lord's Supper is to us, not only a sign of something, but the thing itself of which it is the sign; that what we offer to God in it and receive from God in it is not a memory or memorial only of Christ, but is Christ Himself alike the object of our faith and the substance of our life. As a word of man cannot do more than represent, a word of God on the contrary cannot do less than be. That which from any one else could not be more than figurative, from God cannot be only figurative. Suppose that all Christians could and would in the truest and best sense simply and sincerely take God at His word; that their faith could take His gifts as being what His word makes them. Suppose that every baptized man should know himself to be, and by the power of God in Him through that knowledge truly undertake to be, one with Christ Himself in all the reality of His divine Sonship, what would be the consequence? Would not all the truth now too much lost to the Christian Church, and so much sought after outside her pale, be at once restored to her? Men want a Gospel which is indeed the power of God unto salvation. They need indeed to know first what salvation means, but that rightly understood, they have a right to an experience of salvation which will leave them in no doubt that it is from God. Why have they not that assurance in the Church? Is it not because we do not believe God? Not that we do not believe in God, but that professing to believe in Him we do not believe Him. If Christ means anything at all to us as the Word of God, He means God in us as in Him, He means God our own actual righteousness and our own actual life. If Baptism means anything at all to us, it means the oneness of Christ with ourselves and of ourselves with Christ. It means the reality of Christ's death as ours and of ours in Him, the reality of His resurrection as ours and of ours with Him. If it means all this, how much of all this *is* it with us and in us? Why the immense difference and distance between what our Christianity is and what Christianity means? Is not the fault all, not in what God is to us in Christ, but in the response which our faith makes to Him in Christ? Now if we are to begin to take God at His Word—that is to say, to believe in Christ in ourselves and ourselves in Christ—*what* are we to take as the exact content of God's word, as the substance of what is ours to be and to do in Christ? Surely not what any one may individually and of himself conceive Christianity to be, but what our Lord Himself has given and gives in the sacraments as divine conveyances to us of Himself and His life. This is what St. Paul sets us the example of doing. Baptism into Christ not only means to him but is to him that personal incorporation into Christ which actually makes what is Christ's his own, which is in him too the very power and reality of Christ's death to sin and Christ's resurrection from the dead. Let one make this entire sixth chapter his own, not merely to appreciate the clearness of its theoretical conception of the real and vital relation of the Christian to Christ, but to feel and share its practical sense and actual experience of the living results of that relation in his own quickened and risen self.

4. NOT UNDER THE LAW
BUT UNDER GRACE

Is it possible, and if so, how is it possible for a moral being not to be under the law? How can it be possible for one like ourselves to be released from the natural personal obligation of being his own true, right self? And the law to a man is nothing but the expression to him of that obligation,—of what he ought to be and the moral necessity upon him of being it. There is an additional feature or element in the law; it not only declares to us what we ought to be, and impresses upon us the moral obligation of being it, but it emphasizes the fact that the being it must be our own. It is our own conscious, voluntary, and actual being ourselves that constitutes us persons and that attaches any value or worth to our being such. There is no better place to insist upon this highest and purest conception of law than in the part of the Apostle's argument that lies just before us. Elsewhere and in certain connections St. Paul speaks of the law in lower and more partial senses, as Jewish, ritual, or ceremonial, formal or literal, etc.; but here it is the law pure, essential, and universal. And indeed with St. Paul there is but one law—the law of God, the law of things, the law of persons. There are many more or less partial aspects, expressions, forms of law—mental, ritual, moral forms— but at bottom or in themselves all these mean one and the same thing, and it is only our misuse or perversions of them that rob them of the deeper understanding and higher respect that properly belong to them. There is no single aspect, or form, or even letter of law that our Lord Himself and St. Paul after him did not reverence, for there is not one which does not in itself mean what all law means—right being, right doing, rightness, righteousness. But here at least, I repeat, we shall see that St. Paul cuts himself loose from all partial forms of law, and has in his mind only the universal, the essential. How then is it possible that we shall be released from the obligation which every moral being cannot but be under to his own law, the law of his own true and right self?

Let us remember that it is that very law—and the more in proportion as it is conceived by us in its highest purity and truth, and in the inviolability of its absolute claim upon us—that is the author of our curse and the minister of our death. It and it alone is the instrument of our judgment, condemnation, sentence, execution. That which in itself, if fulfilled, is the most inherently essential condition and constituent of life, cannot but be, if unfulfilled, the cause and condition of death. And this is the more so the more distinctively the life and death in question are personal, spiritual, moral; that is to say, the more consciously, freely, feelingly, the law of life or death is but the mode of the self-activity of their subject.

In the illustration which the Apostle is about to give, let us keep in mind that the point to be specially elucidated is, In what sense and in what way may we be released from the natural action, or the natural reaction in ourselves, of our own personal law of righteousness; seeing that that action or reaction is within ourselves sin and all its fatal consequences, spiritual, moral, natural or physical? The duality more or less latent or patent in every moral personality which the argument before us now begins to unfold is neither an invention nor a discovery of St. Paul. It has been in one way or another taken into account by every deepest thinker upon human nature and human life. It exists in us in natural potentiality prior to any fact or experience of sin. So far, therefore, from being sin in itself, it is the ground and condition, as of sin too, so no less of holiness; for it is the ground of the possibility of any personal or moral activity and character in us at all. St. Paul's distinction between the natural and the spiritual man in us is not one in itself of sinfulness or holiness. If there were not the spiritual man we should of course be incapable of holiness, because the spirit is the organ of holiness, or of God in us. But if there were not the natural man we should be incapable of either sin or holiness, for the natural man is the organ of the law, by which alone moral distinctions exist for us at all. The original—not fault but—fact of nature or of what we call the natural man, what St. John calls the will of the flesh or the will of man, is its deficiency or insufficiency. It is not a sin of the flesh, or of our nature, or of ourselves in the flesh or in our nature alone, that while we can conceive our law, or form ideals of ourselves, we cannot fulfil our law or realize our ideals. It was not intended that our law should of itself be able to make us perfect or our ideals to realize themselves in us. They are intentionally deficient or insufficient in themselves, because they are neither all nor final. One might say, then, that it is a fallacy of the moral consciousness to hold ourselves accountable or to charge ourselves with transgression or sin. But we do do so, and cannot but do so; and so far from any even true theory or conception of the deficiency or insufficiency of our own powers excusing or absolving us to ourselves, the true progress of the spirit is both to deeper experiences of human inability and to higher conceptions and sense of human obligation. If there is paradox in this, it is a paradox which is our dignity and our glory. The Christian explanation is, that our nature is deficient because it is made for the supernatural, to be more than it can become of itself; that our wills are both necessary and insufficient, because while we can be ourselves, or moral, or personal at all, only through our own wills, yet we can be any of these in the truest or highest or best only through something infinitely other and more than our own wills; that, therefore, however paradoxical it may be, the necessity not only of being ourselves but of ourselves so being must, because it does, coexist and be consistent with the truth of our experienced impotence of ourselves to be ourselves. Let it be paradox, or antimony, or contradiction, or what not,—whatever is essential to the highest actual facts of our freedom, our personality, and our spirituality, or our transcendence of our nature and ourselves through union with God in Christ, that God has made possible, whether or no it is so in itself or we can see it to be so.

Nature, the flesh, ourselves, are ordinarily spoken of by St. Paul as sinful—not, therefore, because they are essentially or in themselves so, but because they are so actually and in us all. It is with us now not only ourselves and God, but our sinful selves and God. But as within every natural man there is a spiritual man, potential or actual; so in every sinner there is a saint, in possibility if not in actuality. And every man, developed up to the point, and not sunk below the point, of spiritual sensation and perception, may be and is more or less conscious of the two men within him—in both stages, of natural and spiritual and of sinful and holy. For as there is no man without the possibility of God in him, so let us hope there is no man without something of the actuality of God in him. The man who is unconscious not only of the coexistence but of the conflict of the two selves within him has not entered upon the reality of human life, for it is just that conflict that gives reality to life. There can be no human life at least that is not a choice, a probation, a decision, a renunciation of one thing for another, a victory of one thing over another, a life of one thing through the death of another. And the one thing or another is one self or another, one or the other of the two men in each one of us. There are always two masters of whom only one can be served, two lives of which only one can finally live, two men, one or other of whom must die for the sake of the other.

This is so universally and necessarily the case, is so much the very *essentia* of human life, that our Lord Himself was not truly man if He were an exception to the rule. And that He was any such exception is the thing of all things most contradicted by the whole tenour of New Testament record or interpretation of him. He was in express terms the transcendence of the natural in us by the spiritual; the victory of the spirit over the flesh; the reversal of the law and overthrow of the reign of sin and death, through the establishment of the kingdom of God and Heaven, of holiness and life. All such expressions of the human significance of Jesus Christ can be understood only by acceptance of the following principle of interpretation: As it is impossible for any man to know himself except in the light of the divine revelation of him to himself in Christ Jesus, so is it impossible for Jesus Christ to be known by us except in exact terms of ourselves as revealed in Him. To know Christ as the spiritual man must be identical with knowing the meaning and truth of our own spiritual manhood; to know the process or *way* of spiritual manhood in Him, we must know precisely what we must go through, must suffer and do and become, in order to be spiritual men; what He went through and accomplished in becoming what He is, is in exact terms what humanity needs to go through with and accomplish in becoming like Him. This mutual interpretation of ourselves by Christ and of Christ by ourselves is the simplest key to the understanding of our salvation in Him. When we say that He was that in our common humanity, the being which was its justification, its sanctification, and its glorification, its redemption, completion, and perfection, we have said enough to satisfy all possible conceptions both of His person and His work; and we have at the same time so expressed it in terms of ourselves and in language of our own—ideal but realizable—experience and spiritual possibilities, that He becomes to us the comprehensible truth of our own salvation, because of our actual human life and destiny.

We may proceed now to St. Paul's illustration of the point for which we have been preparing, the crucial question of our possible release from the natural action or operation of our own law. The law, we are reminded, has dominion over a man as long as he lives. How can a man be absolved from his highest obligation, or be divested of his highest characteristic, in the fact of that obligation? How can it cease to be his duty to attain and exercise his highest manhood, or can he be relieved of accountability or responsibility for failing to do so? How can that which reveals to him and calls him to his highest activity and life not judge and condemn him when he fails to accept the revelation or respond to the call? If obedience and realization and fulfilment by himself of his law is the condition, constituent, and content of life and blessedness for him, how can disobedience, non-realization, and defeat of his law be or be made anything else to him than death and a curse? All these are questions involved in the nature of things and not of mere arbitrary suggestion or solution. How may a man stand both acquitted and released in the presence of his own inviolable and violated law?

The only possible way is the one which begins with a distinct consciousness of the facts as they are. The knowledge of sin is the only beginning of salvation. The knowledge of sin as sin is a moral and not only an intellectual conception; it is an attitude not only of the mind but of the affections and of the will with respect to it; it is a hatred of sin. But there is no such thing or possibility as a mere negative hatred of sin; there can be no hatred of sin that is not a positive and definite love of holiness. The sole and indispensable condition of human salvation lies in the only right attitude possible for man towards the two things that are his personal alternatives, the matters of his moral choice, the determiners of his spiritual destiny, the makers and the make-up of his heaven or his hell. God and Heaven are a Spirit, a Law, a Life; the Devil and Hell cannot be done away with, as at least symbols of an indisputable actuality,—a counter spirit and law, not of life but of death. Now I repeat that the only right attitude towards sin possible for man in his present condition is that whose beginning is repentance and whose end is the putting away of sin, and that the only possible attitude towards holiness or God is that whose beginning is only faith but whose promise and fulfilment is the "God in us and we in God" of Jesus Christ. How are these beginnings to attain their actual ends in us; how is repentance to be an actual putting away of sin, and faith to be indeed the life and holiness of Christ?

The law has dominion over a man as long as he lives. Only death can release him from it. A woman who is married to a husband is bound by the law of her union and oneness with him as long as the husband is alive. Only the death of the husband could release her from that bond and justify her in uniting herself with another man. In our first or natural manhood we are indissolubly united with and under the law of the natural man. It is only in him, subject to all his conditions, bound by his natural necessities and his moral obligations, that we are men at all or can live human lives. The moral obligation to obey or fulfil our law is the most imperative and inviolable of all the conditions of human life. Obedience to it is in itself life, and violation of it is death. When we say that nothing but death can deliver us from the dominion and operation of that law, it is manifest that the death which can so release us cannot be the simple natural fact of physical dissolution; it therefore devolves upon us to define what that death is. The death of the first husband is the death in us of the natural man; and the natural man is regarded in his special and highest relation to the moral law. What is that relation, both in what it ought to be, and in what it actually is? Is he living in it,—in the sense in which it not only is said but is true that, He who doeth the law shall live in and by it? If not, then there is but the one alternative,—he must die by it. But, while it is impossible that we shall be saved in the life, or by the obedience of the law, there is a way in which we may be saved by its death, or by the death which it inflicts. Suppose that the law, while it has failed to secure obedience and so to confer life, has nevertheless, in the very act and by the very fact of convincing and convicting us of sin, taught us the meaning and the obligation of holiness; suppose that it has so brought us into the foretaste and experience of sin and its consequences, as to impart at least a suggestion and prevision of holiness with its immunities and rewards; suppose it has gone yet further and has nursed and nurtured in us the sense of need and the ardent longing for holiness and life,— if the law should go no further, will it not have already put us upon the road and created in us the necessary condition of salvation? But suppose it should have gone further,—have gone as far as it can, and have accomplished its perfect work; suppose that under the discipline and experience of the law we shall have been brought to the extremest knowledge of the completest consequences of our condition under the law; the very end of our natural resources and limit of our natural powers and possibilities;—how then shall we characterize or describe the point we shall have reached? To have come to the end of ourselves and of all potentiality within ourselves; to have made full experiment of our law and of the principle of our own personal obedience to it; to have been tried by it and found wanting, to have sought life by it and found death,—does not this bring us fairly up to that death of the old man, the death in ourselves, which is the one opportunity of divine grace, the one condition of human release and redemption? To have learned the lesson the law was commissioned to teach; to have been brought to the point nature and ourselves were predestined to reach; to have been thus prepared for God's part and our own eternally predetermined activity in Him, this is the way in which the law, not through its life but through its death, has performed its part in bringing us life.

What we mean, then, by the death of the old man, the first husband in us, is this: As long as we were in our old selves, or our own selves, we were under the dominion of a single moral alternative—either to live by our law or to die by it. That is to say, we were under the moral necessity either of realizing, fulfilling ourselves in accordance with the principles and conditions of our moral perfection and blessedness, or else of experiencing the consequences and suffering the penalties of something more and worse than merely having failed in and lost these. For moral failure or loss is something different from mere natural failure or loss; and its penalties are different. It is a failure that brings with it condemnation and a loss that involves in it guilt. The death of the old man in us consists in part in our full realization of our failure and loss in him; but it consists in yet greater part in our full sense of sin and guilt in him. Fellowship or participation in the death of Jesus Christ, the realization within ourselves of the meaning and reality of His death, is an actual experience of the deadness of ourselves in ourselves alone, in union with mere nature, the old man or Adam, the first husband, the flesh. It is something more, however, than that mere sense of impotency or deadness to the requirements and activities of the real life of the spirit. The impotence or deadness is not of our mere condition, it is of ourselves. Consequently, the death of which we are made conscious in Christ is the death not of mere deadness but the death of sin and sinfulness. The adequate consciousness of that death in ourselves to which we are brought in Christ, the fellowship it gives us in His attitude towards it, is the beginning and the condition of our deliverance from it. The consciousness and sense of being sinful is an experience of the death that sin is; but that very knowledge or experience that sin is death is already such a death in itself for sin as carries in it the death to and from sin. Jesus Christ Himself encountered, came face to face with, experienced, not only all the deadness of humanity in itself, the flesh, for the life that is higher than itself; but all the sin necessarily involved in a life lived only in it. His human immunity from the sin of the flesh was purchased only by that perfect sense of the sin and death necessarily involved in a life in the flesh, which I have described as being such a death in consequence of as to be a death to and from it. He felt himself in his humanity involved in the sin and death of humanity; He saved Himself from sinning and dying with it by so dying to its sin as to rise out of its death.

That death and resurrection of Jesus Christ was an act not only in humanity but of humanity. If our faith can meet and answer to God's grace; if we can see in the act of Him the act of us, because the act of God in us,—then not only may we, but must we, say that with Him our old selves, the old husband, in union with whom we sinned, is crucified, dead, and buried. It is not only that he has died from us, but we died in him; for in him we have felt and known the full weight of his sin and his death; we have experienced the death for what we were in him, which is the only way to the death to and from what we were in and with him.

As the wife can marry a new husband only if the old husband is dead, and her union with him and life in him have come to a lawful and rightful end,—so we can be in lawful and gracious union with Christ only as we are dead in ourselves, only as in the old self we have known his sin as sin and have suffered his death as death. But if we have truly known the meaning of Christ's death to the flesh or old man of sin, then indeed are we no longer under the dominion of the law. We are no longer under its condemnation or subject to its penalties; for have we not already in and with Christ endured the one and suffered the other? Have we not already died not only for but to and from our sins, and been raised out of and from our death? We have died in the old man and the old life of the law and of sin and death, and we are alive now in the new man which is Christ and which is holiness and eternal life.

5. THE LAW OF THE SPIRIT

From this point on we may be occupied with the more positive and detailed construction of that life in Christ which, according to St. Paul, constitutes, or is, human salvation. There is but one truth of the being in Christ, but there are stages or degrees in the realization or actualization of that truth. There is an objective being in Christ even prior to faith, which is indeed the condition and content of faith; for how shall we realize or actualize by faith our being in Christ, unless our being in Christ is already a fact to be so realized? Faith does not create a fact, it only accepts one; the effecting or creative cause in our salvation is in God's act, which comes first and consists in His placing us in Christ for salvation. Our act of faith is only the apprehending or realizing cause, and could not take place at all if there were not already in God's act the thing to be apprehended and realized. In the truest sense of distinctively Christian faith, Baptism may be said to properly precede Faith; just as in every case the act of adoption, or the active adopting, is prior to the passive or acceptive being adopted. The act and truth of Christian Baptism furnishes from God the matter or content of Christian Faith, whose sole function is to realize, to make actual or real, our baptism.

Not only is there a being in Christ prior even to our faith, which faith does not effect but only accepts, but even in the very first act of faith, or of spiritual apprehension and appropriation on our part, there is already the beginning of a subjective real, or realized, being in Christ, which, as St. Paul holds, is the earnest and pledge to us of our complete real being in Him. But these earlier stages of being in Christ will themselves be better understood if we follow our principle of defining the thing at once by what it is not in its progress but in its completion. The complete being in Christ means the complete being of Christ in us. The branch is completely in the vine only when the life of the vine is completely in the branch. The life of Christ, or the life in Christ, is best understood in its perfection in Christ Himself, or in us conceived as complete in Him.

In Christ Himself, then, or in ourselves as we shall be complete in Him, we come to study the law of spiritual manhood. St. Paul calls it The law of the spirit of life in Christ Jesus. He might equally well have said The law of the life of the spirit in Christ Jesus. There may be this difference: The law of the Spirit of life, or The law of the life-giving Spirit, emphasizes the universality and the divine personality of the One source and substance of all life, the Spirit of God; whereas when we speak of The law of the life of the spirit—especially as, in the case of ourselves, involving a contrast with the life of the flesh— we mean more immediately and emphatically the spirit as our own. But what is our own spirit but the organ of the universal or divine Spirit in us; and what is the law of that life-giving Spirit in us but the law of the life of our own spirit in Him?

By the law of a thing we mean the mode of the thing's own proper operation or activity,—how it acts or operates when it is true to itself, or to its appointed nature and function. The true activity or function of the spirit is spiritual life. We cannot define ontologically the *what* of the spirit or of spiritual life, any more than we can define that of natural life. What we can do, and all that we need to do, in both cases, is to define the mode or law of their actual or phenomenal action; that is to say, we can determine and express the particular activities in which life spiritual, as well as life natural, normally and properly manifests itself, and in doing so we are stating its law. The law of the Spirit of life, then, as it is revealed in actual operation in Christ, or as it is manifested in an accomplished human salvation, is the exact and actual form or mode of God's activity in us in making us spiritual men. Or, putting it the other way, the law of the life of the spirit in us, as manifested in our salvation in Christ, is the form or forms which our spirituality assumes in union with Christ and in the actual process of our salvation in Him. We are dealing thus only with the observable phenomena of spiritual life; as to the essential matter or substance of the life of the spirit, I have only to say, that as it is the life of the Spirit of God in us, so we only know that it is the life of our spirit in God. The life of God as a Spirit is communicable to all beings who, by virtue of spirituality in themselves, are capable of relationship or participation with His spiritual nature or personal disposition and character.

I am more and more convinced that St. Paul gives an exhaustive as well as exact inventory of the proper activities or functions of the human spirit under the familiar terms, Faith, Hope, and Love. A perfect faith would perfectly relate man to God, and the life of man to the life of God, as the objective perfect cause of all perfection in himself. A perfect hope would furnish the necessary subjective condition of man's adequate or complete self-comprehension and self-realization in God. A perfect love would contribute all the substance, or matter, or content of the entire life of God in man, and the entire life of man in God. The perfection of God in man, which is the object of faith; the perfection of man in God, which is the object of hope; and, in the third place, not alone the perfect being of God Himself in man, or of man himself in God,—but, by consequence of that, the perfection in man of that which is most essentially God, and the realization in God of all that is most distinctively man, which is the divine principle and ultimate reality of love or goodness,—what outside of or more than this can constitute or dignify or bless the true life of the spirit of man!

What has been said thus succinctly, and somewhat mystically, of faith, hope, and love, as comprehending all the proper functions or activities of the life of the spirit of man here upon earth, is capable of being said not only more in practical detail but in more scientific form and in terms of more common experience. And first with regard to the principle of Faith: There is no disposition in general to underrate the part and power of faith in the business of life. In one sense or another, under one form or another, all of us recognize and admit that the pith of enterprise and success in action comes from the faith with which we act. Giving it at once the widest application, he who has the most faith in things as they are in the world is in the condition and attitude to make the most of, and to derive the most from, things as they are in the world. In the application of this practical principle we are disposed to emphasize one side of it to the extent of saying that, for the effectiveness of life, it is a secondary matter what we believe; the point is, how we believe it. But, when again we look at the matter in its largest view, no one surely will deny that it is more effective for life to have faith in the true ends, or end, of life than to have never so complete a faith in those ends that are false and delusive. And surely, too, to have a perfect faith in and to work with things as they are in the world, as they are in reality friendly and assistant to the true ends of life, differs by the whole heavens from taking and using them, with all possible conviction, as they are not. I conceive the function of faith to be, to bring the personality of man—his mind, affections, and will, and so his life—into understanding, sympathizing, and co-operating attitude and relation with the truth and beauty and goodness of things as they are. I think we should cease from trying to prove the unprovable, and take to knowing the entirely knowable fact that the universe in which we are is a personal universe. The realities of it are not the mere elements or rudiments of matter and mechanism, but the highest activities of spirit and life. Like everything else, the universe itself is to be defined by itself at its highest and not at its lowest, not by its lowest constituent elements but by its highest constituted whole of divinest worth and value. The ultimate reality of things as they are is the highest good of the spirit, which is identical with the highest spiritual good of goodness, or love.

Now, then, let us look at the distinctively Christian faith as it is portrayed for us in this great eighth chapter of the Epistle to the Romans. We are brought in the faith of Jesus Christ into the most complete not only understanding but unity with the entire working of all things as they are in the world. We see the meaning, purpose, and glorious end of things; the painful but necessary and salutary process of things; the seeming and superficial enmity but deeper and real friendship of the things of life for all who understand; the actual working together for good of all things to those who enter into the divine purpose and unite themselves with the divine co-operation; the already assured more than victory for those who, however deeply and darkly involved for the present in things as they are, yet know themselves to be one and at one with the spirit and reason and issue of things as they are. Quite apart from the question of the objective correspondence of reality with the contents of such a subjective faith, one must feel the advantage and power of such a feeling, if not knowing, ourselves upon such terms of amity with the world with which we have all to do. Such a faith in itself, apart from its warrant in fact, is assuredly the best equipment for doing the most in the world and making the most out of it. But how would the power and advantage be multiplied by the addition, that the subjective conviction of faith is, in the spiritual order of the world, the ordinary and necessary means and condition of the personal acting in it of a world or kingdom of actual objective spiritual reality and fact! More important to us than even the power and advantage that comes from faith in the truth of things, is that which comes from the truth and reality and actual operation in us of the things of faith.

As to the question of the objective validity in fact of the subjective contents of faith, I can only repeat words already used: for the things of the spirit we need a more distinct and separate method of their own. The things of sense experience are all without us and need to be brought and proved *to* us in order to be known. If we make the kingdom of God similarly an order without us, like that of nature, then similarly, too, it will depend upon proofs or verifications *to* us of the same kind. But the kingdom of God is made up altogether of what we ourselves are; not of what things are to us or in their action upon us, but of what we are to things and in our reaction with them. It is the kingdom of our own attitude towards and relations with our world of environment. The revelation of God in Christ is not designed to add anything to our natural or scientific knowledge. It is a revelation of nothing *to* man, but of everything *in* man. We see all God, all truth, all beauty, all good and goodness, *in Him, in man*— and that is all we see. No more in Jesus Christ than in us is God visible otherwise than within Him, in the quality and character of His visible manhood and consummate personality. These things of the life of the spirit itself can never be proved *to* the spirit; they can only be proved *in* it. They cannot be known by proofs; they can be proved only by knowing. When our Lord says to us, I speak that I do know and testify that I have seen; or when St. John after Him says, What we have ourselves seen and known of the Word of life that declare we unto you, here is the testimony of spirit to spirit of the supreme reality of things which are true only in the kingdom or world of spirit. Knowing beyond all peradventure and with the only immediate certainty possible for man—the certainty of his own interior personality—the essential things of the spirit, we may infer and deduce connections of it with the things of external and natural fact,—but the moment we do so we must, in the sphere of the natural, submit ourselves loyally to the principles and laws and tests of natural knowledge. If the spiritual man is sole judge in things exclusively of the spirit, so in the realm of natural fact around us there must be no spiritual interference with the autonomy of natural observation and conclusion.

Let us sum up the true spiritual contents of our faith in Christ. First, there is the unqualified truth of the perfect being of God in man,—not an immanental being in him which is as true of one man as another and as true of things as of men, but a transcendental being in him, realized first in Christ and through Him to be realized in us, a being in us in union of persons and not mere relatedness of nature.

This is the primary truth of the kingdom of God within us, and it is as verifiable by us from within as it is unprovable or undisprovable to us from without. The Life that was manifested to the world in Jesus Christ is a life in which we are called to share, and just in proportion as we do share it, as we approximate to His own perfect participation in it, can we too say like Him, I speak that I do know and testify that I have seen.

The second truth of our faith in Christ is the revelation and realization we have in him of ourselves in God. Christianity reveals God not merely as love, but in the highest personal form of love, as universal and perfect Father. As the supreme perfection and blessedness of God consists in what He is, in the unsurpassable limit of His divine selfhood or personality, so the supreme activity of God in the world which He has made not Himself is that of His divine Self-communication. To *other* Himself in others than Himself, that is the highest work, the divinest act of love, of which even God Himself, or Love itself, is capable. So Christianity, without ever adequately saying or knowing why, yet forever reiterates and insists, that God in the Godhead itself is essentially and eternally Father, and in the Kosmos, in all the infinite creation, is everywhere Father, and in the nature and destinature of man is at last and forever to be known and crowned Father. Fatherhood is love concrete and eternal in God Himself. It is love ἐυδιάθετοδ—love inherent and essential in the divine nature and action. Sonship is love προφόρικόδ—self-reproduced, no longer in itself but in another,—the other, a veritable other-self, with whom it is one not in a numerical, natural unity, but a new, personal and spiritual unity. The eternal Sonship which is divine in Christ becomes human through Him. It extends and imparts itself to embrace and include humanity, and in humanity the whole creation of which it is the head and end. To know ourselves in Christ, then, and in Christ to know ourselves sons of God and heirs of His own eternal life, is indeed to know ourselves with a knowledge that transcends all human science and of which faith is the only possible human vehicle or expression. The difference between fatherhood and sonship is extended into that between love and grace; sonship is the father *in* the son, grace is love in its object—what we might call *applied* love, love in energy or actuality. We speak, therefore, of the love of the Father and the grace of the Son, the one standing for what God is to us, the other for what God is in us. The one is love in itself, in its source or origin, the eternal divine disposition toward us; the other is love with us, in act, in divine operation within us.

As the first two truths of our faith in Christ might be called simply those of the Father and the Son, so the third may be designated that of the Spirit. Or, to put it in the other way, as the first two may be called those of the divine love and the divine grace, so the third may be named that of the divine *koinonia*. This word is not adequately represented by communion or fellowship. St. Paul objects to the word *mediator* in the phraseology of Christianity, because a mediator is not of one but of two; whereas God and man are not two but one in Christ, and there is nothing, not even a mediator, between them. So I object to the words communion and fellowship simply as not going all the way of that unity of God and man in Christ which is the truth of the Holy Ghost. The truth of the Spirit of God is the truth of the spirit of man. The *koinonia* is not real or complete so long as the spirits are two and not one. We have it in its completeness only as the eternal, personal Spirit of God is the actual personal spirit of the man. We have it at all, in its beginnings and growth, only to the extent to which the Spirit of God has become our own spirit. God is indeed in the truest sense with us; but without us or within us no man hath seen or can see God otherwise than in what God is in himself and as himself—that is, in what he himself is and the spirit he is of in God. The truths of faith, then, are these three: the truth of God Himself in us, the truth of ourselves in God, and the truth of the perfected not merely external relation but internal unity or oneness of God and ourselves.

Having given so much attention to the principle of faith as the first great function of the spirit, we may deal more briefly with the other two. I make the great point of distinguishing the action and part of hope from those of faith because the meaning of the one has been too much lost in the overshadowing light of the other. Faith has to do with the infinite not-ourselves or about-ourselves that is without us; hope is properly concerned about ourselves. It is a just charge against Christianity that it has been made too much a doing for humanity from without, and too little the doing of humanity from within. It is a waiting upon other powers to take the place of our own and determine our nature and destiny, if not independently of ourselves, yet with only a negative and passive part in it of our own.

Nothing is more necessary for our Christianity than to make it clear to us that there is no such thing as a grace for, which is not also a grace in, us; that God works in us to will and to do in the matter of our salvation not in mere co-operation but only in actual identity with our own working out every jot and tittle of our own salvation, through His grace working not merely with but in us. As faith is not enough in itself or alone, and apart from the objective reality of its objects, so hope is a real power only in conjunction with the inherent and essential truth of its object. The only proper object and end of Christian hope is what we ourselves may be and do and become in Christ, that is to say, in God. We do indeed discard or lose ourselves in and for God in Christ, but it is only to re-find ourselves in all God is in us and we in consequence are in Him. Christianity does indeed say, with Christ Himself, I can do nothing of myself,—but only to add, *Because* not of myself, because of God in me, therefore I can be all things and do all things and endure and overcome and become all things. It is a right and a great thing, as to believe that God is all things to and for us, so to hope that in response we can be all things to and for God. We do not in Christianity reduce our hopes and desires to zero for their vanity and futility; rather, for the glory and the certainty of them, do we raise them to infinity in Christ. We enter upon a career which means in the end that is assured to us—perfect as our Father in heaven is perfect. St. Paul says: If God be for us,—there is his faith: if God is for us, all is for us, and all things are in reality, no matter what the appearance, working together for our good. What then? Why, if God is for us then what can be against us? What can separate us from Him or defeat us in Him? In all that can possibly befall us we are already more than conquerors through Him that loved us. There is his hope—a hope assuredly not in all things done only for him, but equally in all things to be done in him and by him.

The permanent, essential, and eternal function of the spirit is of course that to which faith and hope are but the entrance and introduction. To know God in ourselves, to know ourselves in God, is but the beginning of knowing *what* God is in Himself and us. Unhappily there is here again a practical divorce—not indeed between the knowing and loving God and the knowing and loving what God is, because that were impossible, but—between very much supposed knowledge and love of God, and any real knowledge and love of what He is. Is it not something more than a theoretical inquiry—a serious question indeed of practical fact and import—which of two men is more personally acceptable with God, the man who not having faith in God as a Person, nor knowledge of the hope set before us in Christ, nevertheless sincerely loves the Thing that God is and gives himself to it, or the man who, devoted to the Person of God, and zealous in His cause, does not love nor live the Thing that alone God is and that alone is God either in Himself or in us? Surely it is neither amiss nor unnecessary to insist, as St. Paul for Christ and Christianity so much insists, that not a true faith in the truth of God, nor a true hope in the truth of ourselves, is after all the ultimate thing and function of the spirit, but that reality alone which *is* the truth of God and of ourselves.

6. THE MIND OF THE SPIRIT

What has been said of the law of the spirit's activity, both as the law of the divine Spirit of life in us and as the law of the life of our own spirit in God, may seem to be beside the immediate course of the Apostle's reasoning which we profess to be following. I return to it in the analysis of that *mind of the spirit* which the Apostle describes as being *life and peace*. The mind of the spirit, which St. Paul contrasts with that of the flesh, is in the first place, according to him, based upon the reality of an objective fact,—the fact of a consummated and accomplished act in Jesus Christ. When just before he had summed up his vivid account of man's natural condition in the exclamation, O wretched man that I am! who shall deliver me out of the body of this death?—the great change of mental attitude and feeling found instantaneous and decisive expression in the words, I thank God through Jesus Christ our Lord. The new spiritual status is accepted as solidly founded and completely established in an act or fact which has existence as yet solely in the personal experience of the One Man who before God represents all men. Jesus Christ had in Himself, in the unique achievement of His individual manhood, broken the bands and abolished the slavery of sin and death.

The second point in the mind of the spirit is necessarily the recognition of the significance of that objective act or fact for ourselves, or the relation of our spirit or spiritual status to the deliverance or redemption wrought in our common humanity by the individual act of Jesus Christ. The truth of the relation in question may be expressed as follows: The act of divine redemption wrought in Jesus Christ is—representatively, potentially, and really—an act of God wrought in humanity; and conversely the act of self-redemption accomplished by our Lord in His humanity is in all respects similarly an act of humanity wrought in God; that is to say, in the love and grace and fellowship of God, as realized and manifested in the person of Jesus Christ. This relation of Christ and His act of redemption to us, and of us to Him and it, is, according to St. Paul, the divinely significant truth of Baptism. Baptism is an act of God relating us to Christ and to Christ's redemptive act. It not only makes us one with Him, but it makes His death to sin our death to sin and His life to God our life to God. This, one might say, is only representative. But God never merely represents; His representation is always at the very least potential of reality; and in this case all it wants and awaits is our realization through faith to make it reality in ourselves. St. Paul knows himself after his baptism only in Christ; but he knows no Christ but Him crucified,—Christ's death not only the representation but the power and the reality of his own death to sin, as Christ's life is of his own risen life to God. The substance of Christianity is indeed to realize our baptism.

The mind of the spirit cannot but recognize two senses, or at any rate two widely separated stages of meaning, in that word *to realize*. In its entirety, and in its fulness of meaning even here, it means to bring to reality or to make real. What a truth it is that we realize ourselves, accomplish our end and destiny, in Jesus Christ! What a meaning it gives to faith to know that there is positively no limit to its function and power to realize or actualize God's Word to us; that God's Word to us, which is Christ Himself, is not only as full of meaning, but as full of power, and not only as full of power or potentiality, but as full of actuality or reality to us and in us, as our faith will make it, or will suffer it to be! It is literally true that in the things and life of the spirit it is with us precisely and exactly *according to our faith*. Our faith is the measure of ourselves. There would be no impossibility in an instantaneous sanctification or even glorification, if there were none in an instantaneous perfection of faith. But faith like every other human faculty is a thing of growth and progress. We might be made like Christ in a moment, if we could know Christ in a moment or a day. But to know Christ is to know ourselves and sin, and God and holiness. To realize, then, our baptism in the fullest sense would be to bring to reality through faith all God's grace to us in Christ, not only a representative or potential but an actual and completed death to sin and life to God; nothing less than that can be the meaning and end of all true repentance and faith. But seeing, in the thing itself and in ourselves, the impossibility of such an immediate realization of God's gift of life in Jesus Christ, we fall back necessarily upon a lower form of realization, a realization, as I have expressed it, not in the attainment of fact but in the proleptic appropriation of faith.

To know oneself is not necessarily to know oneself unto perfection. There is none of us who does not know himself, as himself, although the best of us knows but little of his whole self. So any one of us may not only know his life in Christ, but may know that his life is complete in Christ, although as yet he may know very little of all that is to be known of either Christ or himself. It is not a spiritual impossibility, or even difficulty, to know this much; that the change from spiritual death to spiritual life has got to take place in ourselves and to be an act of ourselves; that it has to be an attitude on our part towards sin whose meaning and end can be nothing less than a death of sin to ourselves or of ourselves to sin, or on the positive side an attitude towards God and holiness whose only end can be the life of holiness in ourselves; that that is just precisely what Jesus Christ not only means but is; and that Jesus Christ is not only God's revelation to us but God's realization in us of all that He is in Himself. What do we mean when we say that repentance and remission of sin are preached to us in His name, or in Him? Is it not, that we see in Him a divine grace and power of repentance unto the death to sin, and of faith unto the life of holiness? What do we mean when we speak of Him as the Baptizer with the Holy Ghost? Is it not that we are baptized in Him with a divine grace and power to die His death to sin and live His life to holiness and God? What though an eternity may be profitably occupied with bringing this truth to its full reality, to being perfect as our Father in heaven is perfect, to knowing Christ as He is and being made like Him,—what we may be thus forever realizing in fact may we not at once realize in at least implicit and ever unfolding thought in a faith that shall be forever shining brighter and brighter unto the perfect day? It is this forereaching power of faith, to see the end already in the beginning and to possess the gift in the promise, that religion makes such valuable use of. What if we had to wait for the possession and enjoyment of its gifts until the end! On the contrary it is only through foreknowledge and desire and pursuit and assured confidence and ultimate attainment of it, in other words it is only as it has been from the beginning an end of faith and hope, that the end itself can become to us at last one of actual realization in fact. So it is that our present spiritual status is one of faith and hope, and that not alone our justification, or perfect acceptance in Christ for all He is, but everything that is to be ours in fact in Christ is already ours in faith in Him; and in the confident faith of man as in the assured grace of God, whatever may be predicated as true of him is predicable *as though* true of us. God's Word to faith and God's Spirit working in and through faith will as assuredly fulfil themselves in the realm of spirit, as when in that of nature God said, Let there be light, and there was light.

The mind of the spirit rests upon an objective fact, upon an act of life which has been accomplished before it and for it, and which carries in it not only the full meaning but the efficient potentiality and the ultimate realization and reality of its own actual life in God. The relation of the human spirit to that act of life in Christ is one primarily of faith. It is the privilege and province of faith to see in Christ God revealed in the life of man and man realized in the life of God. There is nothing that can intervene between the spirit and that fact, except the spirit's own want of faith in it. Where the faith exists, nothing separates it in degree or in time even from the completeness of the fact but its own finite limitation and its need of growth from finitude to infinity. But faith is already fact, where it rests upon fact however at present above and beyond it. We are partakers with Christ, we are partakers of Christ, if we hold the beginning of our hope steadfast unto the end. But the mind of the spirit is no mere quiescent or acquiescent state; it is no resting still and satisfied in a condition of objective salvation, a salvation for or instead of its own. It is the highest energy or activity of the spirit itself. It is, as the Apostle describes it, the actual working within us of the law of the Spirit of life, or of the law of the life of the spirit. Life is the busiest and most active thing in the world, and the life of God in the spirit of man has a great and endless task before it,—nothing less than to know Christ and be like Him, perfect as God Himself is perfect.

However inchoate and imperfect the present life of the spirit, it is already not only life but peace, when it knows that it is working straight along the lines as well of the perfect truth of itself as of the eternal truth of God. Faith, as we have seen, is then indeed the greatest power when it rests in that which is itself the greatest power to the truest ends of life. And not only such a power but the only such power is the power of God working through human faith unto human salvation. And human salvation is nothing else or less than living the life of God and working the work of God. It may be very pertinently asked, What *is* the life of the spirit here apart from the life of the flesh?—using the flesh, as I think we may, not in its acquired bad sense, but as St. Paul himself, for example, uses it when he says, The life I now live in the flesh I live in the faith of the Son of God who loved me and gave Himself for me. I think we may illustrate how we may live the life of the spirit without withdrawing from the flesh, or from the world, in their truer and normal sense, or without taking refuge in so-called otherworldliness. Is there anything overstrained in our Lord's demand that in all things we shall seek first God's kingdom and righteousness, and in His promise that then all things else shall be added to us? There are in every act in the flesh or in the world, in their indifferent or colorless sense, two parts— the act itself and the spirit of the act, or what the *act* is and what the *man* is in the act. Now surely no one will deny that in any act or human activity the important thing is the man himself, or what spirit, or spiritual quality and character, he is of. Can any other greatness or success in the act really compensate for its not being a right act, or for the man being unrighteous in it? So far from life in the spirit, while we are where and as we are, meaning a life of abstraction from life in the flesh and in the world, I hold that any such life is for us as inconceivable as it is impossible. Life in the spirit means abstraction from the flesh and the world precisely in the sense and in the degree in which these are actually sinful, or are contradictory of the real and true life of the spirit or of the man himself. To go yet further, I have contended that as we are constituted and placed in the world our holiness or divine life are as much conditioned by one actual attitude, as our sin and spiritual death consist in another and the opposite attitude, towards the flesh and the world as they are. In other words, so far as our experience and knowledge can yet go, our present relation to the flesh and the world is as necessary to our holiness or our life of the spirit, as it is the cause or occasion of our sinfulness or our indulgence in the lusts of the flesh.

How life in the spirit is in itself life and peace will perhaps better appear if we consider how life in the flesh is in itself death. That life in the flesh is sin does not mean that the flesh in itself is sinful. This may be made clear by an analogy. Men of modern scientific mind speak of what we have called original sin as "our brute inheritance." Accepting, for the sake of illustration, the phrase and what it denotes,—what of brute or animal nature man inherits as the raw material of his earthly life is not in itself evil. On the contrary, it is quite the proper stuff out of which to make himself or his manhood. Whether one makes a man or a beast of himself depends upon the use he makes of identically the same material. Just the same appetites, desires, affections, and passions which controlled by freedom and conformed to reason make the man and invest him with all his virtues, not so controlled and conformed keep him back in the life of his brute ancestry and constitute what we call his bestiality. Our vice does not consist in the fact that we are first animals, but in the fact that we do not become afterwards men. Virtue consists in the addition or application of reason and freedom to the life and activities of the animal nature. Quite in analogy with this, Christianity stands to us for a yet higher reach or stage of human life. As our natural manhood consists in our no longer living in or according to our lower animal nature but in or in accordance with the higher human endowment of reason and free will, so the spiritual manhood imparted to us in Jesus Christ consists in our no longer living in ourselves, in our natural or mere human power, but in the completeness of personal oneness with God into which in Christ we are admitted. The natural manhood which we thus renounce for the spiritual one is no more sinful in itself or in its order than the animal nature that preceded it. We do not say that the flesh, in the sense of our natural manhood, is sinful, but only that no man can in the flesh be sinless. However blameless an animal is in doing so, the man who abides in his animal nature cannot be other than a vicious being; and however necessary and high a thing man may be in himself and in the exercise of his human endowments and powers, the man who remains in these and will not go up higher into personal union and alliance with the divine and universal Source of all holiness, righteousness, and eternal life, condemns himself to live in a lower world of sin and death. The mind of the flesh is death, for the simple reason that the things that make for and that constitute life are not in or of or by the flesh but come from beyond or above it. The soul that knows nothing of faith or prayer or grace, of that union and communion with God which becomes visible to us and participable by us in Christ, of the holiness which is God's own Spirit and nature and breath of life in us,— knows not all that of which, as the knowing is in itself life and peace, so the not knowing is of itself sin and death. To know God is the only real life as to serve Him is the only true freedom.

7. THE REDEMPTION OF THE BODY

The Apostle begins a discussion in which the body is the leading subject with the words, If Christ is in you, the body is dead because of sin, but the spirit is life because of righteousness; and ends it thus, We who have the first-fruits of the Spirit, even we ourselves groan within ourselves, waiting for our adoption (the consummation of our sonship), *to wit,* the redemption of our body.

However real and thorough one's spiritual apprehension and acceptance of Jesus Christ, however complete one's spiritual self-identification with Christ, the new divine life of the spirit is not *ipso facto* or at once communicated to and made that of the body. A man may be full of an initial faith, hope, and love, which are the signs and activities of the Spirit of God and of the new life of his own spiritual self; he may have so appropriated to himself the righteousness of God in Jesus Christ as to be before God justified through Him; and still he not only may but will long be aware that the new life of his spirit is very far as yet from being correspondingly the life of his body. On the contrary, he will, and the more in proportion to his earnestness and sincerity, discover to his cost that however the spirit in him may be life because of righteousness (because as yet of the righteousness of Christ, not his own), the body in him is still dead because of sin. But, the Apostle goes on to say, if the Spirit of Him that raised up Jesus from the dead dwelleth in you, He that raised up Christ Jesus from the dead shall quicken also your mortal bodies through His Spirit that dwelleth in you. We cannot exclude from the ultimate operation of this promise the physical resurrection of our bodies in a future life; but the promise has a much more immediate application than that to the spiritual business of our life now and here. Taken in its narrower bearing within ourselves it is a promise to the natural in us too that it shall be taken up into the glory of the spiritual. And taken in its wider sweep of prophecy it means that the whole natural order of which man is the head, in what we call Adam, was predestined and is destined to be taken up and included in the higher spiritual order of which man is still the head in Christ.

With regard to the narrower view indicated above, or the assurance that if Christ is in us spiritually He will also be in us naturally, or in other words that He who has given us spiritual life in Christ will also quicken us into natural or bodily life in Him, it is to be observed that the agent in both these acts or operations is the Spirit of God and of Christ. This would seem to indicate that the promise to the body is, primarily at least, not that of mere physical continuance of life after death but that of spiritual participation, here and more perfectly there, in the higher life of the spirit. In other words, the promise is that the life of God revealed and communicated to us in Christ, into which the spirit of man may enter at once through faith and hope, or what we call justification, shall by another and slower process, which we shall have to describe as sanctification, become the life of the body also. And the body thus sanctified or spiritualized will be the spiritual body,—any physical change or progress to ensue in "the body that shall be" being intimately associated with the spiritual change that has preceded and induced it.

There is an older analogy which may assist our understanding of the process just described. There is nothing of rationality or of morality *in itself* in our animal nature, and yet by the exercise in it and upon it of the higher human reason and freedom the animal nature may be rationalized and moralized. According to Aristotle the reason and the free personal will are or constitute the *man,* as such, or as differentiated from his lower, vegetable and animal, natures. There is a pure or intellectual, dianoetic, virtue of the reason itself— the rational faculty, by means of which we see and know things as they are and as they ought to be—and this pure virtue of the reason we may call Wisdom. But there is another, practical or applied, virtue which does not reside in the reason itself, although that is its origin and source, but within the animal appetites, desires, and passions, to which it has been communicated by discipline and habit. So that in the truly virtuous man not only is the reason itself a right reason, and the will a strong and free will, but the very animal nature itself has become, as I said, rationalized and moralized, or made virtuous. Such a man has not by the continuous exercise of his reason and will to make or keep himself moral or virtuous. The animal in him has itself become so, and is so of itself. And that process is the making of the man. The animal nature is the stuff or material out of which in the exercise of his personal endowments of reason and freedom he constructs himself, he molds and shapes his life, his character, his destiny.

Let us apply a similar reasoning to the matter before us. As it is the function of the reason to rationalize or moralize the animal in us, so is it the function of the spirit to spiritualize or sanctify the natural in us. The right reason or wise man sees and knows things as they are and ought to be, but the man is actually rational or wise only as he has impressed his reason or wisdom upon the raw material of his animal nature, that is, upon his appetites, desires, affections, and passions. The reason is the man,—but not so long as it is with him only the abstract or theoretical reason. It is the man in proportion as it has become concrete and practical in all his body, parts, and passions, for apart from these the man has no real existence. The meaning of the spiritual in us is well expressed by the poet, whose language we take the liberty of extending or generalizing a little: Ourselves are ours, we know not how; ourselves are ours to make them God's. Through reason and freedom we become ourselves and our own. Through the Spirit and our own spirits we make ourselves and our own—God's; and so make God our own and ourselves. It is necessary that we shall become ourselves; but it is then no less necessary that we shall transcend ourselves, for in fact we never become ourselves until we have grown up from ourselves into oneness with God. The spirit, or the spiritual, in man sees and apprehends in Jesus Christ God in himself and himself in God. Jesus Christ is to him God his righteousness, God his life. Yet more truly than that the reason is the man, may we say that the spirit of the man is the man; the reason is the man in himself, the spirit is the man in God. What the spirit of the man is, the man is; and when the man in spirit, or in faith, truly sees and knows himself in Christ, God sees and knows him in Christ. But a mere ideal or theoretical faith or being in Christ goes no further than a mere intellectual wisdom or pure reason. It is only applied faith, as it is only applied reason, that is of any practical account. The faith that holds Christ in itself but cannot impart or impress Christ to and upon the nature and the life is not a real faith. And what is the nature or the life of man? Is it not all the animal and the natural or what St. Paul calls the psychical in him? We know nothing of a purely or abstractly spiritual manhood. The spiritual man is a spiritual *man,* not a spiritual something else. He is a man whose manhood, whose animal and human constitution and nature, have become spiritualized by the indwelling and sanctifying Spirit of God and of Christ, and in them of ourselves. If God in Christ is truly in our faith, and so in our spirit, then He will be in our bodies and in all the motions and activities of our natural lives. It is not in being holy outside and apart from our bodies and bodily lives that we are spiritual men; it is only by becoming holy in and through these that we act by act and step by step become spiritual men. Our bodies, parts, and passions are still the stuff out of which we shape and fashion ourselves. Saints and sinners are made, by opposite processes, out of the same material. Whatever our future bodies are to be, the part which the Holy Spirit has to perform in determining them takes place largely here, and it consists in the daily discipline of spiritualizing our natural affections, our bodily lives, our earthly and human selves. We look for a Saviour, the Lord Jesus Christ, who shall fashion anew the body of our humiliation, that it may be conformed to the body of His glory, according to the working whereby He is able to subject all things unto Himself. But the fashioning anew of our bodies into the likeness of His is not a future act of physical new-creation, but an ever present act of spiritual new-creation.

We are at once then, psychical or natural men and spiritual men—just as we are at the same time both animal and rational men, however the two may pull apart in us—and the function of the spiritual is not to sever itself by scission from the natural but to subdue the natural to itself and take it up into its own higher activities and life. Our bodies, too, are members of Christ and temples of the Holy Ghost. The business of human life is to compose the strifes which are not only incident to it but are determinative and constitutive of it. Whether a man shall be animal, or rational and free and human; whether a man will be natural and earthly and of himself only, or spiritual, of God, and divine also,—these are not merely questions, they are the essential and determining issues of human nature, life, and destiny. Man is made to be ever going up higher, taking with him his whole self and leaving behind only the temporary, the accidental, the incomplete, abnormal, or sinful. The natural, the body, in a true sense the flesh, are part of us, and the sin in them consists only in their non-subjection to the spirit. There is no spiritual step, no new breath of the Spirit, no participation of the life of God, no access of holiness, no act or attainment of divine righteousness, that does not require and exact of us some submission or sacrifice of the body, the flesh, our natural selves. This must needs be so, for the reason already given: As sin consists for us only in yielding to the lusts of our fleshly natures or the desires of our earthly selves, so holiness or spirituality originates or exists or acts for us at all only in subduing these lower passions in the interest of higher and holier affections. There is literally no rising for us into our higher selves except over the bodies of our dead lower selves.

The question with any man is not whether the spiritual and the natural man do not coexist and strive for the mastery in him, but only this, which part he himself is of in the strife. Of many, let us hope, there is no doubt of their being on the right side. God knoweth them that are His, and we are encouraged to believe knows many more than are visible to us. Of many, alas, there is too much doubt, or too little doubt, on the wrong side. There can be no question but that in the inevitable issues that so vitally determine our very selves a man must be definitely of one part or the other. If *we* are in doubt, God knows, and as it is with us so it cannot but be for us; we are the determiners of ourselves and our destinies. To be on the one side or the other of that question is to be in the flesh or in the spirit. If we are in the flesh or are living according to the flesh, we are, the Apostle says, going to die,—because the life he speaks of is only in the spirit and through the Spirit of God. If, on the contrary, we are, in the spirit and by the Spirit of God, subduing the flesh or the body, and when necessary mortifying its evil deeds and extirpating its sinful lusts, then we shall live,—because it is in just such victories of our higher over our lower selves that our life affirms and accomplishes itself.

To be ever so little in the spirit must *mean* to be all. If it does so mean, then in God's sight it *is* all. The least of the Spirit of God in us is earnest and pledge of the whole. The first word of the Spirit to us is assurance of the fact of our sonship to God: The Spirit beareth witness with our Spirit that we are children of God. The earliest consciousness and utterance of that fact is properly an infantile one—a cry—Abba, Father! Thank God, we have not to wait to know all it is going to mean and to involve to be son of God in the end in order to be already sons of God in the very beginning. It is through being sons of God that we are enabled to become sons of God; if, on the contrary, we had to become in order to be, we should never be sons of God. For it is a far and a long cry from the Abba, Father of our infancy in Christ to our maturity in Him, from the small beginning of our faith to the final attainment of our fruition. But if we are children, we shall be heirs. All that we are in faith only we shall be no less in fact also. All that sonship now only means to us it shall completely be to us. The inheritance which now is Christ's only, but shall be no less ours also when we shall have learned to know Him as He is and been made like Him,—it is no mere participation in any outward state or condition, it is no physical transformation wrought from without in ourselves or our environment; it is what we ourselves shall be when Christ shall be no longer faith to us but fact in us, when God shall have wrought in us what He has wrought in Him—in Him as only the first-fruits of ourselves, the first-begotten from the dead, our forerunner and leader. For observe carefully the condition upon which we shall inherit: If children, then heirs; heirs of God and joint-heirs with Christ: if so be that we suffer with Him, that we may be also glorified with Him.

As to the sufferings with Christ which are not only the conditions but the means of our being glorified with Him, we are to remember that it is only in the light of our Lord's own sufferings, and of the new meaning and virtue He gives them, that they are spoken of as they are in the Gospel. As the sufferings of Christ abound unto us, even so our comfort also aboundeth through Christ. Sufferings are not in themselves, and by no means to all, means of exaltation. Only in one way or event do they become or are they made so,—when they are used by God and received by ourselves in the direct line of their final cause or purpose. The difficult or painful or variously trying experiences inseparable from human life are the sole conceivable, if not the sole possible, means of determining as well as of testing or proving the personal or spiritual quality of human life. As has been more than once said, so far as our own spiritual characters are concerned, as touching the vital issues of vice or virtue, sin or holiness, the conditions of one are identically those of the other. Virtue and vice, or holiness and sin, are opposite attitudes and actions towards the same things, and it is only in relation with the things which occasion them that, for us at least, they can originate or exist. If there were no occasion for cowardice there would be none for courage, and there could be no courage. If there were no powerful temptation to sin there would be no powerful incentive to holiness, and we should not know what holiness means. To Christ, and to the spiritual man, all the experiences of life, so far as they are trials at all, are simply parts of the one question of sin or holiness, which is the question of life or death. The so-called mystery of evil precisely as it is in the world is the only solution, because it is the necessary condition, of all the true good of the world. For good, spiritual, moral, or personal, is the overcoming of evil. We shall not know Jesus Christ or ourselves, until we learn for ourselves that all the comfort of life, all its strength, victory, and blessedness, comes only through the sufferings of Christ.

The sufferings of this present time are indeed not worthy to be compared with the glory that shall be revealed. The affliction seems light and but for a moment which is working for us more and more exceedingly an eternal weight of glory. But this is so only as, with our Lord, we are looking not at the things that are seen, but at things that are not seen. That is to say, as we are seeing deep into the meaning and looking far to the end of human experience. For—the Apostle goes on to say—the earnest expectation of the creation waiteth for the revealing of the sons of God. The creation here is the natural creation, or what we call nature, meaning primarily at least the natural part in ourselves. We ourselves, which have the first-fruits of the Spirit, even we ourselves groan within ourselves, waiting for our adoption, to wit, the redemption of our body. Our adoption, meaning here the completion or consummation of our divine sonship, waits upon the final release of the body too, the admission of all our natural selves into the liberty of the holiness and life of God. Christ in faith, or in the spiritual man, waits upon and is only complete in Christ in fruition or fact, in the natural man,—meaning by the natural man all that is essential and permanent in our natural selves, the reason made right and the will become free, the desires all purified and the affections refined and sanctified. For I repeat that we shall be no longer ourselves or men, if to be spiritual means to cease to be natural, and is not rather the spiritualizing or divinizing and so the glorifying or spiritually perfecting of the natural, which is ourselves.

The natural in us, our nature, became subject to vanity not of itself but through us, or by our act. Sin originates not in our nature, or in our body, but in ourselves. It is distinctively not a thing or quality of the nature but of the person. But sin immediately and deeply involves the nature or the body, because while it is not of these it is in and through them. They are the sole means and instruments of it, and reap the corruption and curse of it. The promise and the hope is that as the body or nature was subjected to sin and made the instrument of it, not of itself or its own will, so by being subdued to and made the instrument and servant of holiness it shall be delivered from the bondage of corruption into the liberty of the glory of the sons of God. That is the burden of the Apostle's earnest exhortation to us, Let not sin therefore reign in your mortal body, that ye should obey the lusts thereof; neither present your members unto sin as instruments of unrighteousness; but present yourselves unto God, as alive from the dead, and your members as instruments of righteousness unto God.

St. Paul would seem to teach that what the spiritual is to the natural in ourselves, spiritual humanity is to nature in general. The whole natural order is but the body and organ of a spiritual order which it exists in order to serve. Even what we call natural evil, the seeming sin of nature, exists not for itself but for spiritual ends beyond and above itself, of which we can see enough to divine if not always interpret the rest. Spiritual good would be impossible in a world in which there was nothing of natural evil; that is, of what we call natural evil, for natural evil is often the truest spiritual good, if not the condition and means of all spiritual good. Suppose that instead of things as they are, or as they appear, there were on the contrary not only no evil in fact but—what one would then suppose ought to and would be the case—none in semblance. Would there then be any virtue or any righteousness? And if it is answered that there must always be the semblance, if not the possibility or actuality, of evil,—then I say that that semblance is itself the evil and a very real one.

But in reality there is nothing evil but spiritual evil, but evil in the spirit or in the will. The whole world of nature, of natural creation, becomes evil or good with ourselves. It is all evil because we are all evil, and it will become all good when we are all good. As long as we are sinners, it is the condition and occasion and instrument of our sin; when we change our attitude and relation to it, it becomes not one whit less the condition and opportunity and instrument to us of all our holiness and righteousness and life. Let us be indeed children of God, and all nature and the whole natural creation shall in due time be delivered from the bondage of corruption into the liberty of the glory of the children of God.

8. THE PROCESS OF DIVINE GRACE

We cannot know the Spirit of God otherwise than in ourselves, as our own spirit,—any more than we can know the divinity in Christ otherwise than as it is revealed in the quality and character of His humanity. We have seen that the first evidence or expression of the presence in us of that Holy Spirit which is the spirit at once of God, of Christ, and, however inchoately, of ourselves, consists in the sense or consciousness of our sonship to God as realized and revealed to us in Christ. We have also seen, however, that there is a great distance between the initial relationship of sons as it begins to exist in faith, and the final consummation of the character of sons as it needs to exist in fact. Everywhere the business or function of spiritual or personal life is to convert meaning into reality, potentiality into actuality. Because we are in a sense rational and free by nature, we have in another sense to become rational and free by act and character. The having been made sons of God does not absolve us from the lifelong task of becoming, or making ourselves, sons of God. The task of realizing ourselves presupposes selves in us to realize, but we shall never be ourselves without the self-realization.

The process of realizing our sonship to God, through the grace of God working with us both objectively and subjectively, is portrayed in the chapter we are studying. On our part there is first the incipient act of faith, the apprehending that for which we were apprehended by Jesus Christ, the seizing in advance by faith all that is to be made ours by act and in fact. However clear and real this first-fruit of the Spirit is in us—indeed just in proportion as it is clear and real—we at once begin to groan within ourselves, desiring and expecting the realizing and consummation of our sonship, *to wit,* the redemption of our bodies. We have entered upon the rightfully difficult task of making our bodies as well as our spirits members of Christ and temples of the Holy Ghost,—that is to say, of becoming, through all our natural selves *de facto* as well as *de jure,* sons of God. It is rightly a difficult and a painful task, because the difficulty and the pain are a necessary part of the process. We become persons at all, we attain all the virtue, the holiness, the glory and the blessedness, of personality, only through pain and difficulty. St. Paul does not exaggerate the necessity, the wisdom, the power, the glory of the Cross. He does not insist too constantly or too strongly that we shall only be glorified with Christ as we know here how to suffer with Christ. He only declares that all the possible suffering of this present time is not worthy of consideration when compared with the glory that shall be revealed in us; that these light afflictions which are for a moment are working out in us a far more exceeding and eternal weight of glory. As long as we are here we are necessarily under stress of the process of becoming, of making ourselves even as we are being made, sons of God. We are saved in hope, by faith not by sight. But if we really believe in and hope for that which we cannot see, then can we with patience wait for it.

Meantime, with us as with our Lord before us, the gloom that shuts out sight and throws us back upon faith and hope will often so thicken as to obscure even the immediate next step. We will not know so much as what to pray for as we ought. Our voice will be incapable of uttering anything more than inarticulate groanings. But the darkness that is so dark to us is no darkness with God. The soul of the believer is sometimes in heaven and sometimes in hell, but it is as safe in one as in the other: If I go down into hell, behold, Thou art there also! The point is that the process of our redemption is not all our own, and it goes on by methods not all or always understood by ourselves. We are often nearest when we think ourselves farthest off, and farthest off when we think ourselves nearest. God reads order where we see only confusion; our groanings that cannot be uttered are the intercessions of the Holy Ghost to Him for us, and however unintelligible to us it is all clear to Him whose, after all, are all the wisdom and the power of our salvation.

The function of the Holy Ghost is to bring the soul to God, to prepare it to enter into His love and purpose concerning it. The soul thus touched with divine love and admitted into the eternal meaning and purpose of God and itself, all things else must of necessity work with it for good. From the subjective preparation by the Spirit the Apostle passes to the objective array of the all things that from without work together for eternal life with the soul so prepared to work with them. And first of all there is the great objective fact of God Himself eternally and infinitely for it and with it. From the eternity of the past stands first on our side the fact of the divine foreknowledge. The creation of which Man is the manifest head and end exists from and for Intelligence, Reason. We may trust God equally for having known what He was about from the beginning and for having entered upon nothing inconsistent with Himself. His foreknowledge or wisdom was not divorced from His love.

Next, therefore, for us and with us stands the divine forepurpose. Whom God foreknew them He also foreordained or predestinated. Their end was as clear before Him as their beginning and was just as much the concern of the eternal love which is Himself. We are no more objects than we were products of chance. Human personality is too great and precious a thing to have been brought into existence through the travail of the ages without a definite and predetermined purpose, without a destiny commensurate with its acquired and inherent possibilities and promises. Jesus Christ is the sole adequate expression of the divine reason, meaning, and end of human personality. Whom God foreknew, He also foreordained to be conformed to the image of His Son. He is in Himself the realization and revelation of the divine sonship which is the meaning and proper destination of us all, the heavenly pattern shown us in the mount after which our common humanity is to be builded into the tabernacle of the eternal divine presence and indwelling. But Jesus Christ is revelation to us not only of the fact of our divine sonship but of the process by which that sonship is realized. His death and resurrection is the necessary baptism of that new birth; through it alone is He the first-born among many brethren, and through it alone can they share His new birth and life.

Whom God thus foreknew and foreordained, them He also called. There is a deep significance in the fact of the divine call as a necessary moment in the process of human salvation. It is the reference of the matter of eternal life to the action upon it of the man himself. Salvation must needs come to us as a divine invitation or call; it must needs be subject to our own acceptance. Our part, however secondary and subordinate to the divine part, is nevertheless the determining factor. But both parts, in all the necessity and importance of each, are emphasized in the nature of the call. With St. Paul Christianity is in every moment of it a call—a call from God and a call upon ourselves. Not only was he himself called to be an apostle, but every believer is called to be a saint. As there is no official apostleship so there is no personal sanctity except such as comes from God, that to which God calls and appoints or admits us. But equally there is none for us which we do not ourselves accept and assume. The called according to St. Paul are only those in whom both these conditions have been fulfilled, who have been not only called of God to life or office or task but have heard and responded and are in possession or in discharge of that to which they are called. There is no word of God, in the strict or proper sense, except such as is addressed to intelligence or will. A word, properly as such, must be not only an expression of these but an expression to these. The Gospel, which is Jesus Christ Himself, is the final and complete word of God to us, because it is the perfect call, the perfect address and appeal, to everything that is within us, reason, affection, will, character, life, destiny. How all these may be our own, to determine for good or ill, may be incomprehensible to us, but the fact remains. Every true call of nature or of grace is a call to the self that is in us, and a call in respect to which all depends upon the how we hear.

It is only the highest instance and illustration of this, that our Lord is said not to have taken His highpriesthood upon Himself, but only as He was called of God to it. We glorified not Himself to be made a high priest, but He that spake unto Him, Thou art my Son, This day have I begotten thee. His glorification to the highest honour and exaltation of our humanity was indeed His own act and achievement. But, if we may express so glaring a paradox, it was His own act only because of the fact that it was not His own act, but the act of God in Him. His achievement or attainment in our nature of the perfection of holiness and life was an act only possible for even Him in our nature—first because He was called to it of God, and, secondly, because He perfectly heard and perfectly obeyed the call. It was humanity's supreme act, in Him, of perfect faith and perfect obedience—the act by which it at once was made and made itself one with God.

The call of God to us in Jesus Christ is a call first to something immediate and secondly to something ultimate and final. The first is a present status or relation to God which St. Paul describes as this grace wherein we stand, our access or entrance into which, he says, we have had through our Lord Jesus Christ by faith, and the expression of which on our part he describes as a present peace with God. The truth which St. Paul's own use warrants us in designating *justification by faith* turns upon two points—the first being that God's act of human redemption and completion in Jesus Christ is revealed to our faith as potentially the redemption and completion of us all; and the second being that it is the function and obligation of faith to see ourselves so redeemed and completed in Jesus Christ. God's Word, which is explicitly Jesus Christ Himself, is the all-sufficient ground of the obligation of faith to see and accept what God reveals and gives in Him. What is true of us in Christ, who is the truth of us all, is to us as though it were already true of us in ourselves. The immediate effect of this is that where our faith truly answers to the divine grace, we are to God even as Jesus Christ Himself is, in whom He already sees us. Or rather in Jesus Christ Himself even prior to our faith God already sees us, and we have only to open the eyes of our faith to see ourselves there also. He who has this divine vision, whatever the warfare of present condition with him, enjoys already the peace of the faith which brings distant things near and makes future things present. We are not to God only what we have first made ourselves, but what God has by His own grace first made us in Christ, that we are thereby in Him enabled to make ourselves. We are not accepted as sons and righteous through being so, but are enabled to become sons and righteous through being made and treated as such. Of all that is Christ or is Christ's we have divine warrant for saying that we have only truly to believe or to know that it is ours and it is ours. As truly as our Lord could say, All that the Father hath is mine, so truly have we the right to say that all that He Himself has or is is ours.

As whom God calls He justifies, so whom He justifies He glorifies. St Paul knows only, in this positive account of the process of our salvation, the call that is effectual, that is both given and accepted. Consequently he knows of only an effectual justification, where the sonship or righteousness is, in Jesus Christ, equally given and received. Where we truly by faith know ourselves in Christ sons of God, there we cannot but truly in fact and in ourselves become sons of God. True justification cannot but result in true sanctification. Sanctification is the making ours in actuality all that justification has made ours in potentiality. It is the becoming in ourselves all that God has made us in Christ. That which once for all was made ours and us in Him we need time and process to appropriate and convert to ourselves. Salvation can operate in us only through the natural and spiritual organs and activities of ourselves, our reason or intelligence, our affections and desires, our will, our acts and habits and character and life. The law of the action of all these requires all that time and environment have actually to offer to human experience in human life as it is. Our actual experience is just what we need to become all ourselves in Christ, and our actual environment is just what we need for that experience. There is a divine fitness and propriety, not to say necessity, in all that our Lord had to undergo in order to be perfected in our humanity, and that fitness and necessity applied to Him simply because they pertain to us who were perfected in Him. St. Paul is describing the successive steps or moments in the long process of our salvation in absolute or finished terms, and so he speaks not of our sanctification but of our glorification. But it is an old and true interpretation of the words as used by him to define sanctification as glory begun, or in progress, and glory or glorification as sanctification completed. The whole drama of human spiritual destiny as realized and revealed in Jesus Christ may recall the words of Irenæus with regard to our Lord, *Longam expositionem hominis in se recapitulat.* In Him the whole course or process is covered, beginning with the divine foreknowledge in the past and ending in the all-accomplished predestination in the future.

What, then, shall we say to these things? The new light that God sheds upon the divine purpose in Christ Jesus reveals the whole creation a connected and consistent scheme having for its end the spiritual evolution and destination of humanity. If God be for us, who or what can be against us? Instructed and enlisted in the divine meaning and purpose of things, there can be nothing that does not definitely and positively work with us and for us. The need is that we be so instructed and enlisted. And the prime difficulty is encountered in the divine mode of human exaltation,—in other words, in the offence or stumbling-block of the cross. If the mystery of wisdom and love, the meaning and process of divine fatherhood and human sonship, has its expression for us in Jesus Christ, how can we account for it that He who is the revelation to us all of the way, the truth, and the life should have been subjected to all, should have been spared naught, of such a human experience as was actually His. The point of the mystery lies just in the fact that God spared not and spares not. That God spares us nothing of all that the actuality of the world has to subject us to is the supreme act and expression of the divine love and wisdom. That there is no real good but personal good, the good of personality, and that, for us at least, there is no personal, spiritual or moral, good that is not the actual conquest and survival of evil— that is the revelation in Jesus Christ with regard to human life and destiny. For our Lord to have been spared the least of all He endured and overcame, would have been to abridge by just so much the completeness and perfection of His attainment and exaltation. And it was the truth for Him because it is the truth for us, of whom He is the way, the truth, and the life.

The answer to the question of the cross for Jesus Christ, is the answer for us of all questions of the no longer dark or insoluble mysteries of human life. The love that spares not, means on our part the faith and the grace that can endure all and overcome all. Without the former we should never attain the latter, and it is the attaining the latter that is the divine process and test and measure of our human exaltation. He that spared not His Son, and through not sparing glorified and exalted Him, how shall He not, in and with Him, by the selfsame process of unsparing love, bestow upon us all real, spiritual, and eternal good? Jesus Christ is the only and the all-sufficient theodicy. In Him all meanings are revealed, and all divine means justified.

There are two further questions pertaining one to the beginning, the other to the end of God's method and process of grace with us. Who shall lay anything to the charge of God's elect? What if God in His love takes sinners, and the chief of sinners, to Himself? The answer is not merely that God in His sovereign choice justifies whom He will; He reveals more of His secret to us than that. His elect are those who in the exigency of their own hopeless strife with sin and death come to find in Him His grace sufficient for them. Because His grace *is* sufficient, because in the new relation of their present attitude towards Himself He is become their righteousness and their life, therefore He not only sovereignly pronounces them, but potentially makes, and actually will make, them righteous. His justification of them is justified not merely by His arbitrary will, but by all the gracious facts.

And who shall condemn those whom God has so chosen and taken to Himself? Has not Christ died, and risen again? And does not that mean their own death to sin, and their own life to God and holiness? Is not Christ's presence at the right hand of God as their representative and advocate God's pledge and assurance that sin in them as in Him has been condemned and abolished and that there is no longer any ground of condemnation to them that are in Christ Jesus?

One further thought concludes the Apostle's survey of the eternal and infinite grace of God in Jesus Christ. There is no hint or suggestion that the earthly experiences, the cross, of Christ are something instead of their own, and not also their own. The hope and assurance is only that in experiences that are His and ours, ours as well as His, nothing shall separate us from Him; that in His temptations we shall know His power and victory; that having suffered with Him in His death we may be raised up and reign with Him in His life. Who or what shall separate us from the love of God which is in Christ Jesus our Lord? The promise is not exemption from His experiences but salvation and exaltation through His experiences.

III.

THE GOSPEL IN THE GOSPELS (1906)*

The Synoptic Gospels, Matthew, Mark, and Luke, may be seen as the Churchly Gospels, to use a favorite expression of DuBose, because they describe the institution of the Lord's Supper and Baptism and conclude with the disciples acting together as the Church. The Gospel in the Gospels may, therefore, be seen as DuBose's theological reconsideration of the scriptural basis of his Churchly phase. DuBose divided The Gospel in the Gospels into three sections that considered the earthly life of Christ, the resurrection, and the incarnation. There is a correspondence between these divisions and the three levels described in the introduction to this volume that are characteristic of DuBose's theology. DuBose concludes the last section on the incarnation with a chapter on the Trinity that summarizes his system. This chapter has been placed at the conclusion of the present volume.

All of the following selections have been taken from the first section of The Gospel in the Gospels, and they set out DuBose's view of Christ's humanity and his interpretation of the Beatitudes. In DuBose's view we are blessed when we experience the adversity that Christ's human nature experienced because this is the way we become like Christ. In considering the perfection of Christ's human nature and our human nature together, these selections illustrate DuBose's reconceptualization of the incarnation and the Church as a process.

---

* The original text that follows is from *The Gospel in the Gospels* (New York: Longmans, Green, and Co., 1906), pp. 1–41, 51–130.

148

INTRODUCTION

The question of the present is, and we may safely assume that more and more the question of the future is going to be—What is Christianity? There was probably never a time when more, and a more real, interest was felt in the truth of Christ and Christianity. There was certainly never a time when so many and so conflicting conceptions existed as to the meaning of Christ and Christianity.

When the necessity was first laid upon Christianity to define itself, the process by which it did so was one of gradual and progressive but strict and thorough-going exclusion. Not only was nothing permitted the name which contradicted the nature, but nothing that fell short at any point of the totality of the truth of Christianity, as Christianity understood itself. It was not only the truth and nothing but the truth,—it was the whole truth or nothing, the highest or none. Whatever may be said of the spirit or temper in which to too great an extent this process of exclusion was carried out to the bitter end, from no point of view can we with propriety deprecate the result of it. God may have made the wrath of man as well as his zeal and devotion to praise Him, but humanly speaking no other spirit or temper, and no other method, could have effected the working out to its logical conclusion and expression the principle or truth implicitly contained in Christianity.

Unquestionably truth is one, and only error is manifold. Truth is one and is a whole, and not seldom we can say that that which is less than the truth is as untrue as that which is contrary to it. But, for all that, there may be a time when for the truth's sake a very different temper, and a very different and even an opposite method, may be most proper and most useful in dealing with it. I propose—with what right or propriety only the result can determine—to treat the sadly vexed question of Christianity by a process the reverse of that which was necessary in the beginning, by a process of inclusion rather than of exclusion. So far from saying that only that is true which is the whole truth, I bring forward the complementary and not contradictory fact that that which has in it any part of the truth is so far true. I hold that the Gospel of Jesus Christ is so true and so living in every part that he who truly possesses and truly uses any broken fragment of it may find in that fragment something—just so much—of gospel for his soul and of salvation for his life. In testing and illustrating this fact, if it be such, it will not be necessary for us to examine each one of the parts into which Christianity is broken up in these days. There are a few stages or degrees of faith in Christ and Christianity in one or other of which every phase worth considering is contained and under which it may be sufficiently considered for our purpose.

In the first place, there is many a profoundly religious—and shall we not say Christian?—soul, including now some of the greatest upon earth, whose faith in Jesus may be expressed somewhat as follows: They will not undertake to say anything of our Lord, theirs as well as ours, before His appearance by birth in the world or after His departure by death from it. On such points as these they are at the best, or at the most, agnostic. But between these two points of birth and death, in the earthly life lived in common with us all, in the simple fact that Jesus Christ was the man He was and lived the life He lived, they find as much of gospel and of salvation as, they think, humanity can or humanity ought to receive on this earth. What or how much that truly is, it shall be our first task carefully and sympathetically to examine and measure. Let us call this gospel, or so much of the Gospel as this, the gospel of the earthly life, or of the common humanity, of our Lord.

In the second place, in reading the Gospels and trying to understand them according to their intention, it cannot escape the attention of most of us that, however essentially and completely human we see the life of Jesus to be, still we cannot but also see that as human it transcends the ordinarily possible limits of the human. There is no one of the Gospels, there was no Gospel before the Gospels, which does not end necessarily, which does not from the beginning mean to end, in the resurrection. But it is not only that;—in our Lord's own clear consciousness, in the unquestioning concession on the part of all the records, of His personal sinlessness, we have a fact which as much transcends the powers and limits of all other earthly life as His resurrection does. The Gospel from the beginning was not at all that Jesus most perfectly represented our common nature or illustrated our human life, but that He brought with Him something into our nature and life which was not there before, and raised them into something which was not themselves or their own, and to which they could attain only in and through Him. What that was was expressed in the Christian consciousness that Jesus Christ is the human, but the divine-human, conqueror and destroyer of sin and of death. Let us call this second phase or stage of the Gospel the gospel of the resurrection.

In the third place, however sincerely and genuinely human we may regard the life and life-work of Jesus, when once we have recognized in His accomplishment or attainment as man that which transcends human accomplishment or attainment—however it may be in the line of man's higher nature and destiny—we have raised inevitably a further question. How does this man break through or pass beyond the possibilities of universal human nature as it is? How does that which is born of the flesh become in Him more than flesh? The immediate answer was and is: The work wrought in humanity through the life in it of Jesus Christ was no mere act of humanity, however exceptional. It was a work wrought by God in humanity. If, on the one side, it was humanity fulfilling or completing itself in God, it was only so because, on the other side, it was equally and primarily God fulfilling and completing humanity in Himself. How then was the so unique or exceptional personality of Jesus to be accounted for or explained? Was He only a human individual exceptionally blessed or graced? Or, while perfect man, was He, just because perfect man, something more than man? Perfection is no mark of our common humanity, and needs a very high accounting for. So from the beginning begins a questioning which Christianity answers for itself in the gospel of the Incarnation.

There is no form of faith in Jesus Christ true enough to be called a gospel or vital enough to be a salvation which, measured by its own self-limitation, may not be classed under one or other of these several "gospels," or phases or stages of the one Gospel. I claim for each that, if it be real and vital and true so far as it goes, it *is,* so far as it goes, a gospel, and brings in it just so much of salvation.

Our interest in these days in so far undertaking an advocacy of partial truths of the Gospel is no, true or false, sympathy with partial truth, but interest in the truth itself, whole and perfect. The fact of which we are not yet fully aware, and against which we have not yet sufficiently guarded, is this: that the so-called *whole* of truth is quite as apt to ignore or pervert the parts, as the parts are to be blind to the other parts and to the whole. So true is this, that it is a common fact that in larger and more catholic forms of Christianity not merely aspects but important truths and even living powers of the Gospel are so lost to sight and use that we may have to go outside to find them at all, perchance in some fragmentary sect which has been driven outside by its overpowering sense of the importance or necessity of knowing and using them. It is no weak concession then, or condescending charity, that ought to lead us to do full justice to what we consider mutilated or incomplete conceptions of Christianity. We ought to go to them in humility, to learn of them sides and uses of the truth which it may well be they understand better than ourselves. So I go, for example, to the gospel of only the earthly life and the common humanity of our Lord to learn many a lesson and catch many a vision and inspiration of the truth as it is in Jesus, which I am sure is lost to those of us who in the higher ignore the details of the so-called lower side of that divinely human life.

We are to study the Gospel as it is to be found in the Gospels. And there is a threefold view of the Gospels somewhat corresponding to the three stages of the Gospel which we have been considering.

The first and main function of at least the Synoptic Gospels would seem to have been purely reportorial. By far the larger part of them is pure record. They are reports, without note or comment, of our Lord's appearance or appearances, where He went, what He said and did. Never were there writings in which there was so little of the writers, so clear and uncoloured an impression of their subject. But this is not absolutely or entirely so. Before our Gospels attained their present form there had been no little reflection upon the whole earthly appearance, and no little interpretation of the words, the work, and the person of Him who had left so deep a mark upon the world. Now the time has passed when men are able to question the historical personality or identity of the man Christ Jesus. And the time has passed too when they can depreciate the uniqueness and permanence, not to say finality, of His impression upon human history and human destiny. No less is the time past when our Gospels can be resisted or rejected as in the main truthful and true reports of how Jesus appeared and what He said and did in His life on earth. But there are men, among the greatest, and scholars the most learned, the most conscientious, the most devout, who, while able to accept so much of the Gospels as is of pure record, find themselves unable to receive what they conceive to be the results and additions of later reflection upon and later human interpretation of the actual facts of the Gospel.

No one can deny that it is legitimate for a properly equipped criticism—by which I mean a criticism competent to judge of spiritual as well as natural facts and phenomena—to apply the strictest historical tests to the historical facts of Christianity. Making the best, which means also the most critical, use of their materials, profound and devout students construct out of the records as we have them the truest, completest, and most self-consistent conception they can of the person of the great founder of Christianity. In doing this they pass by or reject those elements which seem to them inconsistent or incongruous, as not belonging to the objective fact to be reported but originating in the subjective impression and interpretation of the reporters, or of later believers generally. Such a mode of treatment is not only not to be condemned, but it is not to be avoided. But it will be a long time before a critical acumen sufficiently true and adequate, spiritual enough as well as scientific and philosophical enough, will be generally developed to give us permanent results on this line. Meantime each succeeding and temporarily successful such attempt will be subjected to the tests of time and ever-enlarging experience, and will survive or perish according to its truth or falsity. Still we shall never attain to the larger and truer criticism of the future except as we are trained in the cruder and confessedly still imperfect criticism of the present. And it is only through the growth and discipline of the critical faculty and function, of the powers of discrimination and judgment, that we can be educated to a higher understanding, appreciation, and enjoyment of the highest truth. In the first stage, therefore, of our study of the Gospel I shall follow, as best I may, in the track of the critics. I shall endeavour to admit nothing in the Synoptic Gospels and as of the Gospel which the best present criticism will not admit as pure record, as being of the objective truth of which they are the truthful reporters.

We have recognized the fact that beside the bare record or report of objective fact which constitutes the bulk of the Synoptic Gospels, they all more or less abundantly contain matter that may or may not be objectively true also, but that is the subjective conception and interpretation of the objective facts on the part of the writers, or of the Church which they represent. This Christian or Church interpretation takes two directions and assumes two forms. It is first an interpretation of what we call "the work" of our Lord, meaning by that the purpose and result of His whole human life—as, for example,

atoning, redeeming, new-creating, etc. It is often, of course, difficult to separate between pure record and subjective interpretation,
inextricably intermixed as they are. As an instance, the account of
the intimate connection between the successive ministries of John the
Baptist and Jesus is doubtless largely simple report of the facts. It is
common to all the Gospels and seems to have been from the first the
starting point of the public life and of all the stories of Jesus. Yet I
think we shall see that in the form which the narrative has uniformly
assumed there has been already embodied, in the contrast between
John and Jesus, and more especially in the significance of their re-
spective baptisms, a statement and interpretation of the whole work
of Jesus than which nothing could be more comprehensive or exact.
With regard to all subsequent reflection and interpretation of the life
and work of Jesus it must be at least admitted that it is separable in
thought from the objectively true facts which it undertakes to explain. At the same time it has itself to be understood and accounted
for. We have seen that the ultimate and complete form assumed by
reflection upon and explanation of the life-work of Jesus Christ is to
be found in what I have called the second phase of the Gospel, the
gospel of the resurrection: Jesus Christ—the conqueror of sin and
destroyer of death, the author and finisher of holiness, of righteousness, of eternal life.

The other direction taken by Christian reflection has to do with
not the work but the person of our Lord. But it was not the less inevitable, and has equal claim to validity. Admit the nature of the
work, and you cannot escape or avoid the question of the person of
the worker. There may be doubt as to whether or to what extent this
question is raised or answered in the Synoptic Gospels. Whether or
no what we call the Gospel of the Infancy is at all part of the record,
or at any rate of the primitive or original record, this at least is certain
about it. It did not belong to the very earliest form of either oral or
written gospel, which began, as in St. Mark, with the public life, and
knows, or at least includes, as yet nothing of the previous private
history of Jesus. When it is later included, it may indeed be so as
fuller record of facts, to fill out a completer narrative from more perfect information. But unquestionably there was a further motive for
its introduction. The question was up of the mystery of the person of
the Lord. It is not answered in the Gospel of the Infancy it is true.
In all the stories of the birth there is nothing which affirms or nec-

essarily postulates a previous personal existence. But at least the line of reflection and interpretation is entered upon which finds no possible or satisfactory close until it completes and expresses itself in the Prologue of St. John,—that is to say, in the Gospel of the Incarnation.

I. THE IMPRESSION OF THE
EARTHLY LIFE OF JESUS

We are, in this part of our work, to study the Gospel upon the lower plane of the common humanity which our Lord shared with ourselves. From the records of which we are to make use we exclude not only the Fourth Gospel, but the Gospel of the Birth and Infancy and whatever other portions of the Synoptic Gospels may reasonably be supposed to belong to a later stage of gospel representation. Confining ourselves then as nearly as we may to the primitive gospel of pure record, we are prepared to make to criticism the following admissions:

In the first place, the historical appearance of Jesus Christ, taken as a whole, was distinctly and completely a human appearance. He made a great, a boundless claim upon human faith and allegiance, but it was not a claim which He Himself based upon any essential personal difference between Himself and the common or universal humanity. He did not demand allegiance upon the ground of His being more than man, but solely upon the ground of what He was as man. He nowhere in His lifetime asserts, or was understood by those who stood nearest Him to assert, His divine personality. The highest claim He admits is that in response to Peter's confession: Thou art the Christ, or Thou art the Christ of God, or—in the fullest form reported—Thou art the Christ, the Son of the living God. These were all alike well understood Messianic expressions. The Messiah was to be in a very high sense the representative and expression of God's presence upon earth, but in no sense, as yet, which implied his own personal deity. Indeed the passive form and signification of the word Messiah or Anointed One emphasized the fact that the essence of Messiahship was humanity indwelt and sanctified by Deity. This is not at all to deny that there was a higher claim involved in our Lord's personality. But the claim did not appear, was not asserted, in His earthly life. The claim of divinity was to rest solely upon what He was and accomplished in humanity, and it waited upon that consummation to assert itself. Meanwhile, Jesus' whole appearance was, as we have said, distinctively a human one,—a man indeed always with God, and with whom God always was, but still always, in His highest knowledge, in His most mysterious powers, a man. Even after His resurrection He is still to St. Peter "Jesus of Nazareth, a man approved unto you of God by mighty works which God did by Him in the midst of you."

Upon what grounds in His lifetime did the Apostles accept our Lord's Messiahship? Not, certainly, upon any which had been anticipated or expected as signs of the Messiah. Not chiefly, I think we may say, upon the ground of His possession and exercise of mysterious powers. To the mind of His time He Himself had to distinguish those powers from those of Beelzebub by an appeal to their opposite quality or character. He deprecated, and trusted not Himself to, a faith that rested only on miracles. I think we may say that what He was really believed on for was—Himself, what He was as man. It was His divinity indeed, but a divinity manifested or visible to them only in the quality and character of His humanity, in the perfection of His human holiness, in the spiritual power of His human life. Why did they cling to Him through every trial of their faith? To whom else, having even imperfectly known Him, could they go? To them He had the words, already to them He was The Word, of eternal life. That was His permanent credential, and that was His only plea.

If we turn to those who still in our own day decline to go for their gospel beyond the earthly life and the common humanity of our Lord—what answer will they give for clinging to His person and finding their salvation in His life? I think we may say that the answer as it has shaped itself to that question is something like the following: Humanity continues, and will always continue, to believe and to find itself in Jesus, because Jesus embodies and expresses to humanity the truth of itself; the truth, the beauty and the goodness of itself. And truth, beauty, and goodness are the sum of what is of value, and ought to be of interest, to humanity. But why and how does Jesus Christ represent to us all that? We do not know; we need not know. He does; we accept the fact, because it is self-demonstrating; we cannot go the length of the explanations, because we believe they extend beyond the limits of our knowledge or proof.

Well, let us go just so far, and no farther, and find in so much the truth and power contained in it. We believe in Jesus because we find in Jesus the truth and good that most concern us, the truth and good of ourselves. Men of profoundest thought and of sincerest life in our own time have, in spiritual and moral extremity, found salvation in Jesus Christ, simply because they discovered in Him what did not exist for them without Him—a meaning and a reason for human existence and human life. The revelation to us, no matter how it comes, of the truth, the meaning, the reason, the good, the value, and above all—the way, the secret, of the infinitely interesting and important mystery we call life, ought to be to us surely nothing short of a gospel and a salvation.

The personality and life of Jesus could never have taken, and still less could maintain in perpetuity, the hold it has upon the world, if it were not true to the facts of the world. If Jesus Christ were not the truth, the beauty, the good sought by all the best thought and touched by all the best experience of humanity—humanity would not have given Him, would not give Him, its highest, its final allegiance. Every knee would not bow to Him, every tongue confess Him Lord. It will be interesting to recall a few of the leading principles of our Lord's life and character, and to correlate them with the best that has been thought or done before or apart from Him.

In the first place, Jesus took definite part with the West against the East in making the distinctive note of life not *apatheia* but *energeia*. Thought, desire, will were not to be abjured and disowned in despair, through the overpowering sense of their futility. Life was not to be reduced to zero through their renunciation, but raised to infinity through their affirmation and satisfaction. The life of Christianity is a life of infinite energy because it is a life of infinite faith and hope. It can be all things, do all things, endure all things. It feels no limit in itself, it sets no limit to itself, short of absolute perfection. It sets no limit to knowledge, because it believes itself made for the truth, and that the truth best worth knowing, the truth of self and of life, will more and more reveal and verify itself to us the more we know and love and live it. It sets no limit to desire, but covets earnestly the best things. It is conscious of an infinite poverty, and finds in it only the potency and promise of an infinite riches and satisfaction. Pleasure and happiness are not things to be denied and mortified. They are to be placed and found in the right objects, and to be swallowed up but not lost in the blessedness of the perfect life. And so finally it sets no limit to will, to activity, to achievement and attainment. If our wills are ours only as we surrender them to the larger will that comprehends and embraces all—our wills are His only as we have made His ours, and have found in His the highest freedom, realization, and satisfaction of our own. And so not only as against the aged pessimism of the East, but equally against the most modern fatalistic necessitarianism of the West, Jesus Christ raises to the highest pitch the universal human sense and consciousness of personal freedom and of eternally and divinely free personality.

In the second place, Jesus Christ makes Himself at one with the earliest and best ethical thought of the West in that He places the issues and decision of life, and the happiness that is the sense or consciousness of life, not without but within us, not in the action upon us of environment, but in our own free and personal reaction upon environment. Environment is the condition, but we are the causes, of life and its blessedness—or the reverse. Aristotle had said: It is the energies, the acts and activities, of ourselves, of our own souls that control, that determine and constitute happiness. Nature makes us nothing; it constitutes us, by the possession and use of reason and freedom, to make ourselves all that in life we, that is we humanly, personally, become. It is the essence of personality that it is made to be the maker of itself. Now Jesus Christ emphasizes and deepens this great fact or truth of life when He says to us: The kingdom of Heaven is within you. He Himself had found and entered the kingdom of Heaven. He had discovered the meaning and had experienced the blessedness of human life,—even such a life as outwardly His own was. We shall see as we proceed, as the essential difference between Him and all others, that all that human philosophy in even an Aristotle could conceive or express, He *was*. More than that, He was all that He Himself taught. The kingdom of Heaven was all in Him, because His life realized and embodied all that constitutes and belongs to the kingdom of Heaven.

In the third place, Jesus Christ is the great, the only, interpreter to us of the meaning and reason of human environment as we find it. It is not only that environment is the condition of life, that we determine ourselves only through our response to its action upon us. If we are to take actuality as we find it, if we deal not with theory but with actual conditions, our conclusion must be that only in an environment of evil can good determine or realize itself. Even in that lower world of mere animal evolution in which there is so much of purely natural or physical evil, and which we pronounce so inexplicable a mystery, can we see how there could have been the evolution of sensuous pleasure only through and in contrast with the sense of pain? But the question enters much more into the field of our experience and understanding when we pass into the world of moral action and life. Within the sphere of finite activity the development of moral good appears to be absolutely conditioned upon an environment of moral evil. To take it at once in its most developed form, there is no holiness possible or thinkable for us which is not a distinct attitude towards, a definite action upon, what we know as sin. If we did not know the one we should not know the other. Jesus Christ was no exception. His holiness was a resistance unto blood to sin. The moral significance of His death was that it was a death to sin. His perfection was accomplished through His personal attitude, His moral or spiritual superiority, to the things He suffered. There ought to be no mystery to us in the outward experiences, in the temptations, the fierce trials, the afflictions and sufferings of Jesus Christ. We ought to know that the moral victory He won, the spiritual height He attained, could not have been won or attained by Him as man except through such an outward experience, except in reaction and conflict with such a world of spiritual and moral evil. The perfect realization by Jesus Christ of all that is true, beautiful, or good in humanity as personal response to all of spiritual, moral, and natural evil that met and assailed Him in His outward life, is God's answer, if not to the full meaning and necessity, yet to His own use in the world of actuality of the mystery of evil.

But, in the fourth place, the contribution of Jesus to the truth and meaning of human life goes nearer still to the heart of the matter. In the "virtue" of the Greek, the "righteousness" of the Hebrew, and the "holiness" of Christianity, we have three types or standards of human conduct and character. With the Greek man himself was the measure and the end. The ideal man was he who the most symmetrically, perfectly, and happily realized or fulfilled himself. As in plastic art he strove to express the perfect balance or proportion of physical beauty, so by a higher spiritual aesthetic perception and measurement he endeavoured to portray the fair features and proportions of the moral ideal, the "beautiful and good" in humanity.

But the ideal man, if he combined in himself elements of both the beautiful and the good, the æsthetic and the moral, inclined very much more in the direction of the former than of the latter. Self-respect, supreme regard for one's "own fair personality" was the dominant if not the sole motive. The ideal was a beautiful one, and true in so far as the highest beauty must necessarily approximate the true and the good. But there was still too much in it of egoism to allow of its identification with these.

The Hebrew saw in his standard and measure of human life and conduct something vaster and more objective than the perfection and beauty of his own earthly personality. The law with him was something more than that of nature or his own finite nature. The Greek or Roman virtue was the following or fulfilling of nature, the realizing of manhood. The Hebrew righteousness was the recognition of a law, and behind the law a personality, infinitely beyond and above himself or his own. The tribunal before which he bowed was not his own right reason or the wider wisdom of the community revising his private judgment. There was a judgment seat more awful than the æsthetic taste of the individual or the public opinion of society. The power not himself that made for righteousness, no matter how it came or how it revealed itself to him, was to him the sum of all reality. We need not in this connection dwell upon this conception of the standard or measure of life further than to remember that it was an objective universal law other than which there could be no rule or principle of obligation in the heavens above or in the earth beneath.

The Hebrew point of view, while relieving the standard of the finite human subjectivity which made man alone the measure, was in danger of the opposite extreme of making the law too wholly objective; and we may add, of separating the power or presence behind the law too far from human life. If the law had needed to be made more objective and universal, it needed now again to become more subjective and more human. It was the problem in process of solution, how to combine the opposite truths of immanence and transcendence. Jesus Christ, by not stopping at the law but going at once behind and beyond it, by recognizing the fact that no objective law can produce subjective life or righteousness, because law is only the outward form, the expression or letter, of the inward substance which we call spirit,—Jesus Christ took the third and final step which completes the account of human life. If the passage had needed to

be made from finite subjectivity to infinite objectivity, equally necessary was the passage made once for all by Him from the infinite
objective to the infinite subjective, from the absolute without us in
the form of law to the absolute within us in the form of spirit. The
essence of the moral teaching of Jesus was the change of venue from
the tribunal of law to that of spirit. The act of humanity in His own
person was most exactly expressed in the words: "Who through the
eternal Spirit offered Himself without spot." In Him eternal law had
given place to eternal spirit, the letter that killeth to the spirit that
giveth life.

We are considering the truth of Jesus just now not from the
standpoint of Christianity but in its correlation with other reflections
and conclusions upon human life. And so we may ask ourselves:
What is this eternal spirit through which Jesus Christ has realized
forever for us the true meaning and end of humanity? Let us try
briefly to answer this question. Science more and more recognizes
the universe as one, and as a universe of order. Now what is the unity
and the order that constitute the reality of the universe? In the order
in which it appears to us, it is first material or physical, and then
moral, and then spiritual. Which of these is the real? In the actual
evolution of our individual selves, we are first purely physical, and
then psychical, and finally spiritual or personal. Which of these is
we? Do we find the reality of ourselves in the physical, the psychical,
or the personal—the spiritual and moral—self? Man is not what he
is in process, but what he is when complete. He is, as Aristotle
teaches us, his highest part. Everything is to be defined by its end,
by what it will be when its becoming is completed and it is perfect.
If we are to interpret this universe as a whole, in the light of that
which is its manifest direction and logical end, we cannot but conclude that the natural order exists as the necessary condition of a
higher moral order, which in turn has no meaning or possibility except as the form or expression of a yet higher spiritual or personal
order. It is absurd to object to this that the moral and spiritual orders
are still so far from existence. There is nothing contradictory or impossible in the immediate existence of a material order, and yet even
that was a matter of inconceivably slow evolution. An immediate
moral or spiritual order is impossible, because by its very nature it
must evolve or constitute itself. As surely as gravitation or evolution
are laws of the universe, is righteousness a law of the universe,—

and behind and before them all is that spirit of which alone righteousness is the law, the ultimate truth and reality of the universe. Jesus Christ is the fulfilment of nature and the realization of humanity because He is the embodiment of the moral and spiritual order, not only the infinite law but the eternal spirit of the universe.

But we have not yet given a real definition of the eternal spirit which Jesus Christ embodied and revealed. His contribution to life was the truth which is at once first and last,—that there is no human good but goodness. We can know good first only as our own. That existence itself, that life or anything pertaining to life, is a good, we can only know as we experience the pleasure, the value, or worth of them for ourselves. But the good which as such we can first know only as our own we can then, by necessary inference, know and will to others as theirs. And this is the origin and essence of goodness. Man is never from the first an individual but always a social being. He has his existence in, with, and through others. He lives and becomes all that constitutes himself only in concrete relationships and in actual personal exchanges between himself and them. A man can be a good man only by fulfilling his natural relations, by being a good son, brother, husband, father, friend, neighbour, citizen. And as this is his only impersonal goodness, so is it his only personal good. He cannot realize himself except in, with, and through others. His universe is so constructed, his life is so constituted, that there is no good for him except goodness. He cannot love himself except as he loves others as himself. He cannot find himself except as he loses himself in others. Jesus saw and not only perfectly expressed but perfectly embodied the fact that goodness or love is the secret and the essence of human life. And of human only because of all life. It is the beginning and the end of all reality. As the natural exists only for the moral, so the moral is only the outward expression, the law, of the spiritual. And the spiritual, which is the real, is infinite and eternal goodness. The real law of the universe is the law of righteousness, and the true soul and life of righteousness is the spirit of love, whom the world calls God.

It follows not only naturally but necessarily from the above that Jesus, calling Himself always Son of Man,—that is, true, essential manhood,—should speak of Himself as having come into the world not to be served but to serve, to be the servant of all, even to the point of giving His life for all. Love, service, sacrifice,—these He has, not made, but revealed in His person and human life to be the spirit and law and reality of the universe.

2. THE GROWTH AND
PREPARATION OF JESUS

We have been considering our Lord's earthly life from the standpoint of conceptions of life in general. We come back now to study it from the point of view and in terms of the distinctively Christian records. If our Gospels are to be supposed to include properly only the report of the public ministry (as defined in Acts 1:21, 22), we must remember that Jesus appears in that ministry at the age of thirty, with full qualification and authority to discharge its functions. There was no apparent question within Himself of Himself, and no questioning of Him on the part of those capable of feeling the force of His authority. It is to the records so limited as though He had come into the world fully equipped for His part in it. But if Jesus was human, He was so not only in what He was at His height, but in the process by which He attained that height and became what He was. If we are to know *Him,* without which it is impossible to know His life or His lifework, we are obliged to take into account the contribution of the thirty years of preparation for His ministry.

The traditions of our Lord's youth later prefixed to the records, brief as they are, are, when we consider them carefully, singularly probable in matter and exact and illuminating in expression. The child Jesus, we are told in St. Luke,—after the circumstances of His birth and the formalities of His circumcision, presentation, etc., have been narrated,—grew and waxed strong, filled with wisdom: and the grace of God was upon him. The general terms are practically identical with those just before applied to John the Baptist: The child grew and waxed strong in spirit. They are in either case descriptive of a normal, purely human, not only physical but spiritual, youthful development. But in the case of Jesus the description is more explicit, as doubtless the growth described was fuller and more complete. In the first place, the child grew and matured *pari passu* in all the elements or parts of a complete human development, physical, intellectual, spiritual. It is added: Filled, or properly filling, becoming more and more full, of wisdom. Emphasis is naturally, perhaps unconsciously, laid upon the inward and outward means and process by which we shall see the wisdom was acquired, and the necessary progress of its accumulation. Wisdom is in itself, as Aristotle defines it, the product only of time and experience. And then, most significantly of all, come the words: And the grace of God was upon him. It in no way militates against the perfect humanness of Jesus to know that from the first, in a more complete way than through the prophets or John the Baptist before or St. Paul afterwards (who believed in his separation from his mother's womb), God was preparing to reveal or express Himself through Him. That, as we have seen, was just the gist of the long promised messiahship which Jesus was later to assume. The grace of God is a quality communicated or imparted. It is something which, creaturely or humanly, we have not of ourselves, for which we are dependent and which we can receive only from the personal source of all personal life. It is identical with the spirit of God, that eternal spirit which lies behind all law material or spiritual, and which is the ultimate reality or fact of the universe. That divine spirit lay upon Him from the beginning, and wrought through Him all that through it He humanly accomplished or became. We cannot for a moment blind ourselves to the truth that God was the objective source and cause, and the objectively apprehended and known cause, of all the subjectively and humanly attained heights of the earthly life of Jesus Christ.

The above account of the beginnings of our Lord's life is consistently taken up and continued in the equally brief description of the incident which throws additional light upon it at the age of twelve. After narrating that incident, to which we shall return, St. Luke proceeds: And Jesus advanced in wisdom and stature,—in wisdom as in age and physical development,—and in favour with God and men. There is definite progress and new interpretation expressed in the last clause. The word here translated favour, and elsewhere otherwise, is the same term grace which we have been just discussing. Jesus advanced in grace with God and men. It is in reality the same grace viewed at different points, first as operating objectively from God upon Jesus, and then secondly as operating subjectively in Jesus towards God and men. The spirit that comes from God as His appears in us as ours. There is no more exact or beautiful designation of the spirit that Jesus was of than is conveyed by the word Grace. As between Him and God it is the response of God within Him to

God without. As between Him and men it is the eternal spirit looking humanly on earth upon men as God looks upon them from heaven. We have in this little touch a glimpse of the spiritual attitude at once towards God and towards men that was growing with the growth of Jesus and that was to be the sole key to the explanation of His whole life and ministry. It already manifested itself in His youth in a graciousness of spirit and manner with men which gave Him favour with them, far as yet as they were from fathoming its true depth and significance. We speak of the sweet reasonableness of Jesus. The peculiar quality we are trying to catch and fix is better expressed in terms of the heart than of the head. The sweet reasonableness rests upon a deeper and sweeter sympathy which drew Him to all men and draws all men to Him if they will but let themselves see and know Him. It is with the heart rather than with the head that we understand and know one another. The pure in heart see men as well as God as they are, and have the sweet reasonableness to deal with them as they should.

Closely connected if not identical with the spirit or temper just described is the faculty of spiritual perception or intelligence which so struck the doctors in their conversation with Him in the temple. The power to "understand"—whether things, men, or God—lies deeper than the mind or than the natural affections. It consists in a universality of spirit that at-ones us with the objects to be understood. Jesus was among the doctors to learn, to be taught. They were amazed at His teachableness, at His quickness to comprehend, His ready response to instruction. There was in Him the opposite of the individualism which is the expression of only one's particular self. The universal and eternal in Him sought to make Him one with all. And so He thirsted and was mature beyond His years to enter into the spirit of those Scriptures which had been not only the literature but the life of God's people from the beginning. In a word, there were in the youthful Jesus all the human conditions of divine knowledge, and therefore there was in Him more and more the fulness and perfection of divine knowledge.

The unity of spirit that characterized the youth and the later ministry of our Lord may be briefly illustrated in one or two points. In St. Luke's first description of His public appearance the comment upon the impression produced is as follows: And all bare Him witness, and wondered at the words of grace which proceeded out of

His mouth. The words of grace, or the gracious words—the meaning includes both. There was first the manner that betokened the spirit, the temper or disposition, which actuated Him in speaking. It was the spirit of God speaking in Him. And then there was the matter of His speaking, than which nothing could better express the substance of His ministry. It was the grace of God bringing through Him salvation to men. It has been remarked that Jesus loved best in the Scriptures the prophet Isaiah and the book Deuteronomy. The lesson He had read in the synagogue was from the former:

> The Spirit of the Lord is upon me,
> Because He anointed me to preach the gospel to the poor:
> He hath sent me to proclaim release to the captives,
> And recovering of sight to the blind,
> To set at liberty them that are bruised,
> To proclaim the acceptable year of the Lord.

"He anointed me to"—that then was the meaning of the anointing, the mission of the Anointed: to bring down God's spirit and grace and salvation, in a word God's eternal life, and establish it in a kingdom of God upon earth.

In the later preaching of our Lord, St. Luke reports Him as saying: If ye love them that love you, if ye do good to them that do good to you, if ye lend to them of whom ye hope to receive—what thank have ye? The word not improperly rendered thank or thanks means something more than that. It is again the word grace: What grace have ye? Not only what thanks or reward, not only what men will recognize and be grateful for, but what is the only motive of any true disposition or act towards others, namely, the spirit and grace of God. Therefore St. Luke reports our Lord as continuing: But love your enemies, and do them good, and lend, never despairing; and your reward shall be great, and ye shall be sons of the Most High: for he is kind towards the unthankful and evil. Be ye merciful even as your Father is merciful. These last words open a view into what was the heart and soul of our Lord's preparation and qualification for His ministry. Rather, they suggest the truth of all that He was to be or accomplish in and for humanity. It has always been recognized that the supreme human act and attainment of Jesus Christ was that He truly conceived and perfectly realized the fatherhood of God and so the divine sonship of men. The growth of Jesus was the development in Him of this conception and the progress of this realization.

When His parents, after their three days' search, found Him in the temple, and reproached Him with the fact that they had sought Him sorrowing, His reply was: Why should they have sought Him? Where should He be but in His Father's house, interested and engaged in His Father's business? All truth was expressed for Him in that divine relationship, all duty or pleasure was contained in the life-long and life-filling task of fulfilling it. Taken alone we might seem to read too much into our Lord's use of these words in this His first recorded utterance. But they are very far from standing alone. When the preparation was over and the great call and commission to the ministry was given and received, the divine recognition of His qualification and fitness for the task came to Him from Heaven in the words: Thou art my beloved Son; in thee I am well pleased. The preparation for the true Messiahship is the realization of the true sonship. The fulness of the divine spirit involves the impartation of the divine nature and the reproduction of the divine life, and that is the essence and truth of divine sonship.

But the preparation was not wholly over with the commission. The awful burden and task imposed by the latter necessitated another, a more conscious and thorough, going over of the whole ground of the former. The entire temptation in the wilderness turns upon the fact and foundations of the human divine sonship of Jesus. He was there on trial as the representative of humanity. There in and upon His person were pending and depending the destinies of humanity. We are to understand that temptation, if we understand it at all, as the supreme test and the decisive if not yet final vindication and establishment of man's sonship to God. This statement will necessitate a partial analysis of the brief story.

The account of the temptation is, in the first place, a report of actual experiences—subjective if not objective—of our Lord in the crisis of His entrance upon His ministry. But, in the second place, the account is given in language which is plainly not literal but symbolical. And this very fact gives it a significance and an application far wider than that of an individual experience; it makes it universal. Furthermore, our Lord Himself expresses the principle and application of each temptation withstood in terms as universal as humanity itself: It is written, Man shall not live by bread alone; It is said, Thou shalt not tempt the Lord thy God. Such maxims of conduct are definitely human, and these Jesus establishes at the beginning as principles and foundations of His kingdom of the divine life on earth. These are that rock upon which, except a man build, his house cannot but fall.

The symbolism of the story of the temptation is suggested by the history of Israel as spiritually interpreted in the book of Deuteronomy. That history itself has always been accepted as symbolical of human life in general: the divine fatherhood and the great salvation; the promise of a land of rest and fruition; the condition and then the trial of the people's faith, the temptations in the wilderness; the failure to enter in because of unbelief. In contrast and reversal of Israel's temptation and defeat we have the picture of Israel's temptation and victory. The particular passage that gives form to the later story is the following (Deut. 8:1–3): And thou shalt remember all the ways which the Lord thy God led thee these forty years in the wilderness, that He might humble thee, to prove thee, to know what was in thy heart, whether thou wouldst keep His commandments or no. And He humbled thee and suffered thee to hunger, and fed thee with manna, which thou knewest not neither did thy fathers know; that He might make thee know that man doth not live by bread only, but by everything that proceedeth out of the mouth of the Lord doth man live. The lesson of life as seen in the Scriptures, Old and New, is in the first place that life comes from its divine source and not from the earthly media through which it is received. And secondly, that life, in all its potencies and promises, can be possessed and enjoyed only through faith. And faith comes only through trial. The highest and latest energy and act of our personality, that by which we conquer the world and transcend earthly limitations and conditions, is not attained easily and painlessly. "That the proof of your faith, more precious than gold that perisheth though it is proved by fire, might be found unto praise and glory and honour." The conception and realization of divine sonship with all its implications is not a plain and easy thing for flesh and blood. Even after the vision of the bared arm of the Lord in his redemption from Egypt, it was not easy for Israel to feel the presence or keep hold of the promises, to remember or exercise his divine sonship, in the land of sand and dearth. Very straight home to him went the temptation: If thou art the son of God, command that these stones be made bread. If thou art,—doubt is the beginning of all weakness, and the certain cause of all human failure. Men enter not in because of unbelief. But how in a world like this

shall we believe that we are the sons of God, with power therefore
to be what God is? Jesus Christ has shown us the way, by Himself
entering in and so opening it to all. It was not plainer or easier for
Him than for us to know Himself son of God, and so to have grace
and power to perform a son's part in the world. If the heavens had
opened and proclaimed Him son, it was only in recognition of the
fact that by faith He had known and made Himself son. Even after
that mighty demonstration and confirmation of His faith, the conditions under which, as He foresaw, He was entering upon a humanly
impossible task were enough to drive Him into the wilderness of
doubt and despair. How should He accomplish the task before Him,
the hopeless task of human salvation? Comparing the means with the
end, how could the temptation not assail Him: If thou art the son of
God, command these stones that they be made bread;—of these
stones raise up children unto Abraham! I do not undertake to say just
what were the elements that entered into this first temptation of our
Lord. Only this I seem to see clearly: the whole question of faith, the
whole human hold upon the reality of the divine fatherhood and upon
the power and the promise of human sonship was at issue in it. If
man is son of God; if there is warrant for faith in that divine fact; if
human faith can and will lay hold upon it and conquer its way to
eternal life,—then that is our gospel and our salvation. And all this
was and is done by humanity in the person of Jesus Christ. He fought
the battle, He proved the possibility of the victory, He showed us the
place and revealed to us the secret of the power.

The lesson of the second temptation was scarcely less important. We are not more apt or prone to want faith, to be ignorant of
the power of God which is ours unto salvation, than, having faith,
or thinking we have it, to tempt God by presuming upon it. We are
constantly expecting of faith, and complaining of not having from it,
not only what it is not its function to give, but what the giving to us
would be our worst undoing. We little realize how much, as believers, we expect to have done for us which we do not do for ourselves.
But it is never the purpose of grace to make us anything which *we*
are not at all the pains, and the pain, of making ourselves. Nothing
indeed can be added to us, in the true sense of us, which does not as
truly proceed from *us* as from the higher source which only makes
it ours by enabling us to make it ours. All that comes to us from God,
and as God's, such as His spirit, His grace, His life, comes to us at

all only as we too have so made them our own that they appear in us only as ours. It is only by the spirit we are of that we may be recognized as children of God. Whose spirit, God's or ours? Only the one if the other. The life of Jesus Christ was the opposite of one of enthusiasm or fanaticism. What He most truly was He was not by miracle but humanly, after the way of a man,—of God because of Himself, of Himself because of God—because a man is only himself in and with and through God. Though it may not appear at once, the outcome of the second temptation was the victory of hope, as that of the first was the victory of faith. Hope is of ourselves as faith is of God, as to their objects. As faith is the realization of all God in and with us, so hope is the realization of all ourselves in and with God. Because we know that all things are possible with God, therefore we know that we can be and do all things. What we want is God in us, in what we are. The religion that craves miracles is a religion that seeks a sign outside itself because it lacks assurance in itself. If it knew God in itself by faith, and itself in God in hope, it would ask no proof outside of that. Our Lord's own religion was one not of outward sign but of inward reality. He demanded to be received for the substance, Himself—and not for the accidents, His miracles.

Without going too much at length into the meaning of the third temptation, I would offer the following suggestions for its interpretation. Our Lord had His own way of entering into the authority and glory of His Messianic kingdom. When the hour for it was come, He lifted up His eyes to heaven and said, Father, the hour is come; glorify thy Son, that the Son may glorify thee! And God glorified Him as He glorified God, in, we may be sure, the divinest way, the way of Gethsemane and Calvary. A few months before, when Jesus was beginning to prepare His disciples for the way in which He was to be glorified, Peter took Him and began to rebuke Him, saying, Be it far from thee Lord; this shall never be unto thee. But he turned and said unto Peter, Get thee behind me, Satan: thou art a stumbling-block unto me: for thou mindest not the things of God, but the things of men. If it was a temptation of Satan to shrink from entering upon His kingdom in the divine way, surely it was Satan himself in the human temptation that assailed Him to establish that kingdom in just the opposite way, upon the principles not of love and service and sacrifice, but of pride and ambition and earthly self-exaltation. To surrender one's soul to such motives as these is to fall down and wor-

ship Satan. Pride, or the worship of Self, is the subtlest, the first and
the last, of human temptations. Even when one has given oneself in
faith and hope to God, it creeps in in spiritual form to poison and
corrupt the joy and exaltation that belong of right to these. Jesus
could recognize and accept the glory which is the reward of spiritual
victory, and in that moment detect and exclude every trace of self-
seeking or self-exaltation. He could perfectly lose Himself in the act
in which He most perfectly found Himself. The only true humility is
that of perfect love. One can lose oneself only in preoccupation with
that in others which takes and fills the place of self. The power to do
this, which is the triumph of divine love, is the only secret of putting
behind that opposite spirit which is of the devil.

Thus the issue of the three temptations was the decisive, though
not yet the final and complete, victory of the three great principles
which are the spiritual foundations of the kingdom of God—Faith,
Hope, Love. As they were the constituents of our Lord's own divine
human life, so are they the constituents of that selfsame life as He
imparts it to us by His spirit in us.

3. THE SON OF MAN

The more we examine into it and ponder over it, the more important grows the question: Why, among various designations, does
Jesus elect so habitually to call Himself by that of Son of man? It
cannot be merely because that had been a more or less common title
applied to the expected Messiah. It was characteristic of Jesus that
He was much more concerned with the realities of the new than with
the figures of the old dispensation. We are still too apt to think we
understand or have explained the realities of the Gospel when we
show that they express and fulfil some figure of the Old Testament.
The figure may have adumbrated the fact; the fact too much transcends the figure to be fully explained or adequately interpreted by
it. We may understand the Old Testament in the light of its fulfilment
in the New. We cannot understand the New in the dim light of its
prefiguration in the Old. The Gospel of Jesus Christ can be seen and
understood only in the white light of its own utter and independent
truth. There was a reason in itself why our Lord selected that term
to express or describe Himself.

When we come to examine and compare all the different connections and senses in which Jesus uses or seems to use the designation Son of man, we do not find the answer to our question so plain
or easy. Evidently He means by it to identify Himself in some very
deep and universal way with humanity as such. What do we mean
by humanity as such? We may adventure a few explanations upon
this point.

In the first place, humanity as such means humanity in its sim-
plicity, its reality, its universality. As such, humanity was not known
among those who controlled its destinies, by its teachers and its rulers, in the days of our Lord's earthly life. It was buried and lost under
a hopeless weight of traditional, conventional, and artificial distinctions and regulations. The institution or the law, social, political, and
above all religious, was everything and the man was nothing. Man
existed for the established order, not the established order for man.
Society, the state, or the church—and they were practically one—
was for itself or its official representatives, and man as man, in his
relation to it, had ceased to be considered. Now, as between these
two, Jesus took His position—not, as we shall see, on the side of the
individual against the established order, but—in behalf of humanity
against a perverted established order. The Son of man for our sakes
became poor; He had nowhere to lay His head; He took to Himself
no special privilege of birth or wealth or class or office. He stood
upon His manhood. And the name by which He called Himself expressed that attitude towards existing conditions. Son of man had indeed in Hebrew usage become about synonymous with man, but it
carried the little additional force of man *quâ* man. That which is born
of man is man, shares the common nature, is to be defined by the
universal predicates. That identification Jesus had taken upon Himself; in that universality, or commonness with all, He knew and
named Himself.

But that identification and self-designation had the effect, in the
second place, of recognizing and emphasizing the true nature, the
dignity and value, of bare manhood as such. There was never a
higher vindication and expression of manhood than in the words: The
sabbath was made for man, and not man for the sabbath. The sabbath, yes, and every other natural or human institution. The great
truth grows until it finds its logical utterance in St. Paul's description
of the dignity of man in Christ: Let no one glory in men—that is, in

human dignities and distinctions. For all things are yours; whether Paul, or Apollos, or Cephas, or the world, or life, or death, or things present, or things to come; all are yours; and ye are Christ's; and Christ is God's.

The conception of the inherent dignity of humanity, universally recognized as owing so much to the attitude of Jesus Christ towards it, has been abundantly vindicated and illustrated by both modern philosophy and science. Kant first demonstrated the philosophical fact that there can be no "end in itself" which cannot be an end *to* itself. Only that which has "being for self," which can know, feel, possess, enjoy, or value itself, can be an end either to itself or to anything else. If we ask what all evolution is for, there is nothing else in all we can know of evolution *for* which it can be but man. It cannot be for itself apart from man, because apart from man it has no self for which to be. It is perfectly legitimate to conclude, not only that evolution as known by science has no further task than the further and higher development of the spiritual or personal qualities and destiny of man, but also that if from the beginning there was any end or purpose in evolution at all, that was it. Some such philosophic and scientific cosmical conception as this, we shall see, underlay the entire New Testament interpretation of itself.

In the third place, Son of man in the mouth of Jesus carries with it the idea not only of universal meaning and of inherent dignity, but also of self-realization. The true Son of man is He who has properly conceived and realized His manhood. By assuming to Himself the title Jesus assumes that He has done this. The Son of man is Lord of the sabbath. This He could claim only for Himself individually. He as man was above the sabbath, above the law, above the temple, above every natural or human institution,—why? Because He was the attained and accomplished end for which they were all instituted. There are two errors against which we have very carefully to guard ourselves. The first is the idea that Jesus set Himself against the established order, against outward institutions, as such. He was the furthest from doing this. What He did set Himself against was the sin of an order or an institution, divinely established to serve an end, setting up itself as the end; sacrificing the true end to itself instead of itself to the end; reversing the divine law by being in this world to be served instead of to serve. He did not object to the visible temple. The zeal of it even ate Him up. What He did object to was that

His Father's house which was to have been a house of prayer had been converted into a den of thieves, that men were making merchandise for themselves out of what had been instituted for the service of God. Every ordinance of God was God to Him. He was indignant not at the consecration of means to ends, but at their desecration to other ends or at their blasphemous elevation into ends in themselves. And so the second error against which we need to guard ourselves is the thought that even Jesus in His humanity could have been above the sabbath or above the law any otherwise than through having obeyed and fulfilled them. Nothing can dispense us from the humble and devout use of divine means except the fact of having through their appointed use as means attained the ends for which they were instituted. This was wonderfully illustrated by our Lord's own acts and attitude throughout His life. He submitted to every ordinance of man or God, except when it was possible for Him to honour its spirit only by violating its letter. When He said, Think not that I am come to destroy the law; I am come not to destroy but to fulfil, there was included in that purpose not only the law in any higher sense but the Jewish law in every essential detail. Not only had He been Himself circumcised but He rose above and beyond the fact of outward circumcision only by fulfilling its inward meaning and purpose. So St. Paul and others, although Jews, felt themselves absolved from the obligation of circumcision, not because it was an outward ordinance, but because in that as in every other respect they felt themselves "fulfilled in Christ; in whom they had been circumcised with the circumcision made without hands, in the putting off of the body of the flesh, in the circumcision of Christ." The law of sacrifice was abrogated only through the true sacrifice once for all, in which all the meaning and the truth of sacrifice is forever expressed and fulfilled. Jesus Christ is the end of the law for righteousness, not because there was or is not the need of a law of righteousness, but because He is the righteousness for which the law exists.

In pursuing our reflections upon the senses in which our Lord used the term Son of man or rather perhaps in this case the sentiments or impulses which unconsciously led Him to take it to Himself, we might make a fourth point of the following. Indeed it is involved in what has been already said, and only needs a little more emphasis. Jesus we say was the enemy of all mere formality or conventionality, which was to Him hypocrisy. But it was not the mere hypocrisy that so deeply troubled Him. It was the inhumanity underlying it that moved Him to the depths. They watched Him on a certain occasion to see whether He would heal on the sabbath day; that they might accuse Him. Perceiving their thoughts, He puts to them the direct question, Is it lawful to do good on the sabbath day? When they held their peace, He looked round about upon them with anger, and then bade the man stand up and be healed. But his anger was not at their legalism in making so much of mere outward observance. St. Mark gives a deeper reading of His heart. He was grieved at the hardening of their heart. What man is there of you, He asks,—and there is in the Greek an evident emphasis upon the use of the word man—Who is there among you with the heart of a man, that shall have a sheep, and if it fall into a pit on the sabbath day, will he not lay hold upon it and lift it out? How much is a man of more value than a sheep! Wherefore it is lawful to do good on the sabbath day. It is not hypocrisy but inhumanity that grieves Him; except that all hypocrisy, all unreality, all shallowness or stopping short of the deep meaning and truth of things, is selfishness and inhumanity. Reality is humanity, because it is love and service and sacrifice.

I said, under the third head just above, that our Lord, in taking to Himself the title Son of man, at once identified Himself with all humanity and distinguished Himself from it. He is the truth of it, and so is Lord of all that pertains to its life. When He says, as He does, That ye may know that the Son of man hath power on earth to forgive sins, I do not think He is merely claiming for humanity at large the divine right and function of mercy and forgiveness. His words have reference to His own Messianic mission, which was, as we shall see, by the taking or putting away of sin, to bring humanity to God, and so bring it to itself. From the beginning of His ministry of humanity He had exhibited His skill and power to deal with human ills. He began with the ills most in evidence, those of the body. But He was not to stop with or upon these. His axe was to be laid at the root of all ill. We cannot suppose that the permanent ministry of Christ and of Christianity was to be the immediate healing, without the use of human means, of the physical or natural ills of the world. His ministry began with these because it was only through the diseases of the body that He could reach those of the soul. But His power to heal the former was only a parable of His power to heal the latter. That ye may know that the Son of man hath power on earth to forgive sins—then saith He to the sick of the palsy, Arise, take up thy bed and walk. Christianity is humanity, and must therefore deal with all ill that is human. It must even deal in many respects with physical evils before it can touch the springs of spiritual and moral evil. But its real mission and function is to reach and heal the natural through the spiritual and the moral. Its permanent method is to treat causes rather than symptoms. If I should attempt to explain humanly the distinctively human right and power of Jesus to forgive or to take away sin, it would be somewhat on the following lines. The inherent right to represent God depends upon the extent to which we inherently represent Him. If one through perfect actual realization of the divine fatherhood should perfectly realize his own sonship, he would be no longer only a servant in his Father's house. He would be a son, entitled to speak in his father's name and with his father's authority. When the son has reproduced the father's spirit and embodied the father's law, then he has not only authority but commandment and obligation to express and administer his father's will. In the perfection of His humanity, Jesus Christ was upon this earth as God. And that perhaps is the explanation why, even before His advent, the Messiah of the Old Testament, while always man, is often spoken of in terms of, and interchangeably with, God Himself. There is perhaps a yet deeper truth involved in that of the Son of man. This, namely: That, if God is ever to be spiritually and personally in the world at all, it will be only through the Son of man; that is to say, through the growing divinity of man. It will be consummated when the Son of man shall be Humanity. The divine Father of all can be in all only as all realize or actualize the divine sonship. But the great truth of our Lord's relation to the taking away of sin, and so at-oneing humanity with God, belongs to a later stage of our inquiries.

In the next place, our Lord speaks most pointedly of Himself as Son of man in those connections in which He is foretelling those most human experiences of the trials and afflictions that await Him, and also of His own victory over them,—especially, His death and resurrection. In a certain place (Romans 5:1–5) St. Paul tells us, in view of what has happened in Christ Jesus, that we ought as Christians to do three things: We ought to be at present peace with God, with whom by faith we see ourselves eternally at one. We ought to rejoice in hope of that actual and entire identification with God which shall be our final glory. And if these two, then ought we also to glory in the tribulations by which He became, and we also shall become, what He is. There is nothing our Lord so insists upon as the necessary relation of the Son of man to the things He suffered. It became God, we may say reverently that it was necessary for God, in bringing many sons to glory, to perfect the captain of their salvation through suffering.

And finally, and perhaps most strikingly of all, it is impossible for any criticism to sever our Lord's own conception of Himself as Son of man from the truth in His mind of His second advent, His perpetual coming in the world, and the great final coming to judge the world. It is in metaphysical and logical sequence with all that has gone before, that St. John should represent our Lord as describing the two great functions of the Son of man as giving life, or raising the dead, and executing judgment. He Himself discharges these two functions because He is Son of man. As the divine end of humanity, its truth and reality and therefore its predestination, it belonged to Him not only to have come but to be always coming. It was His right to foresee not only His true coming begin soon after His apparent departure, but His complete coming consummated in a great and universal final Advent. And in the very nature of it His coming is a perpetual and an everlasting act or process of divine judgment. He came not into the world to condemn the world, but to give life to the world. His proper function is life-giving, a life-giving that is both resurrection and regeneration. But if God sent not His Son into the world to judge but only to save it, it cannot but be that His coming is in itself a judgment. He that believeth on Him is not judged, but he that believeth not is judged already, because he hath not believed on the name of the only begotten Son of God. And this is the judgment, that men loved the darkness rather than the light. We cannot get around that reasoning. In some form or other, in some terms or other, it will always be coming home to us. Stripped of all conventional or ecclesiastical language, Jesus Christ means to every human being the truth, the reality, the worth and the blessedness of himself. That is always with him or before him: for acceptance or rejection, for realization or ruin. All human life is judgment, which is primarily only separation between those who are and those who are not, those who do and those who do not—what it is appointed for all in life to be and to do. If to live, to be ourselves, to do our part, is approbation, justification, blessedness, what can failure to do these be but reprobation, condemnation, and wretchedness?

The truth that final judgment is to be by the Son of man carries this further thought. Nothing is said in the New Testament of a divine wrath against sinfulness as a universal fact or condition. Nothing is said of a final condemnation of human transgression of the divine law. It is recognized that by nature we cannot but be sinners. It is recognized that our highest devotion to and aspiration after the law of God is weak through our human flesh.

There is infinite pity and compassion, infinite mercy and forgiveness, for sinners. Our Lord, or St. Paul, or St. John after Him, have no condemnation for sinners. All their condemnation is for those who are *not* sinners, who do not know themselves to be such, who do not know in themselves what it is to be such, who will not to be, and will not be, saved from their sin.

4. THE KINGDOM OF GOD

Although both John the Baptist and Jesus came in succession preaching in identical terms the kingdom of God, yet they preached it and meant it in a very different spirit. So much so that John to the last found it hard to recognize what he had himself prepared for in his successor. When he sent from his prison to inquire of Jesus whether He were indeed he that should come, or were they to look for another, Jesus answered him with signs of the kingdom, but it is by no means certain that those signs would satisfy John. He was cast in a severer and more legal mould. Jesus, while taking occasion, on the departure of the messengers, to speak in the highest possible terms of John as a prophet and representative of the old dispensation, seems to recognize that he had not been born anew of the spirit, or born into the new spirit, and so after all his preparation for the kingdom of God had not truly seen or entered into the kingdom of God. He was the friend of the bridegroom, who had prepared the bride for the heavenly nuptials, but he did not witness the union. And so Jesus declares that he who within the kingdom of God was least was greater than John.

The kingdom of God must therefore be something very definite and very positive. And yet from Jesus' own preaching of it we find it very difficult to define it positively. Perhaps in this respect too the kingdom of God was to come "without observation," not in word but in deed, to be seen and judged only in its fruits. We must therefore, as before, collect its meaning and frame our definition of it as best we may from the whole tenor of our Lord's teaching and action.

We might say in general that the kingdom of God is simply and literally what the words express, not anything of God but God Himself in humanity. But if we should agree upon this, we should at once disagree upon what this means. With many it would mean no more than the prevalence and influence within each man of his own subjective conception of God. With others who have more of the sense of God as One with whom we may hold objective relations, the kingdom of God will be an actual presence and operation of God in us, as we say, by His Spirit. And still others may go the whole length of holding the kingdom of God to be that permanent and eternal incarnation of God in humanity which we see not only realized in the individual person of Jesus Christ, but to be consummated in the universal humanity of which He is the head. Leaving then for the present so general a definition as that, let us examine the matter more in detail.

Is it possible that that which was John's stumbling-block in the ministry of Jesus was that it seemed to him to lack positiveness and decision; that there was not enough in it of the Law which he knew, and too much of the Gospel which he could not understand? John's kingdom was the kingdom of righteousness, Christ's the kingdom of mercy and goodness. There are many evidences of this in the very different attitude of Jesus from that of John in His dealing with the actual sins of actual men and women. One would say from this point of view that the kingdom of God is the spirit of God manifested in Jesus Christ as pure Goodness,—that is to say, as pure love and mercy and forgiveness. This is manifested from the beginning in the impression of Jesus as one who went about doing good; in His profoundly sympathetic response to the appeal of every form of human misery; in His declaration of His mission as Son of man to seek and to save that which was lost; in His consorting with publicans and sinners rather than with the righteous and the rich. And surely as we saw that our Lord's chosen designation was Son of man, so we may say that the essence of His religion was humanity.

We cannot say truly that the kingdom of God is goodness, un-

less we know clearly what goodness is. Jesus naturally met evil on
the outside, and so He addressed Himself first to the evils of the body
and of the outward condition. But that was not His end or aim. Mis-
sionaries to the slums of a great city or to a crowded foreign heathen
population might go first with relief funds and appliances, with hospitals and improved sanitation and healthier and more decent methods of dressing and living. It is Christian to do so because
Christianity is humanity wherever or however applied. But humanity
that goes no further than that is not Christianity. Christianity is not
Christianity until it is applying its axe to the root of the evil and the
wretchedness of the world, until its business is with sin and with
God's salvation from sin. It is not the Gospel nor the kingdom of
God nor salvation to men that they shall be made the *objects only* of
all the mercy and the goodness of the universe. Nothing can be done
merely to us or for us that will save us. To be loved, to be sympa-
thized with and helped, to be shown mercy and forgiven, to be the
objects of the most unconditional divine grace, are a very great deal.
But these are the merest circumstances of human salvation, they are
not salvation itself. No one saw more clearly than our Lord that life
and blessedness is not in what is done to us, but only in what we
ourselves are and do. He did not mean the story of the Prodigal Son
to be to us the beginning and the end of the Gospel. At least, He did
not unless we include in its teaching not only the perfect and unconditional love and goodness of the father, but, as the consequence,
not cause of that, the complete repentance and self-restoration of the
son. The goodness of God leadeth us unto repentance. Nothing else
can so lead us to repentance or can make repentance so effectual unto
salvation; but it is our repentance and what comes of it in ourselves
that constitutes and is our salvation. Therefore, Jesus quickly and
decisively passes from the consideration of men as the mere recipients or objects of the goodness of God, of which He was the almoner,
to the higher thought of them as the subjects of the divine goodness,
as partakers and sharers of the divine spirit and nature and life of love
and goodness. The creditor who owed ten thousand talents could by
no possibility have discharged the debt, and his lord had compassion
on him and freely forgave him all. But when that same servant
showed no mercy to the fellow-servant who owed him a hundred
pence, what was become of the mercy and goodness that had been
shown him? We can be recipients only as we are sharers and dis-

pensers of the grace of God. And that is not an arbitrary condition upon God's part. All that God has to give is, in the nature of it, capable of being received and possessed and enjoyed only as it is used. And it can be used as God uses it only as it is used, not for ourselves, but upon all in the measure of their claim upon us. How otherwise is it possible to have and to employ and to enjoy God's spirit and nature, and life of love and grace and goodness?

All that God has to give us is goodness, because properly understood that is all that God is Himself. And goodness is *ab initio,* not only what we are in ourselves and do of ourselves, but what we are and do to others than ourselves. But there is no exaggerated or impracticable unselfishness or altruism in that. As we have before pointed out, goodness is our own and our only good. A man's true pleasure or happiness or blessedness or good is to be found in the abundance of his life, which means in the abundance of what he is and does. And what can he be or do except in relation and interchange with others, in mutual offices of love and goodness? The whole tenor of our Lord's teaching and example is to the effect that the *res* or matter of our salvation is not in what God is to us or does for us, but in the result of that upon and in ourselves. It is not the being loved but the loving with a divine love that is our salvation. It is not the receiving but the showing mercy, not our being forgiven but our forgiving, that Jesus Christ is concerned about, not because God is in want of, in the sense of lacking, what we are or can do, but because He knows that that alone is what we want or lack. We do not take sufficient account of the inseparable condition attached to all God's gifts of grace. We can receive freely only what we give freely, and the blessing contained and intended in the gift is to be found by us not in the freely receiving but in the freely using and giving. We need pray to be forgiven our debts only as we forgive our debtors. For if we forgive not, neither does our heavenly Father forgive us. Blessed are they that show mercy, for they shall receive mercy.

The kingdom of God, then, is not a kingdom of goodness as too many of us understand goodness. It is a kingdom not of absolute and unconditioned mercy shown to us, but of divine and therefore unconditioned mercy and goodness exercised by us. In other words, it is a kingdom not only of goodness but of righteousness, or rather of the unity and identity of these. John the Baptist need not have feared that Jesus was going to compromise or relax the law. He was going to magnify it. Except your new righteousness of grace, He was to say to His disciples, shall exceed the old righteousness of law, ye shall not enter into the kingdom of heaven. He was not to lower the standard of personal perfection, but to raise it to its limit in infinity: Be ye perfect as your Father in heaven is perfect. He was not by what so many of us call goodness to put up with human imperfection, to condone human weakness, to let down the demands of human obligation and responsibility. But He was to effect a higher purpose and accomplish a higher result in the matter of all these, not by the old impossible method of exacting a righteousness that could not be rendered, but by the new and practicable method of imparting a righteousness which could be received, and which could and should be none the less our righteousness because not ours but God's in us. That the spirit that I am now of, the new nature into which I have grown, the life I live by the faith of the Son of God, are all not mine but God's who lives in me, makes them none the less mine who also live in God.

The point is that the desire to make the Gospel a gospel of goodness, so called, shown to us, and not of righteousness to the utmost required of us, is the completest possible travesty and contradiction of goodness. The world is slowly educating up to the point of seeing that the worst unkindness to a rational and free personality is the kindness of ministering a natural or physical good at the expense to him of moral or spiritual, by which we mean personal, good. A man's life is not in the abundance of the things he possesses, but in himself. If in increasing his possessions we diminish him, we have wrought him the worst injury in our power. The highest mercy to a man is to spare him no requirement of his own manhood. God spared not His own Son, but gave Him up to all that earth or hell could do against Him. To have spared Him whatsoever of His humiliation would have been to rob Him of just so much of His exaltation. The kingdom of God, then, is not weakness. It is no weakness in God, no lowering of His demand upon us to return to Him with the usury of actuality all that He has committed to us in potentiality, no sparing us any jot or tittle of the labor or the pain that, if we are to be made at all, must of necessity go to the making of us. And therefore, equally, it is no weakness for us. So far from God's purpose in Christ being to do anything for us or instead of us which therefore we are not to do ourselves, it is a call to us to be all, to do all, and to suffer all that Jesus Christ Himself is, did, or suffered. If we are to be near Him in His kingdom, we must have drunk the cup that He drank and been baptized with the baptism that He was baptized withal. We must have died the death He died and attained the resurrection that He accomplished.

The story of the Prodigal Son may be used to illustrate the whole method of the kingdom of God. We will confine ourselves to the most general application of it as giving an account of the return, reconciliation, and restoration of the soul that has been far separated from God by sin. The thing to be illustrated is not a material separation or one of outward space and condition. It is an alienation, a drifting apart, of mind and character and life, a long widening and far widened breach of spiritual sympathy and personal unity. What the son is brought to and experiences in the far country is not the straits and discomforts of physical poverty, but the inherent consequences, the evil and the wretchedness, of sin. Sin is an evil not only spiritual and moral but also natural; and what he felt first was doubtless the natural ills into which he had sunk. But whatever he wished, what he wanted was not relief merely from these. The story would never have been told if its end had been restoration only to that. The restoration was not to outward conditions but to himself, and that through reconciliation or spiritual at-one-ment with the father and the home. How was that internal and essential reunion to be accomplished? The natural first answer would be through the self-reformation and conversion of the son. The change away having been his alone, the change back must be equally his own. Certainly, the father alone could not effect the reconciliation, whatever might be his disposition. In the thing to be illustrated, what is wanted is the change or conversion of the son himself. But suppose that, as is the case, such a spiritual self-restoration is a natural and a moral impossibility. That can only mean that salvation is an impossibility. And so it is, of the son and by the son himself. If it is to be accomplished it must be by the father and the son in co-operation. And that co-operation must depend upon a personal attitude or disposition towards it on both sides. On the part of the son it is not amiss that the most outward experiences of the wretched consequences of his sin should first awake his consciousness of loss and want. But the matter would not go far if that did not lead further, to remorse and repentance and the desire not only to restore his condition but to recover himself. This in turn could not but lead to the consciousness that as it was he who had sinned, so it must be he who should put away his sin. The obligation of his own part in the matter surely could not be felt too strongly. The law must press its claims, and he must feel those claims to the very uttermost. It is only after he has tested to the limit the possibilities of the law, or his own possibilities under the law— that is to say, after he has fully proved his own will to save himself— that he is prepared for further and other conditions of salvation. In the case of our heavenly Father we do not know how far His providence and prevenient grace is operative in our own least and earliest part in the process, but certainly our part must be there. We must have felt the law and tested our own will and strength to obey it before His grace can intervene. When we have come, or have been brought—or properly, *both*—to that point, then may be revealed to us the beginnings of His part in the matter. I say *then,* for nothing can be revealed to us until we are prepared to apprehend and receive it. The philosophy of God's part may be expressed by a return to the illustration of the parable. What could never have come to the son through the law of himself can and does come to him in the end through the grace of the father. Taken back at once and completely, just as he was, into his father's heart and home, all his sin and shame as though it was not and had never been, himself in the best robe and with the ring of perfect not only reconciliation but eternal union upon his hand, treated as though he were already all that his father's son should be, what effect would all that love and grace, all that fulness of fellowship and that atmosphere of goodness, have upon the son? It would deepen his remorse and increase his penitence, but it would go far beyond that. The perfect faith and trust in the father's restoration of him to sonship would give him heart for and hope in his own inner restoration to sonship. The objective fact would create the subjective spirit, and day by day he would not only be in faith and hope, but be becoming in spirit and reality, more and more the son of his father.

If such is the rationale of the only possible true reconciliation and restoration to union of earthly father and son, why shall it not be the true image and shadow of the reconciliation we so sorely need with our Father in heaven? To come back to Him is to come back to our real selves. But however, eternally complete in Him are all the conditions for our return; however our sin has quenched none of His love, nor abated aught of the readiness or the sufficiency of His grace; however He waits to receive us back into full fellowship with Himself and to make our sins as though they had never been,—still even He can go no further unless there be in us the will and the purpose to arise and come to Him, not alone for the betterment of our state, but for the complete and perfect moral, spiritual, and personal union and oneness with Him of ourselves.

5. THE AUTHORITY OF JESUS

The characteristic of our Lord's ministry which made the most immediate and left the most permanent impression was the principle or quality of authority. It is not only that it was perforce conceded to Him by others, but that He unqualifiedly assumed it for Himself. The two aspects in which this authority presents itself to us might be distinguished as the authority of truth and the authority of power.

The authority of our Lord's teaching might be described as that of originality and finality. The originality was the more apparent and striking because it was in such complete contrast with the very principle of all teaching that had gone before. The principle of that teaching had been that of an unquestioned and unquestionable external authority, the authority originally of God speaking from heaven, and then of a long accumulating and consolidating body of traditional exposition and interpretation scarcely less authoritative or irreformable. Instead of that the truth itself was present and spoke for itself in Jesus, and He spoke immediately and directly from Himself as being or embodying the truth. The question arises in studying the Sermon on the Mount, for example, In what capacity, as being Who or What, does Jesus utter that great body of truth? Is He speaking there as God, and with the outward infallible authority of a proclamation from heaven? Or on the other extreme, is it only the highest reach and utterance of wisdom in the heart and from the lips of an earthly sage? On the face of the evidence of the utterance itself, and in the absence of any explanation on our Lord's own part of the authority by which He spake, I would give the following at least provisional and temporary answer. On the one side this teaching cannot and will not interpret itself as the tentative and incomplete wisdom of human reason and conscience so far as they have attained. On the other side, whatever its ultimate source, it does not come to us out of the mouth of Jesus with the immediate or unmediated force of an utterance from heaven. Jesus Christ speaks to us simply in the capacity and with the authority of the inherent and essential truth of the things He says. I speak that I do know, and testify that I have seen,— that is all the authority He will give us. No matter whence or how the truth, the authority of the truth is that it is the truth. Of course our Lord does say always, My truth is not mine but His that sent me,—but what authority had He for saying that, or what proof could He give of it? At the last the only authority lay in the fact of its *being* the truth, and all the proof simply in the power of the truth to prove itself. I repeat, then, that the immediate capacity in which Jesus Christ taught was that of the truth which He taught. That was the truth, whether divine or human or both, but the whole actual truth of humanity, of human existence, human life, human destiny. He was Himself that truth—incarnate, personal, consummated. And He was not only the truth consummated, but the consummation or consummating of the truth; not only the truth and life of humanity, but the process or way by which humanity comes to the knowledge of its truth and attains to the living of its life.

The truth for which Jesus Christ stands is distinctly and definitely the truth of man, of human life. And when He says of it, I speak that I do know and testify that I have seen, He means that what He says of it is matter of His own personal human experience. He has Himself been through the whole of human experience, and is competent to testify as a witness to all that is in it. He knew what was in man, because He was Himself all of man. The fact that from the first opening of His mouth as a teacher Jesus speaks with the authority of perfect truth does not contradict the fact that He had humanly learned the truth. Almost the first step, for example, in His public ministry was to set Himself outside of and in opposition to the whole spirit and principle and method of the religion in which He was born. Shall we not suppose that the grounds of that opposition had been accumulating and the form of it taking shape in His heart and mind long before His public attitude was assumed? At twelve He was deeply interested and concerned with what was going on in the temple, and during the eighteen intervening years He was doubtless more than an annual visitor to what in His conception was, or ought to be, the holy city. If He held His peace outwardly during that time, what was going on within? And so not only with part but with the whole of the wisdom with which He spoke and acted, we shall doubtless have to go further in seeking a reason for its being so far beyond the attainment of all other human experience, but we need not on that account deny it to be the fruit and result of a true human experience.

The difficulties multiply upon us when we pass from the authority of truth to that of power on the part of our Lord. What is this? A new teaching!—they exclaimed on His first public appearance, according to St. Mark. But it is something more than a new teaching,— for, With authority He commandeth even the unclean spirits, and they obey Him. Unquestionably, Jesus was accepted as having power not only over the spiritual and physical ills of human nature, but over disorders even of external nature. With regard to many of the difficulties involved here, we may, so far as our purpose is concerned, quickly dispose of them. The fact or facts, for example, of demoniacal possessions; the commentators do not hesitate to say now of the possessed that one was an epileptic and another a madman. To Jesus they were possessed of demons. What of that? If Jesus Christ, in all the human and divine truth of Him, whatever that be, were come to-day instead of two thousand years ago, would He not speak and think in terms of human thought and knowledge and speech of to-day? If not, then what? In terms of the thought and speech of men two thousand years hence? And if He should think the thoughts and speak in terms of the science of to-day, would there not be the same difficulties two thousand years hence that we have with the thoughts and speech of two thousand years ago? The abiding truth of Jesus Christ is within and behind and wholly independent of the ever changing phases or stages of human knowledge. The setting has from time to time to be altered to adapt it to the changing focus or vision of advancing science, but what is really of the jewel within does not change with it; it is Jesus Christ the same yesterday, to-day, and forever.

We have to meet fairly and frankly the fact that the very conception of miracle is a real and a growing stumbling-block to the thought, and I may say the conscience, of to-day. We have to take account of this prejudice, and do it the justice to understand it. We may say that it is due, first, to the world's growing observation and experience of the inviolability and uniformity of natural law. With that growth miracle has gradually disappeared, not, assuredly, because facts have changed, but because our understanding and interpretation of facts have changed. We assume that if we understood all facts, all facts would appear to us natural. But, secondly, with that change another has followed, or is following, more slowly. We have learned or are learning to see God less and less in transcendences of nature, and more and more in the perfect unity and order and wisdom of nature. We feel that the whole work of God is one and of a piece, that addition or interference or reparation from without would be a confession of imperfection or failure. The natural has become to us more divine than the non-natural or the contra-natural. But more than that, in the third place,—we ought long ago to have been sensible of the positive injury that has come to the world through the misapprehension that the true supernatural is a condemnation or in any respect whatever a supplanting or displacing of the natural. The true supernatural is only the truer and higher natural. It is God not without but within the natural, helping us not to discard but to realize or fulfil the natural, on the lines of its own truer because higher and completer nature. The life of Jesus Christ, because it is higher than nature can carry us, or than we can carry ourselves in our own fulfilment of the law of nature, is not therefore contrary to nature. It is our own highest nature—and that alone is the true supernatural—not to be completed by nature, nor to be able of ourselves to fulfil the law of self-completion, but to find the completion at once of our nature and ourselves in highest union and association with God. The world still wants miracle in its Christianity, to the untold damage of itself and the utter contradiction of Christianity. Was it better that the earth should be gradually delivered from the curse of plague and pestilence by science and sanitation, by the natural process of self-cleansing and sweetening, or that in the stead of that the old so-called Christian method of miracle in response to prayer and fasting should have sufficed, and saved the trouble and expense of the cleansing and the sweetening? And so, in the mass or with the individual, there are natural causes of natural ills which are best dealt with only by natural science, which is the knowledge of natural causes, and by natural art, which is the acquired skill to apply that knowledge. Anything that could and did supplant the necessity for science and art would be destructive of a very large part of human life, and would be a direct contradiction of Him who came that we might have life and have it more abundantly.

The injury that comes to us from the unwholesome demand for miracle is more apparent as well as more real in our inner than in our outer life. Christianity ought to be not only the most spiritual but the most natural life in the world. The life of faith in God ought to be the life of the highest activity of ourselves, and of the completest fulfilment not only of every potentiality, but every relation and obligation of our nature and our natural condition. But there is a not undeserved charge against Christians of weakness, as compared with the more positive and active life of the world. And then comes the charge against Christianity itself, that it weakens the character through relieving the man of the responsibility and the task of self-realization, of working out his own salvation. His life-work has been done for him or instead of him, and "he is contented to be a sinner saved by grace." Is it not true that we are constantly expecting miracle to be wrought in our behalf, that we are looking to God to have done for us or to do in us that the whole benefit of which consists in our doing ourselves? No, Christ is our salvation only because He is the power of God in us to work out our own salvation. If instead of being that, He were instead of that to us, He would be not our salvation but its opposite. Now miracle is something instead of nature and instead of ourselves, whereas the Christianity of Jesus Christ is what we see in Himself, God indeed and the power of God, but God so in nature and so in man that it only completes the nature and perfects the man. There is no Holy Ghost in me save as the spirit that I myself am of, and there is no Christ in me save in what I am myself. And if God be truly in me by His Word and His Spirit, He is so not to supplant or to displace my nature or my personality, but only to complete them on their own lines and perfect them in their own activities. We can see, then, how there may be some ground of prejudice against the conception of miracles, at least as we have misunderstood and abused it.

Yet there can be no doubt that Jesus possessed the extraordinary powers ascribed to Him and performed the works we call miracles. There is less and less disposition to deny that, the more apparent it becomes that there are psychic and spiritual forces as yet latent in human nature of which we know not whereunto the future development may reach. Such powers were existent and manifested themselves in our Lord's time, and, like all other human powers, for evil as well as for good. The devil as well as God could make use of them. It is not inconceivable nor perhaps improbable that there may be a spiritual and divine use for those powers, of which our Lord gave us the highest indication, of which we have not as yet made true experiment, and therefore have not true experience. Assuredly, there is more to be accomplished than our religion or our science have accomplished for the spiritual and the natural ills of mankind through the mind and through the faith of men. On the part of religion, may it not be from a lack of mental and spiritual susceptibility on our part, the absence of a due response of mind and heart, that the truth and the love of God do not work greater wonders in our lives, not only spiritual and moral but physical also? May it not be one more of the many reproaches of our Christianity as it is, that many have to go outside, if not of it, yet of its organized fellowship, to find that power of God unto salvation of soul and body which was its promise to us? Whatsoever lies dormant in us of natural potentiality to be found and healed in soul or body by truth and love acting directly upon mind and heart, let it by all means be awakened and developed. It will not militate against, but rather will work with, the true principle that God's grace and power must work in and with and through ourselves and our own activities, and not simply for or instead of us.

Let us see how our Lord Himself regarded His wonderful powers. Unquestionably, in a very large sense, He considered Himself to be in the world as a divine physician of the ills and the sicknesses that are in it. In how large a sense, I think we can only begin to realize in our later interpretations of His work and person. I believe, as I have said, that our Lord's permanent function was to treat causes, or the cause, and not symptoms; and symptoms only indirectly, as they could be temporarily alleviated, and would be ultimately removed by the removal of the cause. In other words, He came to take away sin, and by consequence all the consequences of sin. But at the first He needed to produce an adequate impression upon the hearts and minds of men of not only His disposition and mission but also of His authority and power to be the divine helper and healer. Of this there was no doubt or question in His own mind, and it imparted to Him that aspect of authority which took away all doubt or question from the minds of those who were the subjects of His power. They *were* the subjects, and not merely the objects, of His power. He carried *them* along with Himself in their healing. On their part it was mind or heart or faith healing. He told them to be well, to arise and walk, to look up and see. And they did it. Could not we in many ways do it too, if only we would believe and know? What we have, first and perhaps chiefly, to note in connection with our Lord's miracles is the way in which He Himself deprecated the element in them of mere sign or wonder. With Him they were simply parts of His mission and power to help and heal. St. Matthew describes them as fulfilling the prophecy, Himself took our infirmities, and bore our diseases. And even as He wrought them there are evidences that all this dealing with outward conditions is but preliminary to a further and a higher aim. The miracles are but parables; the power to heal sickness is but proof of the power to heal sin. But that ye may know that the Son of man hath power to forgive sins (then saith He to the sick of the palsy), Arise, take up thy bed, and go unto thy house. And he arose and departed to his house.

There are other miracles that it would be more difficult to give a reason for or attempt an explanation of; such, for example, as His mysterious sympathy with and power over the operations of nature. However that is to be accounted for, or disposed of, our ignorance need not seriously concern us. At any rate it symbolizes to us this great truth: The more we are at one and are one with God, the more are we so with everything else within and without us, and the more— as we shall perhaps know in the future—have we the sympathy and co-operation not only of our whole selves but of all nature around us.

We were brought just above face to face with our Lord's authority and power to deal with sin. The further question of that must be reserved for our second part, upon the interpretation of His work. Another larger claim, to be similarly reserved, is expressed at the close of St. Matthew's Gospel: All authority hath been given unto me in heaven and on earth. Go ye therefore, and make disciples of all nations, baptizing them into the name of the Father and of the Son and of the Holy Ghost; teaching them to observe all things whatsoever I commanded you; and lo, I am with you alway, even unto the end of the world. But even these are not yet all the ascriptions to Jesus, or the claims by Him of that *exousia,* that divine prerogative, which we have so far only partially traced through the Gospels. In our Lord's last address to His Father, before leaving the world, according to St. John, He speaks thus: Father, the hour is come; glorify thy Son, that the Son may glorify thee: even as thou gavest Him authority over all flesh, that whatsoever thou hast given Him, to them He should give eternal life. And this is life eternal, that they should know thee the only true God, and him whom thou didst send, even Jesus Christ. The eternal life which He describes as His authority and power to impart are spoken of at length as being possessed here on earth; but He goes on to pray, Father, that which thou hast given me, I will that, where I am, they also may be with me; that they may behold my glory which thou hast given me; for thou lovedst me before the foundation of the world.

When we come to interpret these later claims of divine authority, I shall endeavour to show that, while they go beyond the earlier ones we have been considering, and project themselves into all the future of human life, not only here but hereafter, yet they are all, the earliest and the latest, precisely along the same lines and mean the same thing.

6. THE BLESSEDNESS OF JESUS

A study of the beatitudes will give us the highest illustration possible of the leading principles of what we have been discussing as the gospel of the common humanity and the earthly life of our Lord. Blessedness is the highest expression as it is the highest reach and attainment of that life. The life of Jesus would not be a gospel to us if it were not a revelation and a promise of human blessedness. We see in Him the meaning, the value, the worth, which not only justifies to us and reconciles us to our life and its conditions as they are, but enables us to find in it the highest satisfaction of which our natures are capable and the highest enjoyment to which our spirits or personalities can attain. We have already seen that while personal pleasure or happiness or even blessedness can never be the motive, it is in fact the measure and the condition, of the highest activity. Mere instinct or mere duty can never lift us to our height. In the first place, perfect functioning or activity *is* perfect pleasure or happiness or blessedness, as the function is particular, general, or universal, and is lower or higher in the scale. And, secondly, as the perfection of the activity heightens the pleasure, so reflexively the perfection of the pleasure is necessary to the complete heightening of the function or activity. We can be or do perfectly only that which we supremely love, and which therefore it is our supreme pleasure, happiness or blessedness, as the case may be, to be or to do. Blessedness, therefore, let us repeat, is at once the measure and the condition of the perfect life. Aristotle states the principle somewhat as follows: Pleasure, he says, speaking of even the lower true pleasures, completes a function in two senses. In the first place, it *is* its completion; like the bloom on the peach or the cheek, it is the final touch which marks the acme of the act or activity. In the second place, it *causes* its completion, by infusing into the act or activity that without which it cannot complete itself. When, therefore, our Lord comes to speak of blessedness, He is describing His own life, and the life that should be ours, in its very fulness and completeness.

The first question is as to the fact, actual or possible, in human life as it is, of such a blessedness. Our Lord's testimony is to the fact of its actuality, and therefore of its possibility. And let us pause to observe that it is testimony on His part. It is not the immediate revelation of omniscience, but the witness of human experience. He knew that there is a blessedness in human life, because He had found it and was in possession of it. He spoke in the name and with the authority of it, and He declared it that others might seek and find and have part with Him in it. The beatitudes are the revelation of His own humanly discovered and humanly experienced secret of blessedness. There is not one of the human conditions or causes of it which He gives that He had not Himself tested and proved to the utmost. There is not one of the ingredients in the cup of it that He had not drunk to the bottom. It is true here as always, that He spake that He Himself knew and testified to that He Himself had experienced. He had known the poverty which is the condition of the kingdom of heaven, the sorrow without which one cannot experience the divine consolations, the meekness through which He was destined to inherit the earth; He had hungered and thirsted for righteousness and been filled; He had known the mercy to others which is the only mercy to ourselves; through the purity of His human heart He had seen God; in His perfect ministry of peace with God and peace among men He had reached the acme of human attainment, and tested what it is not only to be called but to be the Son of God. He had known, too, and experienced the blessedness of, persecution and reproach and false witness and rejection.

As all the causes and conditions so all the rewards and enjoyments of this blessedness are described by our Lord as to be found within this present life. Blessed are—not shall be hereafter—those of whom He is speaking. For theirs is—not shall be—the kingdom of God and its rewards. Even where He speaks in the future, as He continues to do, it is evident that He is speaking of cause and effect here and not hereafter. Blessed are they that mourn: for they shall be comforted. No chastening or affliction is at the moment joyous; it is only afterward that it yieldeth peaceable fruit. But afterward, in time; if we cannot reap it in time, there is no assurance that we can do so in eternity. St. Paul thanks God that the afflictions of Christ had abounded upon him, not only because thereby he had come to know for himself the comfort that aboundeth through Christ, but because he was thus enabled to comfort others with the comfort wherewith he was himself comforted of God.

Nothing assuredly better than a blessedness that begins in poverty and sorrow, and has its earthly end in persecution, could illustrate the great truth that the issues of the kingdom of God are within ourselves, that it is the energies and activities of our own souls in which the abundance of our life consists, and which therefore control, or determine and constitute, our happiness. It cannot be too often repeated that it is not environment but our own reaction upon environment that blesses or curses us. The same environment is equally calculated to make and to mar opposite responses to it. Identical conditions produce the hero and the coward. The career of Jesus Christ so far as it is a revelation to us from God, or so far as it is a demonstration to us of a fact in itself, reveals and demonstrates to us this truth: that human conditions rightly interpreted and rightly acted upon are the best conditions for the production of a divine human life and blessedness.

If we wish to go more into the details of the blessedness of Jesus, we must analyze the separate beatitudes, and this we shall proceed to do with at least one or more of them. In the two most definite statements by our Lord of the nature and purpose of His earthly mission, the opening address at Nazareth and the reply to John in prison, He repeats an expression which is the keynote of His ministry: He anointed me to preach the gospel to the poor; and, The poor have the gospel preached unto them. As the Gospel to the Poor was the divine commission, so was it the human credential of His Messiahship. Who are the poor? Are they the secularly or earthly poor, or the spiritually and heavenly poor? It is a mixed question in the Gospels, just as we have seen that it is an open question whether our Lord's actual ministry was one of general humanity or for the specific taking away of sin. If we read the whole of the two passages quoted from above, we shall see that all the Messianic functions—release to the captives, recovering of sight to the blind, liberty to the bruised; or, The blind see, the lame walk, the lepers are cleansed, the deaf hear, the dead are raised up—are such as, while they have their material prototypes, may be interpreted as spiritual only, the material becoming mere figure or symbol of the spiritual. We have seen how Jesus Himself strives always to bend the lower to the higher, and the fact that while in St. Luke He speaks of the blessedness of the poor in general, in St. Matthew He limits the expression to Blessed are the poor in spirit, or the spiritually poor, may be only another instance of His desire gradually to spiritualize His mission.

We limit our question, then, to Who are the poor in spirit? Several lines of answer tempt us in different, and perhaps all of them true, directions; the deepest truths are the most many-sided. But let us begin at least by looking for our Lord's own interpretation. The saying must be taken in connection with many others, such as these: They that are whole need not the physician, but they that are sick; I am not come to call—to extend the gracious divine invitation to enter the kingdom to—the righteous, but sinners; I am come that they that see not may see. They that are whole, they that say they see, they that are already righteous, or think they are, are not objects because they are incapable of being subjects of His mission. The blessing of the kingdom is not for them, because they cannot know the blessedness of it. Perhaps the strongest expression of the state of mind that shuts out from the blessedness of Jesus is to be found in the words, Because thou sayest, I am rich, and have gotten riches, and have need of nothing; and knowest not that thou art wretched and miserable and poor and blind and naked: I counsel thee to buy of me gold refined by fire, that thou mayest become rich; and white garments, that thou mightest clothe thyself, and that the shame of thy nakedness be not made manifest; and eye-salve to anoint thine eyes, that thou mayest see.

No doubt the above covers briefly the general ground of the practical application of the first beatitude, so far at least as the first condition of blessedness is concerned. It does not touch the second point involved, the content of the blessing attached. But so far as we have gone, may we not attempt to go a little deeper and touch the philosophy that underlies all the divine teaching? Jesus Christ seems to attach a blessedness not alone to our consciousness of the fact, but to the fact itself, of our natural, or in ourselves, poverty and blindness and sin and death. In the first place, does He not at least exaggerate our natural condition? And if He does not, then how, in the second place, can He consistently call it blessed? It seems to me that the reason of both positions may be made apparent. The religion of Christianity rests on two facts, the one of our nature and the other of ourselves. The first is the deficiency of our nature, and the second is the insufficiency of ourselves. With regard to the first, Bishop Butler teaches us in substance somewhat as follows: We are, as constituted by our nature, deficient beings. That is, in order to be complete, we need ourselves to supplement or add something to our nature. The deficiency is to be supplied by the addition of what we call habit. Habit, which results from our own acts, and forms our own character, and determines our own destiny, is thus something which we ourselves add to our nature, and which as we thus add it becomes a second nature which is only an extension or further completion of the first. Now, the deficiency of our nature at the first is a positive blessing, because it is the condition of our acquisition of the second and higher nature which is that of personality. Suppose we could not become more than merely what our nature makes us. Suppose the mysteries, but none the less surely the facts, of our own consciousness and freedom, our power to determine ourselves by our own acts and habits and character, did not enter into the matter and make persons of us. The deficiency of our nature is a blessing because it calls for and makes possible the higher development of our personality.

There is a second truth no less important to the final and entire ascent of our humanity than the first. If our nature was deficient in itself, it is equally true that we are insufficient in ourselves for the yet higher reaches for which our nature prepares us and for which our personal lives and characters are intended to qualify and fit us. Insufficiency does not absolve us from the obligation of ourselves working out our complete and eternal destinies. It only implies that we can do so only in conjunction with something else. Now to have been complete in and of ourselves would have been to be incapable of becoming more or greater than we are, or are capable of making ourselves. Christianity, on the contrary, holds out to us the promise and the hope of a sympathy and a union with all things, with the mind and spirit and life of the source of all things, which will make us infinitely more and greater than ourselves. It thus begets, or rather addresses and develops, what is already a part of us and only needs to be brought into consciousness by personal experience, the sense of insufficiency and the need of what will alone suffice for the attainment of the fulness of our life. That is it of which our Lord speaks, when He says that He is come that we might have life and might have it more abundantly,—more abundantly than nature can supply it to us, or than we can multiply it of ourselves. He is come to bring God into our lives, and with God all those powers and promises of the kingdom of God, which will suffice to make us not only all that we are but also somewhat of what God is. This is also what St. Paul experienced, when, entreating to be relieved of the mortal infirmity he discovers in himself, he is answered from above himself, My grace is sufficient for thee: for my power is made perfect in weakness. Whereupon he cries, Most gladly therefore will I rather glory in my weaknesses, that the strength of Christ may rest upon me. Wherefore I take pleasure in weaknesses, in injuries, in necessities, in persecutions, in distresses, for Christ's sake: for when I am weak, then am I strong.

I have said before that Jesus Christ nowhere condemns us for the deficiencies of our nature, nor for the insufficiencies of ourselves. He does not find fault with us that, in and of ourselves, we are constant violators of the eternal spirit that should animate us, and transgressors of the eternal law that should regulate and control us. He finds fault that we have not enough of the spirit to know that we violate it, nor apprehension enough of the law to know that we transgress it; that we have not enough of holiness to want it, or of righteousness to hunger and thirst after it. Blessed are they who know their own insufficiency, their own poverty and weakness, sufficiently to feel their need of the powers of the world to come, of the kingdom of God in their souls. And not only so; not only are they blessed who know their poverty and feel their need, but blessed is

that poverty and that need in itself. That we are insufficient in ourselves for the holiness, the righteousness, the eternal life that are necessary to complete us; that only God in and with us can suffice for
them; that without God we cannot compass the spirit or accomplish
the law of our own perfection, only means that God has made us not
for ourselves and our own finiteness, but for Himself and His infinity, and that we are violating ourselves and transgressing our law in
falling short, or in being willing and satisfied to fall short, of that.

The distinction among or between men which the New Testament recognizes and consistently makes, which our Lord Himself
always makes, is not that some are sinners and some are not, but that
some are so content to be sinners that they know not that they are
sinners, while others are so convinced and convicted by the spirit of
holiness of their own unholiness, and by the law of righteousness of
their own unrighteousness, that they are conscious only of sin in
themselves. St. Paul is exactly in the line of Christ when he says that
it was never the end or expectation of the law to make us righteous.
The only righteousness the law could produce would be a righteousness of our own in obedience to the law. But it would be a very low
law that we could obey. When you have made the law as high as God
Himself, you will want God Himself in you to enable you to fulfil
it. By the law, then, is only the knowledge of sin. When the law has
made sinners of us, has convinced and convicted us of sin, it has
discharged its function. When it has prepared us for and turned us
over to God who alone suffices us, or fills up our own insufficiency,
for holiness, righteousness, and life, then it is *functus officio,* and
ready to be abolished, as John the Baptist was swallowed up in the
greater light of Jesus Christ. Blessed then are we even that we are
sinners, if we know our sin; if through knowledge of the curse of sin
we have been brought to the knowledge of the blessedness of holiness, and if through experience of our weakness against sin we have
come to experience the power of God unto salvation from sin.

We are hardly prepared as yet to enter into what I conceive to
be the meaning of the other half of the first beatitude, the nature and
extent of the reward attached to a true poverty of spirit. For all we
have said of the kingdom of heaven or of God, I think we need the
higher interpretations of our Lord's work and person in order to realize all that is ours in the possession of that kingdom. Some one has
said, The kingdom of God is everywhere if we could but see it; and

yet, alas, almost nowhere, because so few of us can see it. The fault indeed is all in our seeing. Jesus Christ has not come so much to create the kingdom of God without us, as to create within us the power to see it. I am come, He says, that they which see not may see. What He saw and what He would have us see is: all the eternal love that God the Father is, *ours;* all the infinite grace that God the Son is, ours; all the perfect fellowship or oneness with ourselves that God the Holy Ghost is, ours. If all this is ours, then all things are ours, and all blessedness is indeed ours.

7. THE BEATITUDES

We may touch more lightly upon the other beatitudes, not so much to give an analysis or exposition of themselves as to illustrate more clearly some of the features of the earthly life and character of Jesus Christ. For from our present point of view that character and life are our gospel and our salvation.

Blessed are they that mourn, for they shall be comforted. It must already have struck us that the grounds or conditions of blessedness adduced by our Lord are largely those which would seem to us rather those of un-blessedness. Poverty, sorrow, persecution, reproach, rejection,—how can these be grounds of blessedness? We have already touched upon this point, but there is something in it the rationale or philosophy of which needs to be brought out more plainly. Aristotle teaches us how, especially in morals, opposites result from the same causes or conditions. Not only out of identical conditions do cowardice and courage arise, as the conditions are differently met, but the conditions of difficulty, danger, pain, and fear, which make cowards of us, are precisely the only ones which could beget courage or heroism in us. We cannot be brave except under circumstances calculated to produce fear and cowardice. So precisely the occasions and opportunities and temptations that yielded to and overcome by are the causes of sin, resisted and overcome are the causes of holiness. They are necessary to the one as to the other. Constituted as we are, we attribute our sin to what we call the flesh. We must just as truly attribute our holiness to that same flesh. For if we have no sin that does not come through yielding to the flesh, neither do we know any holiness which is not acquired by and which does not consist in the conquest of the flesh and its subduing to the spirit. This is easier to see than the fact that even our happiness or blessedness, certainly in the higher reaches of it, cannot be found in freedom from sorrow but only in the enduring and overcoming of sorrow. First for the fact, and then for the explanation of it. As to the fact, assuredly it was so with Jesus Himself. In the world, He said, ye have tribulation; but be of good cheer, I have overcome the world. His own blessedness had been, and theirs must be, one not of conditions but of conquest and victory over conditions. The conditions calculated in themselves to produce sorrow were just those which overcome were necessary to produce joy. Thenceforth to St. John faith was the power to overcome the world,—not only its sin but its sorrow.

The explanation of the necessity of sorrow to blessedness seems to me to be this: The highest blessedness comes to us in the sense of our highest selves. It is the reflex condition of our highest states and energies or activities. Now these can be expressed only by the terms holiness, righteousness, life. Let us take the first of these, the one most distinctive of Christ and Christianity. Holiness, we say, is freedom from sin. For us at least, situated and constituted as we are, that is no true or sufficient definition. Our holiness is no mere freedom from sin; it is a definite relation to, a definite attitude against, sin. It is a hatred of, a sorrow for, a resistance to, an overcoming of, sin— and all these to the point of at least meaning and intending, if not yet attaining, the putting away of sin. I speak only for beings like ourselves when I say that the consummate joy of holiness would be incomprehensible and impossible save through a corresponding and equal sorrow for sin. Lower joys or satisfactions might not be so dependent upon the experience of their opposites, but for us there can be no love of good which is not a hatred of evil, and no joy of what we should and would be that is not born of sorrow for what we are.

Blessed are the meek, for they shall inherit the earth. There is an interesting historical as well as philosophical side to this beatitude. The question is as to the disposition of men towards men, which is the ultimately true and essential one, and which must therefore prevail in the end and possess the earth. It is a curious fact that in all the great answers to the question of human relationship and conduct, the same term has been selected to express the ideal, and that equally in all the inadequacy of the term has been felt and expressed. Men, according to Aristotle, in the spirit and temper of their dealings with one another, should be controlled by a disposition which he calls meekness or mildness or gentleness. The term is the best we have, he says, but it is inadequate; it is not positive or strong enough. Moses stands out as the type of the Hebrew righteousness; he might be said to have been the creator of it. And we speak of the meekness of Moses as though that were his distinguishing trait. But surely we have all felt the inadequacy of the term meekness to express the character or disposition of Moses. Our Lord seems to have selected the same term to express His own fundamental disposition. Take my yoke upon you, He says, and learn of me. For I am meek and lowly in heart; and ye shall find rest unto your souls. And yet we too feel that the word meek is scarcely the one to describe Jesus. We feel even that too much application of that term to Him has weakened the popular conception not only of Himself but of Christianity. It has contributed perhaps to the too negative and colorless interpretation of His great principle of non-resistance. The question is, as I have said, what is the true and perfect temper of man toward man, especially in the difficult and trying circumstances of human life. We may depend upon it that every really great answer to this question will be found to contain some, and perhaps many, elements of the truth. The Greek meekness, as the ideal temper, will rest upon the conceptions of reasonableness and moderation. The right reason, the power to see things as they are, is the natural basis of mutual understanding, and so of harmony and peace. When we add to this self-control, freedom of the will from prejudice and passion, we seem to have both the intellectual and the moral conditions of the ideal temper. The lack is that even in the forbearance and magnanimity of the Greek there is, if not too much regard for the propriety or nobility of one's own attitude, yet too little regard in comparison for what St. Paul calls "the things of the other."

In the so-called meekness of Moses there is a lofty unselfishness, a great humility, a perfection of zeal and devotion, which momentary weaknesses and impatiences scarcely detract from. The Law and the Prophets between them were productive of great types. But the perfection of human spirit and temper waited still for its realization and manifestation. When Jesus speaks of the meek, He speaks of Himself. He speaks of that attitude towards men under all possible conditions of provocation and trial which He had deliberately made His own and which never deserted Him under any temptation to the

contrary. The general attitude or disposition of Jesus towards individual men and towards the world of men was one not without its
natural and mighty temptations to the contrary. When He was sym-
bolically taken up into the exceeding high mountain and shown all
the kingdoms of the earth and the glory of them, we know not what
visions and temptations of greatness and power and natural possibilities and opportunities passed through His mind. But they found
no lodgment there. The prince of this world had nothing in Him.
There were opposite spirits, opposite dispositions and attitudes, that
contended for the possession of Him, but from first to last He knew
but one. All self-seeking, even the highest, the most spiritual, all
pride or ambition or self-glorification of any kind, was of the devil,
and was bidden to get behind Him. The Son of man, the ideal, the
true, the eternal man can know or own but one spirit, one temper,
one attitude or disposition upon earth, and that is, not to be served
but to serve, to be not lord but servant of all. And there was no provocation of private or individual treatment against Himself that Jesus
Christ had not to meet and treat, and He met and dealt with each with
its own application of the universal temper that characterized Him in
all. I do not know how we can define or describe in abstract terms
the peculiar meekness, or what is attempted to be expressed by the
meekness of Jesus. The thing is ever more and greater, and even different, from its best expression. That is why God never gives us de-
finitions or descriptions of things, but always manifestations of the
thing itself. As to the meekness spoken of in this beatitude we can
only say that it is the universal attitude of Jesus Christ, and so the
essential Christian attitude, in all the personal relations of men, and
under all circumstances of possible provocation or trial or temptation. Of course its essential quality is love, the love that never faileth,
that can adapt itself to every case and preserve its identity under
every transformation, that can be all things and yet always the same
thing.

But the interesting point about the beatitude is this: the perfect
assurance of Jesus that the right, the true attitude of man toward man
will be the ultimately successful and surviving attitude. The meek
shall inherit and possess the earth. The spirit and temper and disposition of Jesus, because it is the fittest, because it is that which
alone gives true meaning and value to life, because it is the only bond
of perfect relationship and intercourse among men, will survive and

prevail. And has not the history of our Lord's own throne and sceptre and kingdom on earth, in spite of our unchristian want of faith and courage and devotion in sustaining and extending them, more than vindicated His confidence and His promise? On what other foundations could He have built a surer and more abiding dominion over men and possession of the earth than that He has built upon Himself and His own eternal attitude toward us and among us? The one law of that kingdom is that each of us in it shall be what He is, and that in every possible complication of mutual intercourse or relation we shall be each to each what He is to us all. What would be the consequence if that spirit should indeed inherit and possess the earth?

If one wishes to carry out the principles of the kingdom of Christ by the letter of the Sermon on the Mount, he will doubtless encounter great difficulties. The letter of non-resistance, for example, as there stated without qualification, might be impracticable in actual and general practice. Non-resistance to the evil-doer might be the greatest evil we could render him. But does not our Lord Himself by such sayings as this, Cast not your pearls before swine, lest they trample them under foot, suggest to us that the most unqualified statement of universal principles is intended to be qualified by common sense and by particular circumstances? The one principle underlying all Christian dealing with one another is that in every case we are to consider all "the things of the other," and not merely to assert ourselves against Him. Now the things of the other must include not alone his immediate or his material good, but still more his moral good, or his spiritual and personal good. If one acts with the wisest and best reference to all that, it may well happen that he might be most truly carrying out the spirit in actually violating the letter of the divine precepts. Our Lord shows no disposition to give us dispensation from the use of our own reason and judgment and "perception in particulars." If our Christianity truly possesses that spirit of Christ, without which we are none of His, it can be trusted to deal with the letter of His commands.

In the fourth beatitude we have what is technically if not really the heart and soul of the theology of both the old and the new Scriptures: Blessed are they that hunger and thirst after righteousness, for they shall be filled. With the Greek man is the measure. To stand well with one's self, to be true to one's own norm or standard or ideal, is the end. With the Hebrew God is the measure. To be right with God, to *stand* right with God—but on the ultimate only ground of *being* right with Him—that is the end. The rightness of the universe, righteousness as the universal law, the ultimate triumph of righteousness all appearances or all facts to the contrary notwithstanding, the sole obligation to be on the side of righteousness all conditions or all consequences to the contrary notwithstanding—that was Hebrew theology and Hebrew law. The letter of the Old Testament law, whether natural, moral, civil, or ceremonial, was the truest and best expression of the law of God. Our Lord did the opposite of setting Himself against the letter of the law. There was not one jot or tittle of it that He abolished or supplanted otherwise than by most exactly and completely fulfilling it. It is the highest of rights to be able to say I love,—it is the greatest of wrongs to say that best thing, and then *not love*. It is the blackest of sins to use a rite or a ceremony which says so much, which means so much, which ought to *be* so much, and yet to use it without anything in mind or heart or life of all that it says and means and ought to be. The Pharisee, in making the letter all, made it not merely nothing but very much worse than nothing. In taking the place of, it practically displaced and abolished what it was intended for. That which was made for man, for humanity and mercy, as the sabbath, was made an excuse for inhumanity and the denial of mercy. That which was ordained for God and piety, as the temple, was made a place and a cover for selfish merchandise and earthly gain. The circumcision of the flesh was made to do duty for the mortification and purgation of the spirit. Sacrifice—as in the saying, I will have mercy and not sacrifice—had become the synonym of its own opposite and denial. In nothing else than in their opposite theories and practice of righteousness does the essential contradiction of the spirit of Jesus to that of His place and day manifest itself more clearly, a contradiction which explains the tragedy of His life.

But to forget the false and look only upon the true, and upon the only true! To be right with God, to know His will and to do it! No Hebrew lawgiver or prophet, assuredly, hungered and thirsted more after that than did Jesus. None was more consumed with zeal for His Father's house or His Father's business. It was His meat and drink, a food that again and again lifted Him above the need or the want of earthly food—so that almost He lived not upon bread at all but only upon the word of God. Lo, I come to do thy will, O God!—

by the which will, by the which perfect doing of the Father's will, we are all sanctified. But if Jesus had no less zeal for righteousness than lawgiver or prophet, He had also more knowledge of what God's righteousness is. To say that God is infinitely right, that His law is infinite righteousness, is only a formal statement or truth about Him. It says that what He is is right, but it does not say what He is— or consequently, what is right. Jesus knows better what right or righteousness is because He knows better what God is. God is Love, love of all things, especially love of all that can know and share His love. God loves love because love loves love. The only true zeal for God, the only right or righteousness, is love. That is the only real definition because it is the only one which gives the *res,* the thing or matter or content, the substance, of God or man or holiness or righteousness or life. Love is not only the spirit or law, it is the eternal actuality or reality whose are the spirit and the law, of the universe. And it is that, all to the contrary notwithstanding. All that opposes that is only the opposite out of which that is born, out of which that is surely coming day by day, and æon by æon; is surely coming and will assuredly come at the last to the uttermost. Yet in that age, and in every age, men could and can be consumed by a zeal for God which conceives it its duty and makes it its business to put love out of its heart and to trample love under its feet! Righteousness can set itself against mercy, and zeal against charity!

Our Lord does not say, Blessed are the righteous, but, Blessed are they that hunger and thirst after righteousness. He allies Himself with us with whom righteousness is no fact of our nature nor any achievement of ourselves. It is something we have not and want, something we cannot attain and look for from outside ourselves. We do not hunger and thirst for that which is in or of ourselves, but only for that which comes to us from without and yet upon which our very lives depend. It might perhaps have been otherwise in almost anything else, but in spiritual things it must needs be so. Righteousness is the most personal thing in the world. It is the act and activity of ourselves. It is nothing if not of our own desire and choice and will and entire personal effort and activity. But we cannot supremely want or desire that which is already ours, or which we can easily ourselves get. The relation to righteousness and the attitude towards it expressed in this beatitude is the ground upon which St. Paul's later developed doctrine rests exactly and securely. We are just or righteous before God, not for any actual or possible righteousness of our own, but because we see in Jesus Christ a divine righteousness, a righteousness of God, made ours by grace on God's part, and by faith on ours. Because that righteousness is the supreme object of our desire; because we look upon it as the supreme end and intention of our lives; because we accept it as God's word of promise, of power, and consequently of fulfilment, as regards ourselves; and so appropriate it to ourselves by faith and enter upon the possession of it in hope,— so God accounts it ours already, as He will make it ours in the end.

8. THE BEATITUDES—*Continued*

Blessed are the merciful, for they shall obtain mercy. Our Lord used no more characteristic expression, none that more exactly defined His own spiritual temper or that more completely differentiated it from that of His opponents, than the saying, Go ye, and learn what this means, I desire mercy and not sacrifice. The end of the law, the soul of righteousness, the essence of sacrifice, is love, is mercy. And yet, as we have begun to see, each of these greatest things in the world, the law, righteousness, sacrifice, had come to stand for the opposite of love or mercy. The law meant the letter, not as the expression of but as substitute for the spirit. Righteousness was the scrupulous observance of forms that had killed the life they were instituted to keep alive. And the sacrifices were come, in our Saviour's own mouth, to express the denial and contradiction of that very sacrifice which His life and death so perfectly exemplified. The word and the thing, however misused, can never cease to be the essential content and the essential expression of Christianity. All love or mercy is only so in actual service, and all service is such only in sacrifice. The only true *sacrum factum* in the world is the act of giving ourselves. We may give ourselves in many ways and in many degrees, but it is never real sacrifice unless its spirit is love and its form is mercy. We have seen that that which our Lord encountered, and in opposition to which His whole ministry took shape, in the spirit of His time, was not so much the formality, the hypocrisy, the deadness which prevailed, as that worse thing that underlay it all, the total absence of sympathy, pity, compassion, love. These are the things that fill and constitute and make life. These are the fulfilling of the law, the works of righteousness, the offerings up of sacrifice; and under the consecrated names of law, righteousness, and sacrifice, to be daily performing acts not only devoid but contradictory of these, that was to Him the great and unforgivable offence.

The point of the beatitude, however, upon which I desire most to touch is not the meaning or the importance of mercy, which our Lord's own words and acts ought to make plain enough to us. It is rather this: How the weakening and lowering effects of the being mere objects or recipients of mercy are always by our Lord Himself counteracted and corrected by the condition laid upon us of being subjects no less, or doers, of mercy. The point has been already touched upon, but it is of too much importance not to be again and again emphasized. There is nothing in these days so presumed upon as the mercy of God. We confirm ourselves in our indolence and indifference, in our weaknesses and failures and neglects, in our faults, our vices, our sins, with the thought that God is merciful, that it is inconsistent with His goodness that we should reap the natural consequences of our omissions and our commissions. There are no allowances needed, and there are no allowances whatsoever made for us under the Gospel of Jesus Christ. There was all the allowance in the world needed, and all made, in nature and under the law. Where that was demanded of us which we had not to give, and that required of us which we were unable to perform, there was need for overlooking and passing by and condoning. But Christianity demands nothing of us that it does not give, and what it gives it cannot but demand. Suppose that when our Lord gave to the impotent man by His word to arise and walk, He had not required of the man on his part to arise and walk,—of what effect or account would have been the gift? Christianity gives us all things, but it requires of us absolutely all the things which it gives us. Not to require of us all things would be just so far to fall short of giving us the all things. Of course it requires only as it gives. As it gives only as we can receive, so it requires only as we can render. God does not, for example, give us the whole of His righteousness at once in fact, because we are incapable of receiving it all instantaneously. But He does give it to us all, as it is complete in Jesus Christ, in faith and in hope. God does not therefore require of us in ourselves now the whole righteousness of Christ. But He does require of us supremely to desire and intend it, to believe in it, to hope for it, to appropriate it to ourselves in anticipation, to work for it and to patiently wait for it. He means us to mean righteousness as He Himself means it, for otherwise how can He give it to us?—Whatever God may give and however God may give, beyond our actual reception and use it can only be ours in faith and hope, and within our reception and use it is ours in fact only as these have made them so. So, to return to our text, it is a delusion to suppose that we may obtain mercy otherwise than as we ourselves feel and show mercy. Only so much of what is given or done to us becomes ours and enters into our own salvation as we ourselves give and do of it. All that is not yet assimilated and converted into ourselves is ours either not at all, or is ours as yet only in faith and hope.

Blessed are the pure in heart, for they shall see God. The blessedness promised is the vision of God, and the condition attached is the purity of our own organ of spiritual or divine vision. There was nothing upon which our Lord dwelt more solemnly than upon the conditions within ourselves of the knowledge of spiritual things. The hopeless sin of the Pharisees was their spiritual blindness. They had all but, if not quite, sinned away the power of spiritual vision. They could not see the light because they had no longer eyes for the light. When they had got to the point not only of not recognizing God in Jesus Christ, but even of seeing in Him Beelzebub, and so calling light darkness, then our Lord pronounces them on the brink of the irreparable, the unforgivable sin, the sin against the Holy Ghost. And what is that sin, for which in the very nature of it there is no repentance and from which there can be no salvation? It is the sin of having sinned away the power of repentance or the possibility of salvation. Our Lord says that blasphemy against Himself may be forgiven; indeed, all their sins shall be forgiven unto the sons of men, and their blasphemies wherewithsoever they shall blaspheme; but whosoever shall blaspheme against the Holy Spirit hath never forgiveness, but is guilty of an eternal sin. The blasphemy consisted in attributing to Jesus an unclean spirit, and the guilt lay not in the offence to Him but in the condition it revealed in themselves. To call cleanness uncleanness, and light darkness, and good evil, betrays the last degree of moral blindness, the atrophy and death of the very organ of spiritual vision. We may sin against the Word of God, and even in supposable cases be blameless; because that is a light without us, and we may be honestly mistaken about it. Circumstances and conditions of which we are innocent may conceal it from us. But the Spirit of God is a light within us; it is not the outward light for the eye, but the inward eye for the light; and sin against that is a different thing. Aristotle asks what sort of ignorance it is that excuses a man; and answers practically as follows: An objective ignorance, ignorance of the thing, may excuse; but subjective ignorance, ignorance in the man, does not excuse. Our Lord says, The light of the body is the eye. If thine eye be single, thy whole body shall be full of light. But if thine eye be evil, thy whole body shall be full of darkness. If therefore the light that is in thee be darkness, how great is the darkness! The light that is *in thee*—what is that? It is, not the light for the eye, but—the eye for the light. The Word of God is the principle of objective divine revelation to us; the Spirit of God is the principle in us of subjective vision, reception, and appropriation of the divine light and life. If one stood at midnight and could see no light, it would not be irreparable. The trouble is with the light, not in the eye. But if he stood at midday and could see no light, it would indeed be irreparable.

The clear of spiritual vision are the pure, the clean, in heart. Our Lord calls it the *simplex,* the simple or the single, eye; the eye that sees the thing it looks at because it is not looking at so many other things at the same time. How mixed and sullied are our thoughts of God, our communion with God, our service of God, our very desire for God—with other things! It is the other things—that share us with Him, and take the larger share—that stand between and hide Him from our sight. Seek ye first the kingdom of God and His righteousness, and all these things shall be added unto you.

The seventh beatitude must have had a very deep significance for Jesus Himself. If He meant it with all the meaning it is susceptible of, it includes and expresses within itself the whole of His own divine human blessedness. What was it to Him to be the great peacemaker between God and man, between man and man, between all things that are at variance and in discord in all the world! And it expresses within itself also, implicitly at least, the method as well as the goal and reward of the great reconciliation. It is only in accomplished and realized sonship that God and man, or God and creation, can be and will be made at one. In no other relation than that predestined one of sons, the foreordained end of the whole creation, can the one spirit, the one law, the one life of God reign through all things, and the universe of God be at peace. Again and again we cannot but see that the universal order which is the manifest meaning and end of things is no mere material or natural order. It is an order not of things but of wills; it is a moral order, a kingdom of righteousness. And if a real and abiding order of wills, then it must be something more and higher still, an eternal unity and harmony of spirits, a blessed reign of love. When God shall become the All-Father in His world through all becoming His sons or His Son, then shall love and unity reign, and the task of the great Peacemaker be accomplished.

When St. Paul speaks of God having been in Christ reconciling the world unto Himself, he adds that unto us has been committed the word of reconciliation, the continuation and completion of the mission and ministry of peace. The work of the Peacemaker goes on only through the peacemakers. We are ambassadors for Christ, as though God were entreating by us and beseeching all to be reconciled. As working together with God *we* entreat also. We do not remember as we should that, as God was in Christ reconciling, so Christ is in us reconciling; that all the presence or operation of God or of Christ in the world now and henceforth is by the working in and through us of the common spirit and life of them and us. We now are the incarnation, not only incarnated but incarnating; we are the atonement, atoned and atoning. What is doing upon earth of peacemaking, we are the doers of it. It is the work distinctively not of the Father nor of the Son, but of the Spirit. The love of the Father is complete, the grace of the Son is finished. Only the task of the Holy Ghost remains to be accomplished. And what is that task? It is first to bring us into the fellowship of the life, and then—and *so*—to bring us into the fellowship with the work of God in Christ, which is also the work of Christ in us. I and my Father are one, there is the community of life. My Father worketh and I work, there is the community of work. And the life and the work cannot be separated; the work is the life. We say that this is the dispensation of the Spirit. That can only mean that this is the time for *our part* in the dispensation or economy of the world. Whatever be the place or the part of the Holy Ghost in the divine nature, as the Spirit of Father and of Son, in the world of men the Holy Ghost has no other place or part, He cannot otherwise manifest Himself than in and as the spirit of men. In the spiritual half at least of God's creation, only that is done which we also do, only that is accomplished or attained which is accomplished or attained through us.

There is what we call a *present peace*, which, as we shall see, plays no small part in our immediate relations with God. As the very expression suggests, it is something provisional and temporary. It is the faith and hope which we have, the possession and enjoyment in anticipation, of the real and perfect peace which shall be ours in the future,—that future which means to us, whensoever and where-soever, the attainment of our goal and the consummation of our-selves. For there is no real peace save in real and perfect oneness with God, and in God with all others and all things else. The present peace lies in the assurance that God has provided that and holds it in trust for us in Jesus Christ, and that it is not only ours already in faith, but that it becomes ours in fact, just so fast as we can ourselves make it so. But from the first we are peace-havers, only as we are peace-lovers and peace-makers, and nothing so constitutes us in fact sons of God as peace-loving, peace-making, and peace-having.

I have after all dwelt so long upon the beatitudes because to con-sider them at all convinces us that in them we have the whole spirit, not only of the whole teaching, but of the whole life of our Lord. Moreover, we have clearly stated in them all the conditions, the causes, and the rewards, of the Gospel which it is our object to de-fine. Let us see if we can, in conclusion, reduce all these to a unity among themselves, and so give a more single view of our salvation in Christ. All that we need or want, to supply our deficiencies or supplement our insufficiencies; all that we must be or do or accom-plish or attain for that completeness of ourselves which is synony-mous with our blessedness; all that perfection of relation with God and others, which is necessary to the perfect activity and blessedness of ourselves; all that attitude toward persons and things, toward all the particulars as well as the totality of our environment, which as our own right reaction upon them is the appointed means of forming our characters, determining our personalities, and shaping our des-tinies,—in a word, everything essential to our being ourselves, per-forming our parts, and achieving our ends, we see realized and illustrated in the person of Jesus Christ. Therefore we say that the knowing Him is our Gospel, and the being what He is is our salva-tion.

9. THE DEATH OF JESUS

We come to the last of the beatitudes, the blessedness of persecution, calumny, and martyrdom. I presume that no view of the Gospel could dispense with the death of Jesus. Certain it is that all the Gospels concentrate attention upon that as containing and conveying the meaning of all that our Lord was or accomplished upon earth. The significance of the death has by some been treated as a second thought even on the part of Jesus Himself; as though failing, and foreseeing the failure, of realizing an external kingdom in His life, He fell back upon the conception and plan of an ideal spiritual kingdom to be realized through His death. The Gospels know no such possible change of view. The mind of Jesus as they reveal it is from first to last, and long before those nearest Him could comprehend it, set upon the kingdom as He actually founded it, and set against every temptation to any other conception of it.

Accepting, then, the death as the vital feature in any possible appreciation of the place and part of Jesus Christ in human history, what are the different significances that may be found in it? From the point of view of this first part there can be but one. In it we make the Gospel to consist in the acts, character, and life of Jesus. He was in our human nature, under our human conditions, in our human life, *that* the revelation of which to us is a gospel and the participation in which is salvation. Everything, then, in this gospel turns upon the personal attitude and action and character of our Lord; the manner and matter of man He was; the truth, the beauty, the good He found in or put into our common humanity; the worth, the value, the blessedness, He drew and enables and teaches us to draw from it. This being the case, the significance and value of the death must have lain chiefly if not wholly in the fact that it is only death that sets the perfect seal or places the final valuation upon life. Call no man happy until he is dead, is a very old prescription. And that, according to Aristotle, because it is not enough to have lived well, if one has not died ''accordingly.'' What gives still further significance to the death of Jesus is that it was not merely a death, but such a death as fully tested and tried and proved every quality of His life. The application of such a criterion is necessary not only to the testing and measuring of what has been attained in the life, but equally to the completing and perfecting of what has been so attained. To stop short of the final test is to fall short of the final perfection. For one of the lessons of such a life and death, of that supreme life and death, is that not only are we proved, but we are made and perfected by the things we suffer.

The profit to us, then, of a study of the details of the last hours of Jesus Christ will consist in their perfect revelation and illustration of the qualities that characterized Himself. An analysis of these will be our best review and confirmation in His death of all that we have been learning in His life. Referring to types of which we have spoken of highest human action, and looking for these in the typical attitude of Jesus during the night and day of His final trial, we might say from the Greek standpoint that what most characterized Him was His perfect self-control or self-possession, the mastery and command under seemingly impossible conditions of His reason and His will. Circumstances could not have been rendered more difficult for the exercise of these—in the long night in Gethsemane of apprehension and heaviness unto death and agonized prayer for submission and endurance; in the surprise and panic and desertion of the early dawn, in which life and hope and courage are at their ebb; in the shameful and exasperating dragging to and fro from Caiaphas to Annas, and from Pilate to Herod; in the circumstances that need no recital of His brutal treatment, the weary way to Calvary, and the painful hanging upon the cross. I mention these dark details not to appeal to that sentimental sympathy which has been too large a part of our Christianity, but to call attention to what would be to us the practical impossibility under such circumstances of one's retaining possession of one's whole self and one's best self. The right reason, the power still to see things as they are, in their right relation and right proportion; and the free will, the will uninfluenced and unbiased by selfish passion or personal prejudice,—these were the Greek test and measure of the perfect manhood and its highest activity. We have it perhaps best expressed in what has been so happily characterized as the sweet reasonableness of Jesus. And surely never was there more difficult and therefore more crucial or testing opportunity to exercise a sweet reasonableness than when Jesus, looking down from the cross upon the perpetrators of the typical crime of the world, could feel as well as say, Father, forgive them; for they know not what they do. There is in these words not only a generous sentiment but a just and righteous judgment. Even there there was room for an *audire alteram partem,* a place for the charitable construction, an opportunity for finding excuse and making allowance. And no weak and sentimental complaisance was there in it, but eternal truth, as well as boundless love and pity. There is never a situation, not even in the typical crime, where there is not something of the truth, though it be an exaggerated truth, that *tout connaître est tout pardonner*. To see all the other side in the extremest case of others against ourselves, to make all allowance, to do all justice, is a triumph of something indeed higher and more akin to God than even right reason and just judgment, something without which under such circumstances these would be impossible; but it is a triumph of these also. And so what all His life had illustrated, the death most perfectly and completely confirmed, of the divine reasonableness of Jesus, in thought, feeling, and action. There is not one of the virtues of the Greek catalogue that may not be illustrated, or paralleled on a greater or a truer scale, in the personal bearing of Jesus Christ. Even that most Greek of all the virtues, the virtue of magnificence, the rendering of the great service, the bearing of the great burden or expense, for the public weal or the glory of the commonwealth, and in the greatest way,—what was that in comparison with the act of Him who was all, did all, endured all, gave all, and all for the sake of the supremest good and the highest glory of all! And did it all not for the honor or the fame of it, but at the cost of misunderstanding and shame and rejection.

When we pass from the Greek reasonableness to the Hebrew righteousness of our Lord's attitude under the supreme test, there is much more to say. The principle involved there is that of obedience, the utter devotion of love, service, and sacrifice, to the will and word of God. We have seen that that which might most appropriately have been written upon the earthly life of Jesus are the words, Lo, I am come to do thy will, O God. Without undertaking as yet to define precisely what that will was, there is no question that from the beginning He felt that He had a definite work of God to accomplish. Now, at least, it is as far as we can go to say that that work was the sanctifying of human nature, the righteousing of human action and character, the perfecting of human life, in His own person. And so far as His person can touch and influence all other persons, by revealing and communicating to them the secret, the meaning, and the motive of human life in general, we might say that His work was to be the sanctifying and righteousing and perfecting of humanity in general. At any rate, whatever it might be in its completeness, our Lord's lifelong devotion to the will and work of God is confirmed and perfected in His final sufferings and death. Early in His career He began to perceive that that was what it was obliged to lead to. And Jesus was no enthusiastic or fanatical seeker after persecution or martyrdom. He evaded and avoided it as long as it was right to do so. And when it was no longer right to do so, He went with His face fixed as a flint to meet it, but He went with a natural human reluctance and heaviness of heart. As His hour approached, He prayed to be saved from it; as the cup was presented to His lips, He entreated to the last that He might be spared the drinking it. But all this only shows the hardness of the test to which He was put, and so measures the limit to which His obedience was willing to go. There were other things He loved; He loved life; but above all things He loved the will of God.

It ought not to be hard for us to understand why the will of God should have gone so far and demanded so much; why He spared not His own Son to the very limit, and delivered Him up to the fateful uttermost. And Jesus Himself was wise enough to understand, and great enough to accept. Father, the hour is come. Glorify thy Son, that thy Son may glorify thee! Only the perfect cross could win for humanity the perfect crown. He had a baptism to be baptized withal, and how was He straitened until He was baptized with it! But it was the world's travail, and the world's new birth.

But it was not Greek manhood in the perfection of all the virtues, nor Hebrew righteousness in all the truth of all the sacrifices, that shone most brightly in every act and attitude of Jesus in the day of His trial. It was that which is the divine heart and soul without which virtue and righteousness themselves are nothing, and with which they are made divine. It is the pity and compassion and love of Jesus that, as they had been the supreme motive of His life, so they burn brightest in His death. Having loved His own—and who, on His part, at least, are not His own?—He loved them unto the end. Sympathy, we are told, the bearing one another's burdens, is the law of Christ. Was ever sympathy—leisure from oneself, forgetfulness of self, thoughtfulness for others, carried to such length under such circumstances! The eve of the day is spent in preparing His disciples. In the garden of agony His concern is for them: Watch and pray, lest ye enter into temptation—that is, Keep awake, and give yourselves to prayer, for a great trial is coming upon you. When the surprise and the seizure come, He comes forward and says, I am He whom ye seek; let these go in peace. When Malthus' ear is cut off, He rebukes Peter, and heals the wound. Before the high priests He is only silent because He knows words are useless. In the midst of His own cruel and exasperating tormenting, He has time for a feeling and look of pain and sorrow for Peter's cowardly denial. In the interview with Pilate there is a touch of pity and sympathy for the vacillating governor; he was at least not the most guilty. Under the heavy burden of His cross He could feel and say, Daughters of Jerusalem, weep not for me, but weep for yourselves—in sorrowful anticipation of what the guilty city was bringing upon itself. Under the first agony of the cross, His thought was of His mother, and upon a provision for her future care and comfort; then for His crucifiers, that God would take into account their ignorance of what they were doing; then for the penitent thief, that he should be perhaps the first beneficiary of the pardon He was Himself earning for all the world. And at the very last, in the bitter cry, My God, My God, why hast Thou forsaken me, is there not something which breathes more thought of the possibility of *God's* abandoning than of His own sad abandonment?

There will seem to many to be a vagueness and unsatisfactoriness in the conclusion, that, after we have recognized in Jesus Himself the claim of a very definite mission, purpose, and work in the world, we should ourselves then find nothing in that work more definite or explicit than simply the being the man He was. What more or more definite meaning could He have had for us, what higher dignity or blessedness could He have conferred upon us, than the completing of our nature, the perfecting of our life, the accomplishing of our destiny? But in doing that, He did much more than that. In being the perfect man He was, under the impossible conditions in which He became so, He threw a new light upon those conditions which, practically for us, solves the problem or reveals the mystery of evil. We have nothing to do with a theoretic construction of the universe. Our business is to explain what it is, and not why or how it is, or became, what it is. There is a—in the very highest sense—natural sequence and relation, and therefore a natural fitness, between all that Jesus Christ is in our humanity and all the circumstances, causes, and conditions under which and through which He became what He is. It is not in the power of our human imagination to conceive, or of our reason to suggest, how our Lord could have attained the height of the spiritual and moral manhood for which He stands, otherwise than under the conditions and by the process through which He did actually attain it. The evil that is in the world, just as it is in the world, is there for this reason, that the holiness, the righteousness, the spiritual and moral life, which are our only natural or supernatural completion, perfection, and blessedness, cannot come into existence except through conflict with and conquest of just that particular evil of the world. What more do we want, or what more can we possibly know, than that? When we have said that, through simply being what He was, Jesus Christ has revealed to us what God is, what we are, why evil is, and how good is to be achieved and attained, have we not said enough to explain and justify all the claims that our Lord made or could have made for His divine mission among us? But, for my own part, I am ready to admit that we have not said all that is to be said. What remains, however, must be said from yet higher points of view.

We have completed now what I have called the Gospel of our Lord's manhood and life upon earth, and I wish to repeat what was said in the beginning. In giving so much space to this part of our study of the Gospel, the motive is not to make concession, or even to do justice, to new or modern points of view. It is rather to endeavour to make for ourselves full proof and use of the truth, or aspects of the truth, which modern knowledge, and modern methods of knowledge, have revealed or opened up to us in the unchanged and unchangeable Gospel. That the new light does not change our old Gospel, I hope will be made sufficiently apparent in the remaining parts of the discussion.

IV.

THE REASON OF LIFE (1911)*

The Reason of Life focuses on John's Gospel, and the volume represents DuBose's consideration of the fourth Gospel from the perspective of his Catholic or ecumenical process phase. The following excerpts from The Reason of Life complete the picture of DuBose's spiritual theology, and they build on his previous consideration of St. Paul and the Synoptic Gospels (the preceding selections) to describe human redemption or "at-onement" as a process of grace completing nature through love, service, commitment, and witness.

I. THE PRINCIPLE OF UNITY

Introductory

Revolutions, internal or external, in thought or in action, do not come except in a time or under conditions that have been prepared and are ripe for them. We are expected and commanded to be able to read the signs of the time. It is as criminal not to seize and use beneficient opportunity at its flood, as it is futile to exploit it at its ebb. We are moving now upon a very flood tide of opportunity. The thought of the world is upon and the demand of the time is for unity. We have entered upon an era of reconciliation and cooperation.

---

* The original text that follows is from *The Reason of Life* (New York: Longmans, Green, and Co., 1911), pp. 1–11, 62–102, 115–168, 213–219.

This is evident in the most secular affairs of the world. The abolition of war may be many ages off, but there has never been anything like such a movement in the direction of it as we are now witnessing. So profound and general a raising of the question of arbitration and peace is in itself the surest prognostic of a progressive approximation to its solution such as will be at least the diminution and amelioration if not the actual extinction of war.

So no less with economic and industrial warfare. The clash of capital and labor, of organized and free employment, of privilege and equality, of special and general interests, may be sounding louder than ever, but it is because the knell of all inequitable inequalities, and inevitable consequent strife, has been struck. The movement to meet and treat the disease in its source, to abolish industrial warfare by removing its cause in patent injustice, may not mean immediate and universal equity and peace, but it does mean just as rapidly more of these as the really growing sympathy and fairness of men shall achieve.

But it is the spirit of reconciliation in a wider field—that of religion—with which I am at present concerned. Not that the field of religion is separable from or does not include all these secular questions and interests; nor that any reconciliation, any unity and cooperation, based upon the one only rock of love, of mutual service and sacrifice, is not in itself religion. On the contrary, religion is not, and will not be, either its true self or all itself, until all minds and hearts, all social relations and personal interactivities of men, have become the Kingdom of God: until all life, individual or collective, industrial, political, national and international, has been taken into and become its sphere.

Such a unity, it may be felt, is not for men but gods. But even a pagan philosophy bids us not, because we are mortal, to rest in or be satisfied with mortality, nor because we are human to ignore or neglect the manifest divine that is in us. Neither human reason nor the human conscience can set a limit to itself short of Eternity, Infinity, and Perfection. No matter how we may conceive or define the Divine, human life has no end or meaning but in that unity and completeness which only Love is, and which we can all agree in worshipping as God. There is no impracticability in such an ideal except that of bringing ourselves to believe in and act upon it. That done, we should be quick and certain to find in it the one only principle that would make life really, perfectly, and blessedly practicable and realizable.

But I come down to the familiar conflicts and dissonances of religion as they are popularly understood—such as, for example, that between religion and science. If there be any actual conflict between these, otherwise than in our apprehensions of them, it goes down beneath the thoughts of men (which science and religion are) into the eternal nature and reality of things. The issue, we may safely assume, has passed beyond that first stage of it in which the question was whether in the new light of science there was any place left for religion at all. There is consensus now both as to the objective ground and the subjective need of religion. Controversy has narrowed down to the relation between the immanent presence and operation of God in things, which we call nature, and the transcendent presence and operation of God with and in men, which we call grace. The growing reconciliation between nature and grace is, we must admit, due more to the insistences of science than to the wisdom or reasonableness of current religion. The latter, in its wide separation tending to the divorce of grace from nature, was in a fair way of contracting itself to final exclusion from the world of the actual. In being brought more and more to recognize the essential naturalness and orderliness of grace, it has more than gained in coming to see the co-essential supernaturalness of nature: and so to anticipate, if not yet construe and understand, the ultimate unity and identity of the two. Thus religion, rescued by science from the danger of exclusion from the earth, is enabled to turn and show itself inclusive of all the earth.

It is only an extension of the above to say a more general word upon the reconciliation of the conflicts between the counter truths of immanence and transcendence. These truths we have been brought perforce to see as not only counter but also complementary. The power which is neither nature nor ourselves, but formative and constitutive principle of both, is necessarily immanent and immanently necessary in nature—for otherwise nature would not be nature in its most essential attribute of fixed and reliable uniformity. And it is only in such an objective nature of constant invariability that we could possess or exercise our freedom. But there is no more reason why the power that is nature should not also be a power that is not nature, than that we who are in and of nature should not also be above, or transcend, nature—as we know we do. There are in fact two truths which stand or fall together: One is God in nature and yet transcending nature; the other is human freedom and personality as part of nature, and yet, in the fact and exercise of selfhood, transcending nature. In making God's personality and our own thus dependent upon each other, in our conception of them, we are not making God's personality only what ours is: whatever be the infinite difference, His must include all that ours is.

There is a kindred reconciliation to be effected in philosophy between the rival claims of idealism and pragmatism. Is religion an *a priori* fact or truth, to be ascertained and applied to human life? Or is it an *a posteriori* result deduced from and determined by human life? Is it *whatever* will perfect life and all its functions, as determined by experience? Or is it an antecedent and definite something, the knowledge and realization of which in human life will perfect it and its functions? Is there any reason why it may not be both? It is not a question of what religion is: both agree that it is what perfects life and all its functions. It is only the question of how what is religion is ascertained or known. And with regard to this, whatever may be the value of pragmatism, it is as useless and impossible without idealism as, for example, either deduction or induction would be without the other. We may as well speak of the conflict or contradiction between hypothesis and verification as that between idealism and pragmatism. I have long known that the final and only convincing proof of religion is the experience of what will perfect and complete human life. But pragmatism, I should say, is not a source but only a test of the rival claims that bid for the lordship or mastery of human life. It is a fact that we are practically making truth and life as we go, by incorporating into them in experience the things that make for them. But whence do we derive the manifold material which experience tests and sifts and excludes or includes as it finds it unfit or fit? Experience tries all things and uses or disuses, but never originates or creates. Certainly in that fullest life which we call eternal, pragmatism, as experimentation and determination of values, is in need, for the source and supply of the theories or hypotheses upon which it is to pass judgments preparatory to inclusion or exclusion, of the very highest and purest idealism.

Religion is the most experimental of all sciences. Our Lord was the most thoroughgoing of pragmatists. "Do," He says, "and ye shall know." If any man will live the true life, he will know that the life he lives is the true one by its completeness and blessedness. But he must have an idea, or hypothesis, of the true life as he lives it, and where does it come from? Would it come at all if there were no idealism? We are to "set to our own seal" even to the fact that God Himself "is true"—but where do we get the idea that God is true, to which we are to give the attestation of our experience? Given idealism as a source of ideas, not only of conjecture and adventure from within, but of inspiration and revelation from without—and then pragmatism is not only in order, but is the only true order of human truth or life. God and Christianity appeal to no other ultimate proof of themselves than the fact of their inherent and essential truth as attested by experience. The only convincing argument for God is found in the realized fact that "to know Him is to live, and to serve Him is to be free." The only credential of Jesus Christ is the fact that He is "the Way and the Truth"—the only way and the perfect truth of "Life": the life of God in man and of man in God. Religion can never cease to submit itself to the perpetual judgment of human experience; nor experience to be directly responsible and accountable for its recognition of the reality of religion. They exist for each other, and their unity is the only solution of the question of life and destiny.

There is another conflict just now being waged within the ranks and under the banner of Christianity, which can be settled only by reconciliation, and not by victory or defeat on either part. It is the question between the merely human divinity and the real deity of the person of Jesus Christ. In this controversy each side, in so far as it is honestly and sincerely Christian, is contending for the true half of a really indivisible whole; and the truth in each is included in and essential to that of the other. Christianity is nothing if it is not our identical and common humanity in the person of the man Christ Jesus coming (and come) by the necessary human process into the full realization and inheritance of its inherent divinity and divine Sonship. Nor could Christianity be this, if it were not also and no less, on the other hand, God Himself self-realizing (and realized) in our humanity in the person of Jesus Christ, and there taking us all into a living union and unity with Himself. I can see myself and all humanity in every individual act or incident of the human life of our Lord—but also I can see all of God, and all that is divinest and best of God, in the person of Jesus Christ reconciling and uniting the world unto Himself. How shall I know Him or express Him? As deified humanity, or as humanized Deity? I believe that I can know Him as neither without knowing Him as both. The unity of two must be both and each. If I cannot find God as well as myself in Christ, I can see and know Him nowhere at all.

I might multiply indefinitely these illustrations in part of a general process of reconciliation going on among or around us, but let us go behind them to one that includes them all. The ultimate and essential unity is that of spirit. God Himself is "One, in the unity of spirit." In the first place "God is Spirit—and they that worship Him must worship in spirit and in truth." Spirit is something infinitely more than mere incorporeality, freedom from "body, parts, or passions." The spirit of God or of any other being, "the spirit that one is of," is the totality of one's attitude or disposition towards all other being. It is in this sense that we say that the Spirit of God, or that God Himself, is Love. God as manifested to us is expressed in terms of eternal, infinite, perfect love, grace, and fellowship (or oneness with). Love is Himself; Grace is love or Himself revealed, communicated, and imparted in Christ Jesus; Fellowship is all these received, shared, become ours in the unity of a common spirit, with God and Christ and with one another in Them.

The Kingdom of God is nothing if it is not organized and ordered unity—unity with God and unity in God, unity of spirit, of law, of life. And the Church of God is no living thing if it is not something more than human organization—the divine organism and organ of unity human and divine. Unity is absolutely the first and the one thing: what is Love but oneness with God and with all else in Him? The Church is first "One"—and then, and therefore, "Holy"; for what is holiness but the spirit of unity and love? Then, next, it is "Catholic," for catholicity or universality is the necessary corollary of unity. And finally it is "Apostolic," simply because that which is one, must be so in sequence or time, as well as in extension or space—from beginning to end, as well as from end to end. In no less truth than all this is the Church the Kingdom of God, the Body of Christ, or the Temple of the Holy Ghost.

Expediency, efficiency, economy, success as against failure, very existence as against threatened extinction, the last will and prayer and command of our Lord Himself, every dictate of common sense and impulse of common humanity, ought surely to furnish reasons enough and arguments enough for unity in Christianity. And these considerations have sufficed to turn all the spirits and signs of the time in the direction of unity, and to make it the one problem and task of the age. But it is evident too that we have to go further back and deeper down than all these for the solution of the problem thus raised, for a reason cogent enough to compel and to preserve unity. We need to be brought to realize that religion and unity, that preëminently Christianity and unity, are identical things: we cannot sacrifice or surrender the one and preserve or possess the other. The Church, the Community and Communion of the Saints, the Body of Christ, the Organ of the Holy Ghost, is the unity of Christians with Christ, and with one another in Christ.

The issue is fairly raised between the necessity of Christian unity and the fact of Christian divisions. The subordinate reconciliations that have to be effected before the oneness of the spirit shall find practical and visible expression in the unity of the Body of Christ, it might be discouraging to enumerate. The old question of the one and the many, unity in diversity and diversity in unity, will have to be practically settled in this large and difficult application of it. The adjustment between objective divine claims and subjective human verification and consent, between corporate or catholic authority and personal or party rights and liberties, and many other such issues, will have to be met and dealt with in detail. The first step, which will alone make the others possible, seems to be the only one at present proposed, and may be formulated as follows:

First. Let unity be accepted by all as the principle and essence of Christianity, and faith in it, hope of it, and effort for it become the duty of every Christian.

Second. Let each separate name or body of Christians realize and emphasize as much as possible what it has in common with the one whole Church of Christ, and efface as far as possible all divisive and individual or party elements, badges, or expressions.

Third. Where differences are felt to be vital or important, let them be held in trust for all and not arrogated as the possession of a few or a part.

Fourth. Let there be as much as possible of Christian intercourse, interchange, and cooperation; and in all conferences let there be the utmost of plain-speaking with as much as possible of mutual understanding and charity; let all the truth be spoken as each sees it, but let it be spoken in all the love of Christ.

The present volume has no practical solutions to offer for the problems touched upon in this chapter. It goes before them all, and would only prepare and propose the spirit and temper in which they should be undertaken and may be solved.

2. GRACE TO BECOME SONS

The love of God, the grace of our Lord Jesus Christ, the fellowship of the Holy Ghost!—it is not too much to say that, expressed in terms of their essential natures and functions, God is Love, Jesus Christ is Grace, the Holy Ghost is Fellowship. In these three terms we have all the divine constituents in human life: that is to say, we have the full expression and description of what God is in His relation to our own personal life. In what fulness and exactness of meaning do we say that God is our life—not natural now, but spiritual and personal? The life of God, as distinguished from His mere being or metaphysical nature—what we venture to call His personal life—is best and fully expressed in terms, or under the specific designation, of that which is not only His most characteristic activity, but is the spirit and principle of all His activities. There is only one word that really defines or expresses God; all others applied to Him are only formal, not real designations of Him. To say, for example, that God is truth, is only to say that God is "that which is"; it does not say What He is. To say that God is righteousness, is only to say that He is right, that He is that to which we are under obligation; it does not tell what right or righteousness is, and consequently what He is. We only tell essentially and really what God is, when we say that God is Love, or Goodness; these are the only terms which have a real and determinate content. Love is the willing of Good; and the willing of good is Goodness.

Now there is no question as to what Good is; every being's nature absolutely determines and defines its good: its good is the fulfilment and satisfaction of its nature. The one real good that, in the whole realm of possibility or actuality, we can know, or possess, or enjoy, is Life in its fulness and its freedom. We know therefore precisely what Good is, and what Goodness, or the will of the good, is. The only other good than life itself is whatsoever truly ministers to life. Metaphysics tells us that there is no other motive or end of desire or of action than either the perfection or the blessedness of life: and that these two things are so exactly coincident as to be practically identical. Good is Life, or whatsoever ministers to life.

Love or Goodness is willing good to others—willing to all others the good which we first know, possess, and enjoy in ourselves. It is the desire and disposition to share with others the good which is our own life and our own selves. When Jesus Christ speaks of "giving His life for many," the word used does not mean literal or merely bodily life, it means His soul, His very Self. The love and goodness of God has but one meaning and one purpose in the world of His creation. He has given to all things to have life; He has given to man to know, and personally to live, life; He has given us in Christ all the fulness and all the blessedness of the Life which is Himself, and which He has constituted us, and now enables us, to know, to possess, and to enjoy.

God is Love; and, next, Jesus Christ is Grace. Grace is love applied, love in operation or in effect. You look for love in the subject of it—in this case, in God; you look for grace in the object of it, in man. Grace is God Self-communicated, Life Self-imparted, Good and Goodness shared and reproduced. In Jesus Christ God has not given us somewhat from Him, He has given us His life, Himself.

Incarnation is something vastly more than immanence; but the difference is not so much in God and His part in it, as in us and our relation to it. God is so much more in us than in the clod, only because we have become so much more than the clod. The full half of the Gospel as the "power of God unto salvation," is not in the coming of God to us in and by His Word, but in the bringing us to Him by His Spirit. Fellowship with God, sharing His spirit, His nature, His life, Himself, His goodness and His good, His perfection and His blessedness, is the sum and the substance of Christianity. It is all that God has to give or we to receive. But the doubt or difficulty in the matter of the divine fellowship is all on our side. It was easier for the Word *aptare Deum homini*—even through descent to the Cross—than it is for the Spirit *aptare hominem Deo*. Nevertheless God, and His life, and His good, can be ours only through that fitting of ourselves to Him, only as we do actually receive and share Him.

Therefore I say that it is only from God the Father, through God the Son and by God the Holy Ghost, that we can so have and know God as to be partakers of Eternal Life. We know God only in Jesus

Christ and in ourselves: that is to say, we know Him only by His Word to us, as the principle and medium of His objective Self-revelation and communication; and by His Spirit within us, as the principle of our own subjective reception and appropriation. Thus the whole matter of Life from God and life in us is expressed in the single comprehensive term Grace.

Grace, which is thus almost the distinctive term of the New Testament, is used (1) to express an eternal and essential disposition of God. Grace was in the world before the Law came: it is older than Moses. It is older than Faith, and was before Abraham. It is older than Adam, or Man: it was in the nature, in the heart and mind of God before the world was. All appearances and all facts to the contrary notwithstanding, the beginning and the end of the world is an act of grace. God created not only by and from but for Himself: the end, which is always before the beginning in rational creation, was and is for divine Self-communication, Self-impartation. God creates only that He may bless; the only sense in which it is true that He created for his own glory is, that His glory is His love, His grace, His divine sympathy and fellowship with His creation. It is true, first and most, in God himself, that blessedness finds itself in giving rather than in receiving. He created in order that He might have whereto to give, wherein to impart, Himself: the end of creation is God in His creation.

If it be asked, how we know this initial and ultimate truth of God—the answer is easy. In the first place, it is written in ourselves, who are not only the creatures, but the children and image of God. The world finds its intention preëminently in us, and that intention becomes ever more and more plain as we learn better to know ourselves, and in knowing ourselves know God. The world foresees that, what it is coming to as the true end and law of its being, is the truth that life and blessedness, with us as with God, and with God as with us, are in giving rather than in receiving, and that the more that principle and spirit and law prevail, the more we fulfil ourselves, and the nearer we draw to God. The true nature and law of things are what they are coming to, and not what they already are. That love, service, and sacrifice are life, and that hate, selfishness, and oppression are death, Christianity has already made a commonplace of thought and speech; when it has made it a commonplace of conduct, character, and life, it will have come to its own.

In the second place, the truth of God and man we are insisting upon is just that which was revealed and given to the world in Jesus Christ. The light was always in the world, but it shone in the darkness, and the darkness comprehended it not. The simple fact that the Son of Man, He who came to reveal to man the truth that was in him, and the truth that is God, came not to be served, but to serve—to be servant of all, and to give His life, His soul, Himself, in behalf of all—that simple fact teaches at once what God is, and what man is.

Grace then is primarily the eternal nature and predestination of God. If it is asked, what there is in it in Him which distinguishes it from simply Love, we answer that, from the first, it is love, if not expressed in, yet at least with the purpose of, action, love that means and looks forward to self-bestowal. All that goes before that ultimate participation in God which is the destiny of creation, is the evolution of being or beings capable of participating in Him. That this capacity should come through eons of preparation, and that this preparation should be through eons of poverty, pain, and toil; that the earnest expectation of the creation should have so long to wait for the manifestation, or revealing, of the sons of God; that it should so groan and travail in pain, while it longs and hopes for deliverance from the bondage of corruption into the liberty of the glory of the children of God—does not contradict the truth that the meaning of it all is fruition, possession, and blessedness in the end. That life in the world should have had to undergo the pangs of birth in the acquisition of reason, self-knowledge, and freedom; that it should have to endure the discipline, the hard demands, and the penalties of law; that it should have to learn to know and achieve freedom through bondage, holiness through sin, and life through death—all this is not without a reason into which we may ourselves begin to penetrate. All things are subject to the law and necessity of making and becoming themselves, just because the One thing up to which they are all moving, and for which they all are, Selfhood and Sonship, reception and reproduction of the life and likeness of God, can only thus, through the long and painful process of self-becoming, become at all. "Ourselves also, which have the first-fruits of the Spirit, even we ourselves groan within ourselves, waiting for our adoption, the redemption of our body."

But (2) Grace as a divine act as well as disposition becomes the special function of that (for lack of a better term of differentiation in the being and activities of God) Person of the Godhead, through Whom are mediated all God's operations in creation, and who is known primarily as the Word of God. It has been intimated that all created being, simply as such, is an act of grace, inasmuch as it is, so far as it is its nature and law to go, self-communication on God's part. Grace becomes more and more, as receptivity and recipient become more—until, capacity and faculty for sonship prepared and provided, Sonship from God comes to fill and satisfy it, by incarnation in it.

Incarnation was no after-thought of God, nor after-need of man. It was part—and highest, therefore latest, part—of the process of creation or evolution, which is one from beginning to end, and whose end was already in, and even before, its beginning. Let it be remembered that, in speaking of beginning, I always mean logical and causal, and not necessarily temporal beginning. Creation has its reason, its meaning, its interpretation and fulfilment in Jesus Christ, in whom at last God is wholly in it, as it is wholly in God. But God is in it with a distinction and a difference between His modes of presence in it first and last. He is in it in Jesus Christ, not by immanence of nature, but, in transcendence of nature, by operation in it of Word and Spirit—which, while also He, are nevertheless to be properly distinguished from Him.

Grace (3), always in the World, comes into it in an eminent degree in the person of Jesus Christ. Just wherein that grace consists, and what form it takes, depends upon the specific nature and needs of those who are to be at once its objects and its subjects. The initial act of grace as Incarnation in Jesus Christ incorporates and expresses a principle which characterizes its entire operation: "Because the children are partakers of flesh and blood, He also Himself in like manner partook of the same." The principle expressed is this: Grace, or Love in action, conforms and adapts itself precisely to its objects or subjects, and to the needs and wants to be supplied. Grace becomes both to us and in us just what we want, and in the form and manner in which it is possible and proper for us to receive it. So Jesus Christ is the life of God, objectively to us, and subjectively in us, in that degree and manner in which we can and ought, according to our nature, to become partakers of the divine life and nature. The acts or processes, in us and by us, through which that can be, are—our at-one-ment with God, our redemption from sin, and our resurrection

from death. All these Jesus Christ accomplished and was in our nature; and accomplishes and becomes in ourselves. What God accomplishes in humanity by His grace, humanity accomplishes in God
through its faith. Jesus Christ as the both divinely and humanly accomplished Unity of God and man, is both God and man in the matter—the grace by and the faith through which we live.

Grace (4) is finally and immediately the work in us of the Holy
Ghost—through Whom, in sequence and conjunction with the Word,
are mediated all those divine operations upon the earth that we might
characterize as subjective: that is to say, all the influences which, in
the beings themselves who are the subjects of them, draw, or fit, or
assimilate them to God, and make them in their measure partakers
of His nature. It is in keeping with this that it is said of the Holy Ghost
that He takes of the things of Jesus, of the objectively revealed Word
of God, and "shows," or interprets and imparts them to us. He
works in us the subjective appreciation, appropriation, and participation of a truth and a life which come to us from without and from
above. It is in this sense that the Holy Ghost is to us "the Giver of
life"—the life He gives being the incarnate Word and Son of God.
Thus the Life that was originally and eternally in God, and was God:
that was mediately in, and cause of, all else: that was then humanly
and personally in the world in Jesus Christ—that life of God and of
Jesus Christ His Son, is in us by impartation and participation of His
Spirit.

How Christ is in us by His Spirit: accomplishes in us and by us
all that He accomplished for us: and so makes us by His grace what
He is, sons and heirs of God—that is just the practical and actual
Christianity which we need to recover and to know. If there be mystery in it, as there is in all divine operations and in all natural facts
and processes, it is not a mystery which cannot be rationally stated
and spiritually apprehended.

The life of Jesus Christ upon earth was a human fact and act. If
it was, taken as a unit and a whole, a life at one with God—and so,
sinless and deathless—it was a human life *made so* by His own redeeming and quickening act in it. There is nothing in that act of human regeneration and resurrection different in kind from any and
every human life, as it is, naturally and supernaturally, constituted
and purposed to be, and ought eventually to be. Our lives are ours
to make them God's, and they are God's only as we make them so.

If God by mere word or power without, and not also by spirit within—that is by our own cooperant act—should make our lives His, they would not be *ours* so made: there cannot be an "ours" without "us." We see in Jesus Christ a human life at one with God, "made God's": and the act by which He made it so, we call an act of reconciliation, of at-one-ment, or atonement.

We see in Jesus Christ human life, not only reconciled or made one with God, but thereby and therein redeemed from sin, made sinless or holy. That again is in no wise contradictory to the proper course of human nature or life in general. Sin or vice is not the proper or true law of human life; on the contrary, virtue is, and holiness and righteousness. The spotless virtue, the perfect holiness or righteousness of Jesus Christ, which was in itself in our nature a redemption from sin, was His own act in humanity, and precisely the act by which alone humanity redeems itself from sin. If humanity cannot be holy or sinless by act of itself, its only redemption from sin is through the death of itself into the life of God.

We see in Jesus Christ humanity raised up out of inevitable death in itself into assured and eternal life in God. And again, this is no contradiction of evolution, no contradiction to the true and essential nature and destination of man: for it is as natural for him to pass from human into divine life, as to have passed from animal into rational and human life. If in each act or process of personal transition from stage to stage, there is involved a putting off of old nature, a dying from one mode of relation to environment to live in another mode of relation to environment and to self: if, as the rational man has to die from the brute or the animal that he was, so the spiritual or divine man has to die from his mere selfhood which nevertheless was a necessary stage of his development—all this, I affirm, is part and essential part of the law of successive natural, rational, moral, and spiritual evolution.

Why this evolution cannot have been all and only immanent: why there needed to come in from without and from above an objective, actual and historical, realization, revelation, and demonstration of human life divinely accomplished, of God manifest in man and of man self-completed in God, is a question to which something of an answer may be suggested as follows: To begin with, if religion, considered only on our part, is a transcendent act, an act of objective attitude and relation, a conscious and free going out of ourselves to a Spirit and Life of the universe which, however it may include and be in us, yet is infinitely without and transcends us—if, I say, religion is thus distinctly transcendent on our part, why must it not be similarly transcendent on God's part? Why must it not be God, as it were, coming forth from Himself to meet us, who—in a relative sense at least, in consciousness and in freedom—are as objective to Him as He to us? How can we, by instinct, by reason, in freedom and in personal act and life, go forth of ourselves to meet an infinite and divine Not-Ourselves, which does not meet and respond to us there? If I speak and God hears, if I cry and God answers: if in any sense, and to any extent, there is spiritual interrelation and intercommunication, then there is real transcendence, an objective correspondence between God and us, each in that respect outside the one of the other. And nothing short of this is really religion, or is what will fill and satisfy the human need and demand for religion.

How was mortal man to enter into and share the life, the personal life, of God? We are speaking no longer now of natural life, we have passed out of the realm of flesh into that of spirit: "The kingdom of God is not meat and drink," it is holiness, and righteousness, and eternal life, in the Holy Ghost. And what is the life of spirit, as such? What are the functions and activities within us, in which the life of spirit consists and manifests itself? We can know them only under the personal forms of intelligence, affection, will, and voluntary action. If religion is not in these, it is nowhere for us, for these cover the whole ground of personal life. To know God, to need, desire, and love God, to will and do or obey God, to be, so far as we may, what God is, to have God personally in ourselves, and to find ourselves only and wholly in Him—in what other terms than these can we express or describe our participation in God?

If this be the sole language or life of our finite spirits, as children of God, then the beginning and middle and end of all living relation to the life of God is that we shall know enough of it to enter into it and have part in it. Without knowledge there can be no desire or will or action, for there would be no object of these. Once, on the other hand, we know what God has shown us and given us in Jesus Christ, once we understand what Christ means and is to us—the end and object, the fulness and satisfaction of all of spirit that we are or that is in us—then we see that, apart from the divine revelation and gift of Him, we were in utter and hopeless darkness.

Now we see in Him the power of God indeed unto salvation—
but the power of God acting *how?* Why, through the knowledge, love
and desire, will, and actual exercise and activity on our part, of
everything that is in the truest and highest sense salvation. To know,
love, desire, will, and serve God is salvation: it is His life, Himself,
living in us. We see this in Christ, we know it in Him, we love and
desire it in Him—and through all these we have and share it with
Him. We see, know, and share with Him—what? The death in and
to ourselves, the life in and to God. As by the birth and action of our
own reasons and free wills we pass from animal into man, so by the
new birth from above of the Incarnate Word and Spirit and Will of
Jesus Christ in us, we pass from human to divine—up through the
reason and will of incomplete, and imperfect, and sinful *self* into the
Eternal Reason and Will that is, of right, all in all.

3. THE PROCESS OF LIFE SPIRITUAL

Christianity may be viewed under a variety of aspects, and expressed in various terms, but it is most exactly described as a life.
More exactly still is it described by our Lord Himself, not as a life,
as though one out of many, but as simply or absolutely Life, or by
St. John as The Life: for the life we are speaking of is but one life
and one thing. It cannot be properly described as a theory or scheme,
or even a doctrine, of life; in direct contrast to and contradistinction
from all these, it is the fact of life, the life itself, about which theories
are mere speculation, and doctrines but explanations and instruc-
tions. It is not an ideal of life, as being even the truest conception
and embodying the most perfect standard of life. It is contradistin-
guished from the ideal, as being the actual and the real. Neither can
Christianity be properly described as an ethical or moral system, as
a precept or law of life. While incidentally and all-importantly it is
this too, as it is all the rest, yet essentially it has to be contradistin-
guished from this too, as well as from all the rest. Christianity is not
a theory but the fact, not a doctrine but the truth, not an ideal but the
actual; and so, finally, not a law or requirement of life, but the life
itself, not merely required, but given, received, and lived.

Christianity is of course the life of Christ: and as such it is necessarily a life like Christ's. But, speaking exactly, it is distinctly not

a life like Christ's in us, but the life of Christ in us: not a life resembling His, but Himself our life. Jesus Christ certainly stands to us in the relation of example, but even more distinctly not in that of mere example, but of source, and power, and of content and matter of our life. *He* is our life, nothing whatever merely from Him, as example, or influence, or direction, or command. "I am the Life" is not the word He spake to us, it is the Word of God which He is to us.

"The Word of Life"—God Himself, Himself-imparting— speaks to us, according to St. John's account of it, in the flesh: not through one sense only, but through all, through every natural avenue of human perception, knowledge, or experience: "That which was from the beginning, that which we have heard, that which we have seen with our eyes, that which we beheld and our hands handled, of the Word of Life (and the Life was manifested, and we have seen, and bear witness, and declare unto you the Life, the eternal Life, which was with the Father, and was manifested unto us)." So this, then, is the witness, the witness not alone of those who saw Him with eyes, and heard Him with ears, and handled Him with hands of flesh, but the witness of "every one who believeth on the Son of God" (to whom God gives to have the witness within him): namely, "That God gave unto us eternal life, and this life is in the Son: he that hath the Son hath the Life": because the Son of God is the Life. What response can we make to this, but to say with St. Paul, "I live no longer, Christ lives in me!" True faith in the Son of God is the death of "me," the life of God in me. Our life is "hidden with Christ in God; when Christ who is our life shall appear, then shall we also appear with Him in glory."

The prime point in all this is, that all our relation to Jesus Christ is of that immediate, direct, and intimate character which is possible for us only with God Himself: "closer is He than hands or feet, and nearer to us than breathing." We live and move and have our being, not by any intermediary between God and us, but only by and in God Himself; and so Jesus Christ is our life, not through anything proceeding from Him at a distance in time or space, but through His own immediate presence and action in us. The now, and always, and everywhere living Christ is the only Christ of Christianity—or, rather, is the Christ of the one and only true Christianity.

We have seen how life from the beginning, from the lowest physical or animal form of it, through rational and spiritual, up at

last to eternal or divine life, is attributed to the Logos who in the end
becomes incarnate in the person of Jesus Christ. Life, which begins
as mere "living soul" in Adam, becomes in Jesus Christ "quickening, or life-giving, spirit." The turning-point in the process may
be described more in detail than hitherto, as follows: Life becomes
rational or human at the moment or in the act in which it is revealed
to itself, when itself becomes objective and an object to it. This reflex or self consciousness is happily expressed in the words of St.
John, "and the life was the light of men." The distinction between
lower beings and men, which we call reason, marks a difference,
leaps and leaves behind a chasm between animal and man, wider
than we conceive. In it reason itself, immanent in all things, ceases
to be mere object and becomes subject, ceases in nature to be thing
and becomes person. There is reason in inanimate things as well as
in life vegetable and animal, but it is no reason of theirs, nor to them.
For the first time, to men is there upon earth a reason visible to itself
in their persons: a knowledge and understanding of the reason and
meaning and purpose and end of things, and chiefly of themselves.
"That which makes manifest is light"; and the light that manifests
to men themselves, and all things, and God, is Reason; which, however, is rather an eye to see the light than the light itself. And yet
too, what but light can see light, what but life can know life? "If the
eye were not sunny (of the nature of the sun), it could not see the
sun." We can know ourselves because we are potential selves, and
become actual in knowing ourselves. We know God because we
have somewhat of God in us, because we are of God, and are sufficiently of His nature to become partakers of Himself and of His life.
Only to him that hath can be given.

There is an intimate and necessary connection between human
self-consciousness and self-determination or freedom: neither could
be by itself, or without the other. It is in the gradual and growing
exercise of personal independence, in the equal possibility of opposite activities, in the fact of choice and the moral distinction we
make in acts, that the selves in us emerge of which we become conscious. It is in the discovery through experience of law, in the fact
of obedience or disobedience to it and the consequences that ensue,
that we come to know ourselves and to understand the reason and
meaning of things. If all law—in that case improperly so called,
since both law and obedience or disobedience are correlatives of

freedom—were simply immanent necessity, if we were moved without reason or by a reason in no sense our own, we should neither know reason nor be conscious of selves which we call our own.

Reason, however it comes—whether or no only in the consciousness and exercise of personal freedom—could never of itself take us beyond ourselves and the world of sense. I do not mean that it could not, from the knowledge we have of ourselves and derived from sense-experience, draw inferences and build up speculations as to matters without us and beyond us. Reason of itself may thus lead us to infer, and may successfully justify its inference of, such a fact or truth as God, and may suggest true speculations as to His being and nature: I am not denying the possibility or rationality of a purely natural or innate religion. On the contrary, if man is naturally constituted for religion, for knowledge and life of God—although I hold that he will never come to these by purely immanent process within himself, that he will never meet God by acts transcending self and sense-experience unless God also meet Him from without these, that however he may, prior to consciousness and freedom, be potentially child of God, he can never become actually son of God except as, through consciousness and freedom, God personally communicates and imparts Himself and His life to him—yet, as necessary precondition of all this, there must and will be in the purely natural man himself instincts and impulses tending Godward. Reason may thus teach us, and teach us truly, many things about God—what St. Paul calls the "invisible things of Him," which "from the creation of the world are clearly seen, being perceived through the things that are made." Reason, I say, may truly reveal to us these things of God, but it cannot possibly give us God. Nothing can give us God but only God Himself, God in some mode of personal or Self communication and impartation, God speaking to us and to Whom we may speak.

A Person can give Himself only to persons, because he can be met and received only by persons. A Person cannot give himself, as such, immanently, but only transcendently. A father can give his nature and many things pertaining to himself to his son, by generation or immanent transmission; *himself* he can give to him only by transcendent, objective, personal self-presentation, expression, and impartation. The personal is only between persons, from without to within.

The spiritual is something more than and beyond the natural, though it wholly presupposes and includes it. Man is in a double sense a spiritual being. First, he is by nature finite spirit: nothing but spirit can communicate with or can be communicated with by Spirit. To say that we are made for God, for union and communion, or for unity with God, means that we are of like nature with God, at least to the extent of that union or unity with Him. But to be constituted for and capable of personal relation and unity with God is not in itself to be in that unity or relation. That God has given us much in nature in common with Himself, in order that He might then in that community of nature give us Himself, that the knowledge of Him might be our life and the service of Him our freedom, is not yet to have given us Himself, or life, or freedom. The endowment for these is not these. Just as there is a difference between being naturally or potentially rational beings or moral beings and being actually and really rational or moral, so there is no less difference between being naturally spiritual beings, or beings made for spirituality, and being spiritual in act and in fact.

Jesus Christ spoke much of knowing the Father, and spoke of it, not only of Himself, but for us. We were to know God as He knew Him, for life; to serve God as He served Him, for freedom; and, in a word, to be to God what He was to God. Now how did our human Lord know and serve God, and what was He to God? He knew Him as Father, He served Him as Son, by simply being as truly Son to God as God was Father to Him: Son not merely by nature, whether human or divine, but Son in act and in fact, Son by one spirit with the Father, as well as by one nature with the Father. It is a general or universal truth, that no man knoweth the father but the son: the only way to know the father is to be the son. The only way to know God is to know Him as Father, for that is the only actual true relation we can bear to Him; the only way we can know Him as Father is to know Him as sons, for we can only know Him in His relation to us by realizing or actualizing our relation to Him. We cannot know God out of true and real relation with Him, and there is only one real relation we can bear to Him—namely, being His sons, not only by bearing His nature, but sharing His Spirit and living His life.

Personal or transcendent relation between God and man does not originate or begin with the historical fact of our Lord's incarnation. The divine Word and the divine Spirit, which are the agents of all such relation, are described in the Scriptures as having been in the world from the beginning. But they could be in the world only as the world was prepared and able to receive them, and they were present in each stage of the world in accordance with the stage. Abraham, we are told, was the friend of God: and he lives still as permanent exponent of the faith by which God is said to be known. Did Abraham indeed know God through faith: then it is possible for men through faith to know God. The extent or exactness or adequacy of the knowledge does not enter into the question. An infant begins to know its mother from its birth. If faith made perfect, as in Jesus Christ, becomes knowledge, then faith even in part, and in smallest part, is partial knowledge. There have been those in the world whom the world has called prophets; has God ever truly uttered Himself through prophets? Then it is possible for men to hear God, and to be real witnesses and messengers for Him to the world. Was God actually with and in these men in the sense and in the way in which they represented Him to the world? It does not follow from God's being with or in them at all that He must have been with and in them completely or infallibly. The mother is just as certainly and actually in the child, and with it objectively or from without, from the day of its birth as in its maturity. The fact and reality of religion depends upon the possibility and the actuality of a transcendent, objective, free, personal relation between God and ourselves. God has given us a consciousness and a relative independence of Himself which are designed to enable us, and which do actually enable us, to know Him personally and to serve Him freely. The end and essence of religion is so to know, to love, and to serve Him, which we do only by realizing Him as our Father and ourselves as His children, by being ourselves what He is, doing as He does, and so sharing His life, and being partakers of His goodness, which is His good.

"God who in divers measures and in divers manners had spoken to the world by prophets, has spoken to us in full measure and in perfect manner in His Son." The turn of expression in which this truth is stated emphasizes the fact that God has spoken, not merely in the person of His Son, but in the fact and significance of His sonship. All that in part Abraham knew through faith, or that had been told through prophecy, has been fully manifested and communicated in the Son of Man who is also Son of God. We know the Father in the Son: we know the Father through being ourselves made sons.

Humanly speaking—and we must speak humanly of our human

Lord: in His humanity His consciousness was a human consciousness—Jesus Christ knew the Father through His own perfect realizing of the sonship to God potential in humanity and made actual in Himself. The human condition of a perfect sonship to God is perfect faith, hope, and love, perfect obedience or service as the expression of these, and, through and in all, the life of God become our life. Our Lord was perfect Son, and so perfectly knew the Father, through perfect fulfilment of the conditions and perfect accomplishment of the process of human sonship. As man, Jesus Christ knew Himself only in terms of humanity. However true His deity—and it was infinitely true, for otherwise His humanity was impossible—it was humanly manifested, and cannot be known or expressed by us otherwise than in what He was as man. That He was the divine Man, the Man from heaven, the Eternal Word, God Self-expressed in humanity, Son of Man because humanity itself realized and revealed—that was manifestation enough of His Godhead. He came to be known in man and as man; and it was neither necessary nor to the purpose that He should be manifested otherwise than as man.

Man is spiritual, as distinguished from rational, not through any amount or truth of speculative knowledge about God, but only through personal relation and association with God Himself. No immanence, or community or affinity of mere nature, can convey or impart that which comes only through personal association, through mutual knowledge, love, service, and interchange of offices and functions. The more immediately important thing even for Jesus Christ Himself was His oneness with the Father, not in nature alone, but in heart and mind and will and act; and the immediately important thing for us is that He attained that oneness for us and therefore as we—not as God but as man, not in the exercise of omniscience and omnipotence, but in the experience of all human weakness and temptation and through the sole power and victory that come from God through faith. In a word, our Lord was spiritual man through all the processes and achievements of spiritual manhood.

The spirit in man is the organ and faculty of the divine, of God in him. It is through it that we are by nature related and akin to God, constituted for Him, and capable of union and unity with Him. But the human spirit, as such and as part of our nature, as mere potentiality and faculty, does not make us spiritual, any more than eyes of themselves, without sun or light, give us sight. They are both media, not sources: spirituality, as sight, comes through a capacity within us, but from an object and source without us. It is only God's Spirit in and with and through our spirit that makes us spiritual. "Blessed are the poor in spirit." The first blessedness of the human spirit is the fact and sense of its own poverty: the essence of finite spirit and the condition of finite spirituality is poverty. What is capacity for God, but want of Him, dependence upon Him, utter emptiness and nothingness without Him? "Blessed are the poor in spirit, for theirs is the kingdom of heaven." What an emptiness is it that only heaven can fill, what a poverty that wants and can only be satisfied with God Himself!

The proper and only necessary functions of finite spirit are faith, hope, and love: given these in purity and integrity, and all else will come, for spirituality or for blessedness. Which simply means that if the conditions exist in us, the causes and operations will not fail from God. Of the three, faith, hope, and love—love is first as well as last: no one has real faith in, or hopes for, what he does not think about, desire, and love: love, if only yet in the form of need or want, determines the objects of faith and hope. But, still more, love is last; for it requires for its fulness and completion both knowledge and possession, and these for us are to be acquired only through the long discipline of faith and hope. Faith is initial, progressive, partial knowledge, as hope is initial and partial possession: faith complete is the only knowledge, as hope attained and satisfied is the only possession, of which our finite spirits are capable. Necessary as it is that love should be first and last, and all in all—since faith and hope are but expressions and energies of it—it is equally necessary that these latter should have their place and time in the process of the spiritual life. To speak of knowing, or loving, or living, or possessing the kingdom of God or of heaven, all at once, without growth or process, or any otherwise than through spiritual evolution, is impossible and inconceivable for finite spirits. God must be long the object of faith and hope before He can be the possession of love and knowledge.

It is vain to think of our Lord's spirituality as not having passed through and experienced all the process of a human faith, hope, and love. What were His temptations but the testing, proving, and making in Him of those essential spiritual graces and qualities? What was His victory but the complete triumph and crowning in His person of faith, hope, and love? It is true that our Lord, in His active ministry of word and work, never speaks of His own faith and hope, while inculcating them continually upon us. That proves much, but what is it that it proves? He never speaks of Himself as a fighter, but He does speak of Himself as the victor, as having conquered in the great battle of life: "I have overcome the world." And who is the victor but He who has fought and won? And what is the victory that overcometh the world? "It is even our Faith: who is he that overcometh, but he that believeth?" To believe in Jesus Christ is essentially to believe in the irresistible power and the certain victory of faith, hope, and love: to believe in Jesus Christ as the Son of God is to believe, not only in the eternal fact of His divine Sonship, but no less in the humanly accomplished act and fact of His human sonship. Nor are we excluded from looking behind the scenes upon our Lord's hard-fought fight in the process of its waging and its winning: the Wilderness, the Garden, and the Cross teach us clearly enough that the work of the spirit, the strife against sin, is won only by resistance unto blood, is finished only in death.

I spoke of life, natural, rational, moral, spiritual, eternal, as all associated with the evolutional increation and incarnation of the Word or Son of God. Eternal life is but the end and completion of one continuous process. Spiritual life is eternal life begun here in faith and hope: eternal life is spiritual completed in faith become sight, and hope become possession and fruition.

4. THE SPIRITUAL THROUGH THE NATURAL

There can be no question about calling Christianity a life, nor about calling it the life of God in the soul—that is to say, in the personality and the personal life of man. Neither, from the standpoint of the New Testament and of historical faith, can there be any question about all living Christianity's being the personal life of the living and present Christ—not anything merely of or from Him, as example, or influence, or virtue, or even grace, or spirit, but Himself in us. St. Paul's "I live not, Christ lives in me" is nothing more than the implicit attitude of the New Testament and of the Church whose expression it was and is. "In Jesus Christ," the baptismal, sacramental place and status of the Christian man, the ego or "I," the old man, the self of sin and death, is dead, and He takes its place and lives in me. That is possible by virtue of what Jesus Christ means and is to me. Just as the brute in us dies into the rational, free, moral man, so the natural man dies into the spiritual. By the natural, as well as supernatural, process of a living faith, hope, and love in Jesus Christ, not alone the virtue, the grace and power, but the very act and fact of His death to sin and life in God, are communicated and imparted to us. The old self dies, and a new Self which is more truly ourself lives in its stead. The very life itself of this new Self in us is the death of the old: living in the Spirit and so walking in It, we cease to fulfil the lusts or to live the life of the flesh. As St. Peter expresses it, Jesus Christ has "brought us to God" through having been "put to death in the flesh, and quickened, or made alive, in the spirit." That act becomes ours only through His becoming "we," taking the place of our old selves and becoming the new and true Self in us. Jesus Christ may no doubt be truly called the Ideal Man, or each man's Ideal Self, but He is infinitely more than that: an ideal, merely as such, is an abstraction; Jesus Christ is our actual and real True Self. Man in the mind of God, in the eternal foreknowledge and forepurpose of God, man "as he shall be when his becoming shall be complete," is not less but more man than in his inchoate beginnings and in his incomplete processes. Our Lord is not our ideal self, He is our eternal, divine, accomplished, assured, and perfect Self. Myself apart from Him who is God in me, the everlasting truth and meaning of me, my eternal life and self, is not I. Losing self and life in Him I find them, and finding them apart from Him I lose them.

There are two truths involved in this, each of which is more than liable to be lost in part or in whole. In the first place, Jesus Christ was Himself not only the Life that was with God, and was God, and was manifested to us; He was also that life made ours and manifested in us. And as such, it was in Him, in His oneness with us, precisely the same in kind with our life now in Him. For Him as for us, in our common relation with the Father, was the "Not I, but Thou," "Not mine, but Thine;" "I can do nothing of myself." "Believest thou not that I am in the Father, and the Father in me? The words that I say unto you I speak not from myself: but the Father abiding in me doeth His works." The Son can do nothing "of Himself," apart from His "oneness with the Father." That truth, in all its human signification and application, our Lord first realized for us in His own humanity, and so, in its converse, too, that "in oneness with the Father the Son can do and be all things,'' He has made it forever applicable to us as to Himself. In Him the perfection of faith grew into sight and knowledge, the consummation of hope became actual possession; the fulness of the life of God manifested in Him was manifest in the fulness of the life that humanly was Himself and His own. The Son of God became man, and the man that He became and was, just as truly and completely, by human act and process, incarnated the Divine Word of God in His humanity, as the divine and eternal Word incarnated Himself in Him. As the Deity in Him became human, so the humanity in Him became divine, and God and man in His person were One. So Jesus Christ was the Way of Life in both directions, from God to manward and from man to Godward: from God to us He was Love, Grace, Fellowship; from us to God He was Faith, Hope, Love, eternal Life.

In the second place, not only *was* Jesus Christ Himself our life in all the human way and order and process of it—through faith to grace, and through grace to glory; but Jesus Christ *is* Himself our life, in all our own progress from grace to grace, and finally to glory. We progress just in proportion as (1) ''it is not we but He in us,'' and (2) as it is not only He but we too, finding and realizing ourselves in Him. The living and present Christ operative in us for life now, is just as necessary a truth as the dead and risen Christ operating for us for life long ago.

We are being, not too often or too much if we take it aright, reminded in these days that the life of God or of Christ in us does not mean life out of or apart from the world, but rather the divinely right life in the world. It is a spiritual life because it is essentially, not only a life of the Spirit, but a spirit of life. One, and one only, spirit characterizes and manifests it. Hereby know we that we are of God, or of Christ, and that we abide in Him and He in us—by the spirit that He has given us. We know that we are of His Spirit, by the spirit that we ourselves are of. That Spirit, or spirit, we know, is Love; and although in a sense it is truly expressed in the words ''Love not the world nor the things that are in the world,'' yet it is not in the sense that the Object or objects of our love are wholly in another world and not in this. We do not perhaps need to be reminded that the contrary is the truth, but how and how much it is the truth, we do need to realize much better than we do. The same Apostle in the same epistle in which he bids us not to love the world and the things that are in it, teaches us that, if we do not love our brother whom we can see, we cannot love God whom we cannot see: which embodies a great principle. If our life is not in our relations here, and is not all that it ought to be in them, it can neither be what it should be, nor be at all, in relations elsewhere. Life is correspondence with environment—its own, actual environment, and not another. Life here may fit us for another, but there cannot be another save through this and as the sequel and result of this. The conditions and circumstances of earth are precisely those that are fitted and suited to develop in us the actions and characters that make up our lives. In bettering them, and making them what they ought to be, we are actually making, shaping, and determining ourselves.

To make this world all that it ought to be, to see that the will of God is done on earth as it is done in heaven, to convert the imperfect and the wrong in all of our present experience into the perfect and the right of a divine standard which God has written in our minds and revealed to our faith, is the only way to make heaven for ourselves, or to achieve that kingdom of God which is the goal of spiritual desire. We complain that the world is made what it is, forgetting that it is not made but still in the making, and that it is here for us to make it what it ought to be, and that it is no better only as we do not make it better. If the world is our proper environment, in reaction with which we are to make ourselves, and in making which we are to make ourselves, how else are we to expect it to be better than by our making it so? The right reaction of life upon environment and of environment upon life is the only mean or hope of either.

We forget how much of the good that Jesus "went about doing" was spent upon human and earthly conditions, and how much He makes the final judgment upon us to turn upon the same way and kind of "doing good." We are to find Him, as we are to find God, in all that needs us, and especially in all who need us, here. To go away from this, or these, in search of Him elsewhere or by Himself, is to seek Him where, for us at least, He is not.

In our fancied spirituality, we are perhaps too much inclined to seek and to find the goodness of Jesus in His concern for the spiritual and eternal conditions and welfare of men. We say that His bodily helps and healings are only temporary object lessons and parables of His permanent mission and ministry as physician of souls: "That ye may know that the Son of man hath power on earth to put away sin''—then, in proof, He put away sickness. Of course, there is much truth on that side, but on the other side too there is this to be said: Spiritual life is not something that can be detached and separated from natural or even from bodily life. The senses, the appetites and passions, all bodily functions, all pleasures and pains, are part of the soul that needs to be saved: and only as they are spiritualized, and sanctified, and so rationalized and moralized, is the soul itself saved, of which they are constituent and determining elements. We are not ourselves apart from all these parts of ourselves; and while some of them may be organs and functions of life only as life is here and now, yet even these in their time and place in the process of life enter not slightly into the determination of what shall be our life hereafter. The bodily and natural life is therefore to be dealt with immediately and wisely and lovingly in the interest of the spiritual life which is inseparably connected with it; and the dealing with it in the right spirit and the right way is a very large part of our present spirituality. Patience, endurance, fortitude, courage, temperance, self-control, self-discipline, and general physical efficiency, have all directly much to do with the body, and are all none the less spiritual virtues and graces. Sympathy, pity, charity, relief, and help, which have even a greater part in our spiritual activities, have scarcely less to do with the earthly and bodily conditions of others.

Indeed, the spiritual in our life is so largely the spirit and temper in and with which we deal with the temporal and the natural, that in the life of Jesus and of the New Testament the danger is rather that of seeing little else or more than that in it. There is, of course, much there of God and of Heaven, but the God and heaven of our Lord and His Apostles are mostly in the world, not out of it. The concern is vastly more with the now and here than with the elsewhere and hereafter. Faith indeed has everything to do with the absent and the future, but its whole function and concern with them is to make them present, in both time and space. In the spirit of the New Testament all our desire and effort should be, not to go to heaven, but rather to bring heaven to us, and to establish it upon earth: the kingdom of God is in need of nothing with Him in heaven; what it needs is to be set up among us upon earth. The things of faith are indeed absent and future, but that is just what they ought not to be, or to continue to be; we shall go to them only through bringing them to us. Our Lord "brought us to God" through dying to all distance or separation from Him, and living in nearness and oneness with Him.

The important question for us then is, What is the life of God, and of Christ, here and now: in what spirit, and by what spirit, shall we know ourselves in Him and Him in us? If we concern ourselves aright with the present and with earth, we may trust God for the future and its heaven. We do ourselves make and determine our future and our heaven, but the earth and the present are our only time and place for making them, and furnish all the material and the means out of which and by which they are made.

If we would study yet more particularly the form which the life of God and of Christ assumes among us upon earth, and the spirit that actuates and characterizes it, we shall find no more exact account of it than in our Lord's own words: "Ye know the rulers of the Gentiles lord it over them, and their great ones exercise authority over them. Not so shall it be among you: but whosoever would be great among you let him be your minister, and whosoever would be first among you shall be your servant: even as the Son of man came, not to be ministered unto, but to minister, and to give His life a ransom for many." With regard to the last clause, we may safely pass by all controversial theology by agreeing upon only so much of common interpretation as the following: The "giving" of our Lord's life, or soul, or self (for all these three are included in the term used), was certainly the cost or price of our redemption by Him, no matter why or how it was by that effected. It was that act of perfect love, service, and sacrifice on His part that in fact redeems and saves humanity. The act was in itself human redemption, salvation, and eternal life: for in it, humanity in His person conquered sin, death, and hell, put all enemies under its feet, and is seated as victor at the right hand of God, as participant in His holiness, righteousness, and eternal life. The admixture of imagery or figure with literal fact in that statement, in no wise impairs its truth, and is of help to the imagination in conceiving it. This supreme act of our Head, of the Leader or Captain of our salvation, of the Author and Finisher of our faith, is accepted by God, and appropriated by us, as ours: because it is ours—not only potentially through the grace of God assured to us in Christ, but actually upon the sole condition of our faith's taking and making it ours. Upon the details and methods of this divine salvation we may differ indefinitely, theoretically or speculatively; and yet, practically and substantially, can agree perfectly in knowing ourselves to be indeed dead unto sin in the death, and alive unto God in the life of our risen Lord.

It is, however, the spirit before and behind all this, of which I wish to speak as the breath and principle of the life of Christ in us. The life of man, as the life of God, is essentially and necessarily a ministry and a service. It lives in giving itself, and ceases to live in ceasing to give. It is a fundamental fact in itself, independently of the authority upon which it is stated, that "it is more blessed to give than to receive." Aristotle says substantially what our Lord says. Receiving, or merely having, is passivity; using, giving, spending, are activities; and life and blessedness are acts and activities—energies and actualities, not mere states, or conditions, or potentialities. The Self in us is at its best and highest in an act of pure love, service, and sacrifice. "Not that which goeth into a man either defiles, or beautifies, or blesses him, but only that which comes forth from him:" for only that is he, which proceeds from himself.

It is not mere giving, of course, that is the true expression of Christ, but giving life, soul, self. And there is no either true giving of self, or true self or life to give, that is not Love. If God can define Himself as Love, can comprehend and express all that He is within the compass of those four letters and that single syllable—it is not too much, nor too little, for us to say that all true life, true selfhood, or true blessedness in us is love. It is not enough, in describing love as the essence and principle of life, as the sole principle of all true and real life, to insist upon its rightness; we must assert, above and beyond that, its absolute and sole blessedness. It is not only the sum and substance of all our duty, the fulfilling of the whole law of life; it is also our highest good and happiness. The "right" is but the rule or law of the "good," the formulation and expression of our obligation to it. The Good, therefore, as an end is higher and more ultimate than the Right as a way or means. If "goodness" itself, which is the activity and natural expression of Love, and is the principle and essence of rightness or duty, is "will of the good," then it would seem that good, as the end, is something above and beyond even goodness, as the will and the way. What then is the Good, to which all ways lead and all means tend? It cannot be conceived or expressed otherwise than as at once the perfection and the blessedness of Life.

If life, which is inseparable and indistinguishable from its movement, its exercise and activity, its use and application, were not in itself a pleasure, a happiness, a blessedness, there is no other sense in which it would be a good. Why should we want it, for ourselves or for others, to be complete or perfect, or to be at all, if it were the pleasure, and so the desire and the will, of no one. Our individual life might be only a pain to ourself, and yet, because it is a duty or a good to others, or the will or law of God, we choose to continue it. In that case, not only has the pleasure, the desire, or the will of others been the end which has determined our action, but that end has determined us only by becoming our own dominant pleasure, desire, and will. We cannot escape the conclusion that pleasure, happiness, blessedness, is not only the actual and universal, but is the proper and necessary end and determinant of life. Our freedom, our responsibility, our wisdom, and our salvation, is in the choice of our pleasures, in the quality and material of our happiness, in the truth and purity of our blessedness. In choosing God and the Kingdom of Heaven we have made the wisest and best possible choice, but we have not chosen God because He is our duty alone, but because He is our highest pleasure or joy, our truest happiness, our essential life and blessedness. Or, if we have chosen Him from duty, then we have made duty our dominant pleasure, desire, and will, or happiness.

Which is the higher and the ultimate, Goodness or Good—good, which is personal perfection and blessedness, or goodness, which is will of the good to others and to all? The answer is that they are one and the same, and neither can be first or second. If good is life, and life is love, and love is goodness—then goodness, and love, and life are identical and are the sole and the only good. It follows that the spiritual, moral, divine end and aim of life is not reached by the surrender or sacrifice of pleasure or happiness, in their true sense, to duty. What we need for that abundance of life which our Lord came into the world to bring and to bestow, is not to deny or mortify pleasure or happiness, but to raise it to its highest place and power. We do this when we learn that the highest good is the being good, and that to be good is to will and to do good. The true goal is yet afar off, it is only in the way and on the way of ultimate attainment, so long as it is to us only the object of duty, a matter only of law and obligation. Loving, willing, being good, are attaining perfection with us in the measure in which they are ceasing to be law and becoming spirit, are ceasing to be duty and becoming a pleasure and a passion, our happiness and our blessedness.

The philosophy of all this is, that the good gift of God to us is the life that is His own. If life is a good, its good is to be found, not in its mere potentiality or possession, but in its use and exercise, in its proper functions and energies and activities. All these are given in the actual and manifold relations, associations, and interactions of human life. Of all these there is one all-embracing, all-constructive, all-sufficient spirit, and principle, and law—the spirit, principle, law of love and goodness. Love is the fulfilling of the whole law of life— that is, only in it is life fulfilled, goodness attained, and good secured.

5. DIVINE LOVE IN HUMAN SERVICE

We need to bring our Christianity down more closely and intimately into the natural and common life of this earth. There is much in our life here, necessary and right now, that will probably not survive with us our present conditions. But even these things have their place and their part in their time, and will survive if not in themselves yet in the use we have made of them and in the permanent effects their use or abuse has left in ourselves. A man's respiration, circulation, and digestion, in so far as they are automatic and parts of a general nature that goes on without him, may not be properly or permanently himself, but they are certainly parts of his present self, and so far as they are in his power and under his control for more or less healthy and efficient action, they are not only himself, but very important parts of his duty and his religion. Upon the action and efficiency of the lower and commoner functions of life depend most directly the vitality of the higher and permanent ones. Every natural impulse, appetite, and passion of the physical life has its necessary and important part, and leaves its permanent influence and impress, in the sum total of the immortal being who originated in it and has lived through it. Religion should begin early, embrace everything, and neglect nothing in the successive stages and long process of human life, for every moment and element in the evolution has its distinct and necessary contribution to make to the final result. The neglect of the earthly life in the interest of a heavenly is a fundamental error.

Marriage, the family, the community, society in general, as a living organism rather than an artificial organization, is older than any history we have of it. States are older than statesmen, just as languages existed before grammarians. Social life as well as physical has its principles and laws antedating our science or philosophy of them. The more closely we follow nature the better, so long as we really follow her, so long as we interpret nature in her highest meanings and follow her along her truest lines. God and nature are not two but One: Nature's determinations and destinations are God's predestinations working themselves out in the processes He has appointed them. There is no natural institution of society that is not infinitely perfectible, and yet none that does more than look toward a perfection that is infinitely far off. It is not God's plan or purpose to create by fiat a perfect social condition upon earth. From the beginning He has created by the action of a law within things, by the interaction of things among themselves. In the world of human intelligence and freedom He has by natural processes instituted a perfectible social state or condition, and devolved upon its subjects the task of carrying on and perfecting it. This devolving the social condition and progress of the world upon its subjects, and leaving it there, is wholly for the sake and in the interest of the subjects themselves, for it is only thus that they become "selves" or "themselves" at all. In using the intelligence that human life requires they acquire intelligence, in exercising their own wills they develop freedom, in restraining and regulating freedom they originate law, in rectifying and formulating law they institute justice and produce righteousness, in perfecting social conditions in general they make themselves or build up personality.

To complain that human institutions, that any human institution is defective or imperfect, to require in thought that things with us should have been or should be made more perfect or less imperfect than they are, is to refute or seek to invert the entire intent and beneficence of nature or of creation: which is not that there should be a necessarily and mechanically perfect world, but that there shall be a world of intelligently, freely, and personally perfect persons, made so or become so, or becoming so, through the long and difficult and painful task and achievement of themselves personally perfecting the world. We are no judges or measurers of the time requisite for such a process, and as to the methods followed or the means used in it we ought surely to know that neither effort, nor pain, nor doubt and uncertainty, nor possibility of error or wrong, nor the fact of evil, nor indeed any one of our actual conditions in the world, could have been spared from among the ingredients. As a matter of fact, not only our wills, as the poet says, but our selves, our conditions, our world, are all "ours, we know not how"; we know not how, but we do know why: "They are ours, to make them God's." God's end in it all is not Himself to make them His, but in our making them His to make Himself ours. In becoming coworkers, co-creators with God, we make ourselves one with and partakers of God Himself.

The impulse to discredit or destroy institutions that go back beyond all memory or knowledge of man—such, for example, as that of marriage—because of imperfections or failures or abuses, instead of reading their slowly unfolding meaning, and looking forward and patiently working up to their future ideal perfection, however far off, is an impatience incapable of cooperation with Him to whom a thousand years are as one day. The divine intent of marriage, as we have seen, is the highest ideal of human relation and association, of social purity and perfection. Discredit of it, leading inevitably to corruption in it, is poison at the root of human life.

The truth we are trying to carry along with us is, that life or salvation is not a way from the natural to the spiritual, but through and by the natural into the spiritual. We are not to love God instead of our neighbor or heaven instead of earth, but to love God in our neighbor and make heaven out of earth. If we have not loved the visible, how shall we love the invisible? If we have not been faithful in the earthly, we will not be so in the heavenly: "If ye have not been faithful in the unrighteous mammon, who will commit to your trust the true riches?" Human life grows up, or is built up, from the ground; it needs to get the proper good of all its stages, in order to have its complete and perfect good in the end.

Moral good originates in and is identical with social good. If goodness is the will of the good, then, since goodness is itself the highest good, it is the will of itself: just as the highest love is the love of Love, so the most perfect goodness is the will, not merely of good, but of that completest good which is goodness. It is the will of goodness, not alone in ourselves, but everywhere and in all: we have shown that true egoism and true altruism, true self-love and true other-love, are not two, much less inconsistent and discordant, but one and inseparable. We are to love other as we love ourself: we are indeed to love other as ourself: we are to take the other into ourself, and to seek and find ourself in the other. So God loves us, and so He bids us love Him—Himself in us, and ourselves in Him. He and we are all members one of another in a common life.

Life is organized, as we have seen, on social lines and exists only in the fulfilment of social relations. It is born in union and perfected in unity. That is why God is Love, and all life is love: because love is the only real and perfect bond or principle of union and unity. The most elemental, earthly, human life rests upon that sole foundation. "Man," says Aristotle, "is a political, or social, animal"—that is his first word, the seed of all his subsequent discourse about him. And he shows elsewhere that the one ideal perfect bond of society—that which lies before, behind, and within all mere justice or righteousness, the soul and life of all virtue or virtues—would be a universal *philia,* his nearest approach to that Love which, over three hundred years after, our Lord came into the world to make the realized and actual bond of all human life.

Natural relations, associations, intercourses, mutual offices, duties and services, are the cradle, the nursery, the school, the gymnasium for any and all human life that may come after, here or elsewhere. Our Lord began His divine office upon earth with the humblest ministrations to the bodies of the poor, the diseased, the repulsive, the ungrateful and undeserving. Almost His last act was to wash the disciples' feet, and to bid them go forth into the world and be in it and to it what He was, the servant of all. When at the last they should come before Him to receive His verdict upon what their life upon earth had taught and made them, the test and the testimony would be, "Had they been faithful in the little, and to the little? Then would they be accepted as faithful unto Him, and in the much." "Had they fed the poor, clad the naked, visited the sick and the prisoner? What they had done to these they had done to Him:" Service rendered to love was rendered to God, and God would recognize or accept none other.

Religion begins with the simplest, the humblest, and the most earthly of duties and offices, and if it does not find God in these, it will not find Him elsewhere. Life is service or nothing with God; and service, like God, is no respecter of persons. God wants the service for the sake of the server, the servant, as well as the served. It is infinitely more to Him that we should serve than that He Himself should be served. He can dispense with our service, but it is our breath and our life: only in it have we Him; only in doing His work of love are we sharing His life of love, and enjoying the blessedness of it.

Life is more a service, and a more divine service, when we recognize and love it as such; but whether we know it or not, or will it or not, it is still so as a matter of fact, and we cannot well live it otherwise. It is remarkable how universally—and in spite of ourselves—we acknowledge the truth in terms, even when we are the most thoroughly contradicting it in spirit and intention. Among all the avocations or occupations by which men earn their living, and in which they practically live their lives, there is probably not one which does not in some way avow or proclaim itself a service. In the necessary division and subdivision of labor in every community, there is no way of living for one's individual self except through some sort of service of the community. To what an extent life is collective and organic, or social, and not individual or particular, we find it difficult to realize, for the simple reason that we dwell so much more upon the little that is ours exclusively than upon the very much that is ours only inclusively or in common with others. It is literally true that "no man liveth unto himself": either he is not living "unto himself," or he is not "living."

The most selfish and dishonest politician is obliged to claim or profess that he "serves" a constituency. He is avowedly in the public service, however he may be using it for private ends or gain. No one denies in terms, however he may contradict it in acts, that "public office is a public trust." But it is so, not only with public office, but with any kind of public business: why should certain large organizations or combinations of capital style themselves "Trusts?" There is no business that does not use habitually the language of service: the merchant "serves" his customers, the insurance company its patrons, the lawyer his clients, the doctor his patients, the master his pupils. Lower down in the scale of service we distinctly apply the title "servants," but who in the universal occupation or business of living or of life is not a servant?

Our Lord did not come into the world to make life different so much as to make it real—to make it what it must be, what it cannot but be, if it is to be life indeed. St. John says of Him, that He was not come to give us a new commandment, but to put grace and truth, spirit and power and reality, into the old commandment which was from the beginning.

In human life, as it is constituted by nature, every act of real service is equally a service to others and to ourselves. In the highest as in the lowest sense a man "makes his living," lives his life, by service. In every act of service there are two elements, motive or purpose, and consequence or result. When we speak of the end of an action, we may mean by it either the conscious intention, or the actual effect of the action. The law of these two, the true relation and proportion that ought to exist between them, may be the discovery or revelation, it is not the creation or invention of Christianity. No revelation of life to us is true because it is revealed, it is revealed because it is true. It is no truth of Christianity that a man's life or self is not to be an end to him. The end and motive of Christianity is not self-extinction, but self-realization. We are not to extinguish desire, but rather "to desire earnestly the best gifts." The self or personality in Jesus Christ is not reduced to zero but raised to infinity, exalted to participation with God. Nevertheless it is a fact and a law in self-realization, that the less self appears in the motive the more it is found in the result of all human action, and the more in the motive the less in the result. That is, the more in any kind of service we are seeking ourselves, the less we are in reality serving ourselves, "He that seeketh his life shall lose it; and he that loseth his life for my sake (that is, he who most truly goes out of or beyond himself in others) shall find it."

This seems plain enough to us in the highest reaches of service and sacrifice: it is certainly in losing oneself in the cause of God and in the interests of humanity that one attains the highest selfhood and enjoys the purest satisfactions. No one will deny a generality like that, but the question is, Is the principle true and applicable and practicable in all, even the lowest, details of our earthly life? We might take any particular business of life, from the lowest to the highest, and apply to it such questions as the following: Who makes, even here, the truest success of his business and of himself, the man who plies the business with the most selfish motive of himself and his own gain, or the man who, with equal purpose and devotion, plies it for

its own high sake as a service, and for the sake of those whom
he is serving in it? As a matter of fact, the common judgment and
sentiment of the world, always so far beyond and above its actual
working principle and practice, sufficiently answers that question.
Its verdict of truth, of nobility, of heroism in action or conduct
or character, turns immediately, if not exclusively, upon the relative proportion in the motive of self-seeking or of other-regard-
ing. We know always what to love and admire in others, what to
celebrate or commemorate, however little we may value or live
by it in ourselves. All natural heroism or nobility is identical in
principle with the loving, self-sacrificing service of Jesus Christ
to God and humanity. He came not into the world to institute a
new principle or law of human life, but to be the resurrection and
regeneration of the old and the only. Even the non-Christian
world's verdict of approval and apotheosis upon Jesus Christ turns
upon the recognition of the fact that "He loved not Himself unto
the death." Those words express, not only the perfection of law
to the followers of our Lord, but the limit of natural perfection
for humanity.

"I, if I be lifted up, will draw all men to me." The Apostle
interprets the lifting up to be that of the cross: "this He said, signi-
fying by what death He should die." It was assuredly not the literal
cross that was the lifting up, but that of which the cross has been
made by Him the permanent and expressive symbol—the spirit and
principle of life and action which, when carried out to its limit,
brings humanity into oneness with deity. Perfect love is the only at-
one-ment. There is a very high sense, the very highest, in which it
is true that all the world loves Love, and cannot but love the Lover:
"I, if I be lifted up (lifted up by that principle and motive, and to
that height, of self-sacrificing love and service), will draw all men
unto me." The world, when it knows, cannot but respond to that
expectation and prophecy. Because He was infinitely obedient to the
one divine spirit and law of love, because He loved not Himself unto
the death of the cross—"therefore God exalted Him and gave Him
the name that is above every name." And therefore also, for that
same reason—"At the name of Jesus every knee will bow, of things
in heaven, of things in earth, and things under the earth, and every
tongue will confess that Jesus Christ is Lord, to the glory of God the
Father."

6. CHRISTIANITY THE UNIVERSAL
MINISTRY OF LIFE

The irresistible and inevitable progress of human society, in all its forms, is from monarchy to democracy. Intelligence, with all its growing activities and powers, diffuses itself downward and outward from the one or the few to the many: its aim cannot stop short of all. Life in all its stretches and reaches must lie open to all who would explore its deepest recesses or essay its highest attainments. Human thought and will, in no part of it, can be kept in nonage, under guardians and stewards, forever. In spiritual things as in natural, the world is demanding that authority must meet and carry with it consent. The order and unity of the authority of one, is of course an easier and simpler thing than that of the consent of all; but the question is, is it a better thing? And the better, and best, has to be sooner or later pursued through whatever of confusion and pain and difficulty. At any rate the easier thing has passed away from among us forever, and will never be possible again; the harder thing lies before us.

The end of Christianity is the unity of human life with Christ in God. The ideal—by which we must mean the ultimate, final actual, the end and goal of the present imperfect actual—is not the unity of or under a head outside and over us; even though the head be Christ Himself. The only true head of a body is that which is equally the life and intelligence of every part and particle of the body. The aim of the Church, which is the Body of Christ, is to be equally alive in its every part, in all the abundance of His all-sufficing life. This does not mean that there is not to be differentiation of functions and division of labor. It does mean the unity and consent of a life which, though distributed through parts, is one and is equally the life of the whole body.

The desideratum of Christianity, then, is that every individual member of the body, in his place and part, shall be and shall know himself actually and always engaged in the general life and work of Christ. This is practicable and possible only through a very much larger appreciation and realization than we now have of the universality and inclusiveness of the life and work of Christ.

A great and important phase and practical working out of this question is just now presented to us in the "Laymen's Movement" going on throughout our country and more or less affecting the entire

Christian world. What is the immediate meaning of this movement, and in what permanent form or forms are its aspirations going to be expressed and satisfied? The principle seeking expression in it is that the work of Christ, that work which He came into the world to accomplish, and the actual accomplishing of which was to be His witness in and to the world—that work of Christ is the work of the Church, and is waiting upon the Church for its accomplishment. That first—and, secondly, that the work of the Church is the work of the whole Church, and can be made so only by its becoming the work of every member of the Church. It is absurd to suppose that Christ is going to be a presence and a power upon the earth, unless the Church will wake up and become a power and a reality for Him— seeing that the Church is the Body of His presence and the instrument and organ of His power. And it is equally absurd to think of a living body in which all the members, the least as well as the most prominent parts, are not alive and performing their proper functions. If the life of Christ is to be the life of all, then the work of Christ must be work for all: faculty without function, life without work, is dead—in fact, is death.

If, coextensive with Church life, there is to be Church work for all, then we must broaden and enlarge our conception of what is Church work; for hitherto the body of the Church, apart from a very limited number of differentiated and specialized "workers," has found nothing really to do. We must first widen Christian or Church work to include all that is done in Christ, or in the name and in the spirit of Christ; and then we must expand what is done in Christ into "all things that pertain to life and godliness." Christianity includes all life in Christ—not only some, or a part. As all comes from Him in creation, so He aims to enter into all by incarnation. He shares all with us, and ministers to all in us—the life of body as well as soul. We cannot, except in the abstraction of thought, sever the continuity that runs through and unifies all life, from the lowest material up to the highest spiritual. So Christ's mission and ministry was to men's body and bodily life; the heaven He brought and preached was a heaven upon earth; the kingdom He set up was God's spirit of love, service, and sacrifice to be manifested and exercised by men among men in the world. All the work of Christ is work to be done here and now. Wherever and however life is lived and service rendered in the name and in the spirit of Christ, there Christ is in the life and in the service. We cannot be or do in Him, without His also being and doing in us.

When then the layman asks what of Christian or of Church work there is for him to do, and ends by finding none, it is the most fatal of mistakes to leave him in the conclusion that there is none for him except as he can take some quasi-part in the official or professional work of the distinctive ministry. What he needs to do is simply to make his own lawful and useful business or profession, whatever it may be, a work and his work for Christ. Let him be doing it "in Christ," in the name and in the spirit of Christ, and Christ will be doing it in him and making it an integral and necessary part of the work He is Himself on the earth to accomplish. He did not spend His time upon earth ministering only to men's supermundane interests or teaching a heaven elsewhere or hereafter; He brought God and heaven down into hearts and lives and conditions here—where they are most needed and therefore best acquired.

I do not mean that laymen are not, upon occasion, and when qualified as many of them are, and more ought to be, to be interested and take part in ministrations and services which are now too exclusively made the business and left to the care of the clergy. A living laity will help and relieve the clergy in many ways, and leave them freer for the more essential parts of their special ministry. But the mistake is in supposing that the special so-called or "proper" ministry is the whole Ministry of Christ, and that one must intrude into that in order to be exercising a ministry or doing Church work. Whereas every Christian is not only a minister but a missionary for Christ, and has his own work and mission to accomplish. And inasmuch as there is no real business upon earth which is not in fact a service of God and man, it follows that one has only to follow the apostolic injunction, "whatsoever we do in word or deed, to do all in the name of the Lord Jesus," in order to know and feel that one is doing Christian and Church work. There is not a man or woman in Christ who ought not to—and, as they truly realize the meaning and the fact of being in Christ, will not—say with our Lord, and as our Lord, "The work which the Father hath given me to accomplish, the work that I do, beareth witness of me, that He hath sent me."

We have seen that there is no living business, or business of life, that does not profess in terms to be some form or part of that "service" or "ministry" for which the Son of Man Himself professed to be come into the world. There is no normal means of one's own live-lihood which is not properly and professedly a service of others as well as of self. We have seen that the actual effectiveness as well as the moral and personal worth, the benefit to self as well as the common good, of all service rendered, is even by the world's judgment measured by the degree in which self is sunk out of sight in the motive, to reappear unsought and exalted in the reflex result. "Wherefore God highly exalted Him"—but God exalted Him only through His own act, and so alone He exalts us: it is always the act itself that exalts us, and ourselves through the act. But the law of the process is, that he most exalts himself who, with least thought of self, identifies himself with and attains his highest and truest self in unity with others and so with God.

Now this process of self-finding through self-losing, of making one's own life as well as one's mere livelihood through living in and for others, is as possible and practicable in one avocation as in another. "The Ministry," professionally so-called, is no more exclusively the service or ministry of Christ upon earth than any other natural and necessary form of living for others. Anything done in love, for the help and furtherance of life, is an actual and material part of the ministry of Jesus Christ, so it be done in His spirit and in His name. All life is His and is He: in His incarnation He enters into it all, in order that by knowing Him in it we may have it more personally and more abundantly.

The man who tills the ground as an act of service to God, and in order that it may bring forth fruit for man, who realizes and feels that he is ministering directly to the most elemental needs and wants of human life—working with Christ that men may have life, and have it more freely and abundantly—will in the first place be a better tiller of the ground than he who sees nothing in his labor but the material betterment of himself. He will increase even his most temporal gains and condition by the higher conception of himself and his work, but what other and truer gains will he not add to himself, if he will in even his most menial tasks and toil see himself a coworker with God and with Christ, an actual steward of God and minister of Christ in the producing and dispensing of life! So no less with any and every other worker in the varied but universal and all-employing business of life. Our Lord was no less engaged in His ministry when He was healing the leper than when He was saving the sinner; and why should the physician of bodies be less a minister of Christ than the physician of souls? Will the physician be a less good or successful one in any, even the lowest sense or respect, if his practice is one of love, service, and sacrifice, and not merely (though that too) for what the world calls "a living"? Who is the truly great lawyer?—he who is the public-spirited and incorruptible servant of justice and humanity, a minister of Christ and with Christ for the equity and integrity of social and corporate life, or he who uses his profession as a facile and powerful instrument or tool for the furtherance and protection of selfish interests?

The point is, If Christ's work upon earth was and is the universal and all-inclusive ministry of life, and includes "all things that pertain to life and godliness," and if the whole spirit and principle and law of life and godliness is expressed in the three distinctive Christian terms, Love, Service, Sacrifice—then who that is engaged in the business of life (as who properly is not?) is excluded by his occupation from that ministry? When the laity of the Church come together in a body, from which there should be no exclusions, to enquire what they can be actively and constantly doing for Christ—what shall be the answer? I am very far from saying that no man shall go outside of his own special business in search of Christian service, for no man should be a mere specialist, and it is well to be called out of our own routine, and there are needs and occasions enough for help in others. But I do say that no man need go outside his own business to find work for Christ and His Church, and that his first and most constant and urgent call is to make his own business distinctively and avowedly the ministry and the mission he is in search of. If it cannot be made so, or ought not to be made so, then it is not a legitimate and an honest business. For, I repeat, all life is in Christ, and Christ desires to be in all life; what cannot and ought not to be in Him is not life.

It so happened that the above words were in writing when the writing was interrupted by the duties of Good Friday, but with no thought at the time of the services for that day, on which our Lord sealed with His death His life of unbroken love, service, and sacrifice. It may be supposed that the following prayer in the service on that day came into mind with a peculiar force: "Almighty and Everlasting God, by whose Spirit the whole body of the Church is governed and sanctified, Receive our supplications and prayers, which we offer before Thee for all estates of men in Thy holy Church, that every member of the same in his vocation and ministry may truly and godly serve Thee, through our Lord and Saviour Jesus Christ!'' Who is there in God's holy Church without his own "vocation and ministry"? And what is there in any one vocation and ministry that is not in essence in all? The Son of Man is the truth and life of every man: and every man is in Him "not to be served but to serve, not to be ministered to but to minister, and to give his life for many.''

It so happened also, that at the very time of the writing of these thoughts the following words appeared in the current number of a religious weekly: "The spirit of business, at its best and highest, is the spirit of service. No business can prosper permanently that does not find its basis and its reason for existence in rendering service to those whom it seeks to reach. There is of course a great deal of business done which is selfish in its purpose and intentions. But there is also a great deal of business conducted by men who, as consecrated disciples of Jesus Christ, are using their energies and their business abilities in the spirit of a stewardship that is responsible to Christ.''

There is no reason why good business, business conducted in a Christian spirit and upon Christian principles, should not be profitable business, in even the worldly sense. Whatever makes it good or better will naturally make it profitable and more so. It is not good or better, for example, that business should be conducted "for charity,'' as we use the expression. If we are conducting our business upon right principles of real service, willing and doing good in the best sense to those with whom we deal, we will not exercise our virtue at the expense of theirs; and the charity which may be the moral good of the doer or donor, we know has too often been the moral weakening and injury of the recipient. The truest principle of business, that which best works the total good which Christianity is in the world to accomplish, is fair and equal exchange. There is room enough and need enough for true and helpful charity, without injurious interference with justice and righteousness.

When our Lord bids us "seek first His kingdom and His righteousness,'' with the promise that the other things "shall be added to us,'' neither the kingdom nor the righteousness of which He speaks is a thing apart from our life and business in this world. How can righteousness originate or exist or appear apart from relations and interchanges of life, from business dealings and associations? It is amid occasions and opportunities and temptations of wrongness that rightness appears over against and in contrast with it, in conflict with and triumph over it. But even righteousness, in and of itself, is but a formal notion, a law and nothing more. As a mere expression and rule of obligation it is a body without a soul. That which gives it content or motive or life is the spirit of Love. There is nothing essentially and eternally right but love, the will of good to all; there is no actual or real love but service, the doing good to all; there is no true service but sacrifice, the spending of life and self in the service of all. That is God, that is Christ, that is the Holy Ghost, that is Christianity, that is the ministry, the priesthood, of every Christian man and woman.

And this ministry is best exercised in just that place and part which is each man's business in the necessary division and subdivisions of the labor of life. It is his part and place in the universal and the eternal, his life as one with that of God and of Jesus Christ. Where the parts are all in the whole, the Whole is in each of the parts. We are seeking God's kingdom and righteousness first, when we put the Whole which is God above the part which is ourself.

When St. Paul bids us "set our minds upon the things that are above, not upon the things that are upon the earth," he is not preaching "other-worldliness." The things that are above are as much with us, if our mind is set upon them, as the things that are upon the earth. If our daily business and dealings and duties and cares are all what they ought to be, and as they ought to be, then the kingdom of God and His righteousness are as truly in them as the promised issue of "what we shall eat and drink, or wherewithal we shall be clothed." And the more truly we put the first things first, the safer we shall be from lacking the last.

7. FELLOWSHIP WITH GOD

Human Life, as it is the subject matter of Christianity, may—and indeed must—be studied from opposite points of view, accordingly as we treat it as our life in God or as the life of God in us. The human life of Jesus Christ Himself must be viewed, separately if not independently, in those two aspects. He was son of David, of Abraham, of Adam, Son of Man, as well as Son of God; and in His former character or capacity His life was subject to all the conditions, laws, and processes that belong to human life in general. There was a natural evolution of human spirituality, as of everything else that is human, from Adam, through Abraham and David, to Jesus. Our Lord humanly becomes Son of God through every link and moment of the process by which it is necessary that man should become son of God. Genealogically He was born of a progressively spiritual ancestry, and only in the fulness of time. Individually or personally He *becomes* son of God by human act and in the human way, as well as *is* Son of God in divine fact. St. Paul, on the whole, more clearly conceives Christ in the aspect of human author of a divine sonship and righteousness; St. John in the aspect of divine revealer and imparter of divine sonship and life. Similarly we must regard our own spiritual life as, in one aspect, a human evolution and inheritance, and a personal act and attainment of our own, though wrought only in God; and, in another aspect, a direct revelation and communication to us from God in Jesus Christ. How to combine these two aspects of one and the same thing is the truth and task of Christianity.

The First Epistle of St. John may be taken as a dissertation upon the life of God as it is revealed in and imparted to humanity. He begins with The Life as it is first manifested in Jesus Christ. There is no, or little, allusion to how our Lord Himself becomes what He is in our humanity; He is simply, in his spiritual human perfection, what God reveals or manifests Himself in humanity: what He wills and purposes, if we will, to become in us all. The Apostle describes the manifested Life in terms, not alone of a natural witness who had had every sensible evidence and experience of the external and historical facts involved, but no less of a spiritual witness who, as fully as any other, apprehended the deeper import and significance of those facts. He sees the life that has come down from God perfected and glorified in Man; and in full confidence and assurance of participation himself in that life, he goes forth, in the joy of it, to complete his joy by making all others partakers of it. "We declare it unto you, that ye also may have fellowship with us; yea, and our fellowship is with the Father, and with His Son Jesus Christ."

The first question for us, is as to the meaning and reality of that fellowship or *koinonia,* in which the life is to consist. What is it of God, or rather, what is God Himself, that we can share with Him? The answer is: that God is Light, and in Him is no darkness at all.

Among the many possible explanations of the meaning of "light" in this connection, we may consider the following: The light is not alone that of the intelligence, as Truth; it is equally of the feeling or affection, as Love; and of the will and life, as Holiness and Right-eousness. We might say that "light" is simply a synonym for "truth," if we include in "truth" that, not only of thought or knowl-edge, but also of feeling or affection, and of will and action. These are the three constituent elements of ourselves, and in each there is a true and a possible false, or light and darkness. The truth of intel-ligence is "the right reason," wisdom, the knowledge of things as they are. The truth of affection or feeling is love, the right feeling for, the right pleasure or happiness in the right things. The truth of the will and activity is true freedom, the obedience of the whole life to the law of truth and love. Thus Light is the unity of the three pris-matic hues or aspects of human life, knowledge or wisdom, love, and obedience or righteousness. Of these, love is the central and chief: it is the substance and content of the other two. In a sense it alone is real, and not merely formal. Knowledge is of "the things that are," independently of what the things are—good or bad. Obe-dience is conformity to a law, equally independently of what the law is. Love is wish and will, not possibly of any thing else, but only of "the good." To wish or will evil, for oneself or for another, is not to love but to hate.

In consonance with this, it is evident that in the Epistle, Light is used in all the meanings of Truth, Love, and Obedience; and that Love is at once the content of Truth, the reality to be known, the "Thing that Is" in the universe; and the object or law of Obedience: it was to the law of love that Jesus was obedient unto death, and that the death of the cross: love is the spirit and life of all righteousness.

We come thus to the main question of our *koinonia* or fellow-ship with God, and here there is a matter of interpretation to be first considered. "God is Light; if, therefore, we say that we have fel-lowship with Him, and are walking in the darkness (of ignorance, or hate, or sin), we lie and do not the truth. But if we are walking in the light, even as He is in the light, then have we fellowship one with another." The point is, Who are the "one another" in this relation: who are the two parties to the fellowship? If we suffer ourselves sim-ply to follow the argument or course of thought, it would seem that the two parties are ourselves and God. If our not walking in the light, which is God, be evidence that we are not in God, or in participation with God, who is light, then the fact that we are in the light is proof that we are in God, or that God and we are in fellowship with one another. The Apostle had already affirmed that our fellowship is with the Father and with His Son Jesus Christ. This does not exclude the subordinate and consequent truth that participation with God is necessarily participation with one another in God. In the case of the Apostle, fellowship with God impels him instantly to the further and completing truth and joy of fellowship with the brethren: "that ye also may have fellowship with us, . . . that our joy may be fulfilled." God in us would mean infinitely less to us if it did not mean God in all, and all in one another.

What, then, have we, or what are we, in common with God? This cannot but include or involve the previous question, What is our natural or metaphysical kinship or relationship with God? Because there can be no transcendent interchange of relations with God, if there is no immanent basis of relationship with Him. Without oneness of nature, there can be no oneness of communion or intercourse. And such indeed is our natural kinship with God that we cannot know or think either except in terms of the other. As we have seen, we know ourselves only under the categories of thought, feeling, and will or action; our "self," or personality, is a compound and unity of intelligence, affection, and volition and action. Now what is God? He is infinite or omniscient intelligence, or Wisdom; He is infinite or perfect affection, or Love; He is infinite or omnipotent activity, or Righteousness and Goodness. Is it not true that God is the Infinite of what we are, and that we are the finite of what God is? The first word of religion is the recognition of the fact that we are in the image of God. To know God at all we have to know ourselves; to know ourselves unto perfection, we have to know God. To be ourselves unto perfection, we have to be what God is. It is a natural and metaphysical fact that we "do not the truth," that we are not the truth of ourselves, are not our real selves, until we walk in the light, and are what God is. There is no other end or limit or goal for man than God. What we want from Him is nothing less than Himself, seeing that He is our own and only perfect Self.

But the truth which St. John is enunciating is not an immanent but a transcendent one, not a fact of nature but a revelation and impartation of grace. Or, if these are essentially the same, it is as one and not as the other that they are here under consideration. If it is our nature, or in our nature, to be saved and completed only in God, it is not only in our nature, or in our only immanent and natural relation to God, that we shall be saved and completed. God will have to make Himself and ourselves known to us by a transcendent act of Self revelation and impartation, before we can realize either Himself in us or ourselves in Him. That, too, is a metaphysical necessity: it is essential to our very being as persons, as finite spirits and children of God, reproduction and image of Himself, that what we shall be we shall be of ourselves. That is to say, what we are to be must be matter of our knowledge, our choice, and our action, if there is to be any selfhood in it for us, or we are to accomplish and become ourselves through it.

It is therefore not as God is in us in nature, but as He is in us in Jesus Christ, by Self revelation and impartation on His part, and by faith and personal appropriation on our part, that we are here described as having with Him something more than is adequately described by the term "fellowship," and for which I would retain the original *koinonia*. That evidently expresses more than association or communion with another: the two are no longer two, but are become one. It means more than sharing something with God: what we share with Him is Himself; when we have truth, and love, and righteousness or goodness, we have God. Love is both Truth and Righteousness, because Love is God—not merely *That which Is,* but the essential and eternal *I Am.*

When we say that "Our fellowship is with the Father, and with His Son Jesus Christ," we mean that we become one with the Father in the Son—that in the sonship to God, realized for us by Christ, God has become to us Father, and we have become to Him sons. The time has come when we may settle by reconciling a controversy which has given rise, not only to rival schools of thought, but to rival types of life. The question has been, Whether we are children of God by nature, or only become children of God by grace—whether we are so by birth, or only by regeneration or new birth—by immanent fact or by transcendent act. Both are true, and neither is truth apart from the other. The confusion or contradiction arises from not realizing that sonship is both a natural and a personal or spiritual relationship; that it partly is, as a fact, and partly must become, as an act. "Because we are sons"—that may be taken as a fact of nature; "God sent forth the Spirit of His Son into our hearts, crying, Abba, Father''—that was an act of grace. The immanent or natural fact would come to naught, that is, would never be spiritually realized and actualized in us, without the transcendent and personal act: what is the relation of son, without the spirit and life of sonship? Regeneration then presupposes natural sonship, and natural sonship is only the ground or condition, the potentiality for regeneration or realized sonship, and is incomplete without it. Because we are sons of God by nature, therefore we must become sons of God by grace through faith, that is, by the Spirit of God working in and with and through ourselves.

As a matter of mere Scripturalness, or the point of view of the New Testament, the position of sonship by grace rather than by nature has the stronger argument. Sonship by nature is only a postulate or presupposition of historic Christianity, which is immediately concerned rather with the realization of humanity through spiritually accomplished sonship in Jesus Christ, than with the unrealized sonship of humanity in Adam—that is, in mere nature or in itself. Jesus Christ is regenerate or spiritual humanity, as Adam or primitive man is the symbol of natural or unregenerated humanity. The sequence and connection of truth in this matter may be illustrated by what seems to be the meaning of an obscure passage in the Epistle before us. In Ch. II. 7, the Apostle is insisting that the truth of which he writes is no new truth, but the old truth that was from the beginning. But, again, he declares, it *is* new: because it has been made truth in Jesus, and in Him has become truth for us. Now apply this to our sonship to God: in a partial sense it is an old fact which has been from the beginning. But in the better part of its truth—in its realization and actualization—it has become what it never was before, and is new.

Quite as important as the truth of regeneration in Christ, is the question of its mode—or "way," as our Lord Himself calls it. It is not enough to say that it is by grace through faith, unless we understand something of the process of each of these. And first with regard to grace and its mode of operation: Grace is indeed a species of power, inasmuch as it is an efficient cause producing a definite effect. But it is a species widely differentiated from mere power, or from power necessarily or inseparably connected with its effect. Grace is never bare operation: it is effectual cooperation. The subjects of grace are only those in whom its working is in and with and through their own working. The perfection of the operation of divine grace in human cooperation is manifest in Him who could say: "I and my Father are one:" "My will is His and His is mine; my works are, of course, mine; and yet not mine, but His in me." The paradox of divine grace can never, any more than that of human freedom in general, be elucidated in logic, while yet it is indisputable in experience. The divine is present and efficient in the human, while the human maintains all its integrity and acts freely in the divine; so that one and the same act is both human and divine; as, altogether, in our Lord one and the same person is both human and divine. The cooperation is not the semi-pelagian one in which each side does so much, in different parts; it is rather that of the hypostatic union, in which each does all, in perfect union, or unity, with the other. The human manifests itself in no positive independence of the divine, but only negatively in the power of noncooperation, and so in the freedom of its cooperation.

Grace appeals thus to cooperation, and is ineffectual without it; otherwise it were not grace, but bare power. It can be resisted, grieved, and even quenched by the unpardonable sin of final rejection: "How would I, and ye would not!" And how can the appeal for cooperation be made to aught save intelligence, choice, and freedom; or otherwise than through all these? The essence of divine grace is divine Self-communication: God gives us nothing less than Himself. And He can give us Himself, or we receive Him, only through our knowledge, love, acceptance and exercise of Him. Only through all these can we of ourselves become what He is; and we cannot be what He is without ourselves becoming it, because the being so through bare power, and not grace, would not in fact be *we* being so.

I would not deny all truth to natural religion without revelation: or, as I would express it, I would not deny a knowledge and service of God based upon mere inference from ourselves and the universe, and our immanent relation to Him, without transcendent communication from Him. I concede, on the contrary, that if there were no natural there could be no revealed religion. Natural religion is simply the potentiality and demand, of which revealed is the actuality and supply.

But, while natural religion may give us a knowledge about God, it would not give us that knowledge of Him which is Himself with us and in us, and which we have only in and through Jesus Christ. Nor can we see how otherwise that knowledge could have come to us than in Him who is at once God and we, God Himself our holiness, our righteousness, and our life. In Jesus Christ we have at once that knowledge of ourselves which enables us to know God, and that knowledge of God which enables us to know ourselves. For, I repeat, we can neither know God at all save through what we finitely are, nor ourselves adequately save through what God infinitely is. In Jesus Christ we have the totality of religion realized—not in ourselves, for that were impossible in the beginning—but in Him as the object and end of our knowledge, our choice, and our will, of our faith, hope, and love, of all our doing, becoming, and real or essential being. How otherwise could God better, or at all, bring us into all that Himself is?

As grace proceeds from the eternal love that God Himself is, and reveals or communicates itself to us in the divine oneness with us that is Jesus Christ, so it manifests itself in us in that *koinonia* of ourselves with God in Christ, which is our present theme, and which is, in fact, the Holy Ghost. The Holy Ghost must, with equal truth, be spoken of as It and as He. As to what it is, when we speak of it as impersonal spirit, it is that character or quality of divine Love, which is the sole principle of all unity, and order, and beauty, and goodness, and real or essential life. Hereby know we that we are of God, that we are in Him and He in us, that He and we are one—that He hath given us of His spirit: "We know that He abideth in us, by the spirit that He hath given us."

If we have not what the Spirit is, we have not Him, and cannot know Who He is. If we have it, we have Him, and know that He is God. There is nothing in God that is merely impersonal. If Jesus Christ was the word or utterance, the revelation or manifestation of God to us, then He was the eternal Personal Word of God, who is Himself God to us. If the Holy Ghost is the spirit of God in us, the mind, disposition, and character of God become ours, then is He the eternal Personal Spirit of God, who is Himself God in us. Our word or our spirit may become detached from us, and become in others only they, and no longer we. We ourselves may, without detriment to them, be not merely absent, but even wholly extinct. But God's Word and God's Spirit are never detached from Himself, but are always Himself both present and operative in them. It is the worst of anthropomorphisms, to think or speak of God's acts or influences or operations as separate from Himself, as ours are. It is the sin of a mere transcendentalism or deism, as the opposite extreme is the sin of a mere immanentalism or pantheism. The true theism is that which does full justice alike to the transcendence and the immanence of God.

The life of God is represented, first, as coming down into us from God, in a series of stages; and secondly, as ascending up in us, into God, in an answering succession of stages. Love in the Father becomes grace or divine Self-communication in the Son, and finally fellowship, or human participation in the divine, in the Holy Ghost, in whom the Spirit of God and the spirit of man are brought into a divine-human unity, which is Christ in us. The answering ascent on man's part is from faith, through hope or anticipative possession, up to and into love, which is actual or accomplished possession. Of course, in both series, love runs through all and underlies all. Just as grace and fellowship are only progressive means and operations of the self-imparting of love, so also faith and hope are but progressive ways and means on our part of our participation and growth in love.

The process of faith, hope, and love may be described some-what as follows: The life of God, to be really ours, must be ours of our own choice and of our own act. The "we," of personal quality and character, must be all in it. God gives us to have life in ourselves: the water He gives us becomes in us a well of life having its source in us as well as in Him. Through faith, hope, and love, Christ be-comes ourselves, and His Spirit our own. But the life of God thus becomes ours, not by a divine magic, but in a human process and order. God in Christ, by His Spirit, enters into us through the only personal channels of intelligence, affection, and volition. We must know life, desire life, will and purpose life, before we can really or fully possess life. Even the earliest of these stages is indeed already a beginning of life, but it is very far off as yet from the end of it. Life must come to us first from without; it must be an object, before it can become a possession: we must know it without us before we can have it within us. And what is all important, we must know it without us *as ours,* in God's purpose, and by God's act, before we can pos-sibly realize it as ours, in us and by our own act. Who will of himself conceive, or by his own act alone undertake, all that to which we are called of God in Christ Jesus? "Whom He foreknew, them He predestinates to be conformed to the image of His Son, that He might be the First only of many, or of all. Moreover, whom He predestinated He calls: Christ is the call to every man, to become what He is. The elect are the effectually called: that is, all who answer and obey the call. Those thus called He justifies: that is, He accepts as being, in grace and in faith, in Christ. And then, by His grace and through their faith, in Christ He progressively sanctifies and ultimately glorifies them." If God be thus for us, and with us, and in us—for us, eternally in Himself as Father; with us, effectually in Jesus Christ as Son; in us, actually and in progressive assimilation on our part by the Holy Ghost, as the common Spirit of His and our life—if God be thus ours throughout the entire process of our attainment of life, what can be against us in it or disappoint us of it? How necessary is it that we should have this objective revelation to us of ourselves and our destiny, of the part of God in it, and of the part that waits and depends upon ourselves! How needful was the divine manifestation of human life in Jesus Christ—"for our sake, who through Him are believers in God, which raised Him from the dead and gave Him glory; so that our faith and hope might be in God!" "The greatness of His power to usward who believe" is measured for us by "the working of the strength of His might which He wrought in Christ, when He raised Him from the dead."

It is thus that the Holy Ghost in us is "the earnest of the promised possession." St. John says that we have "a chrism from the Holy One": what of the Spirit, or spirit, of God and of Christ is abidingly in us, as part of our life and character, is so much of Christ and of God in us, and is both potency and promise of all. Faith is of God and of God's part in our life; hope is of us and our part. It is only, as St. Paul teaches, in the tribulation of life, that endurance and perseverance and survival on our part works in us proof of the sufficiency of grace, and of our own power through it; and so faith passes on into hope, and through both love, the love of God, is fulfilled in us.

He who in the Son sees the Father, who in Jesus Christ recognizes the Life of God manifest upon earth, who by the Holy Ghost appropriates that life to himself and assimilates himself to it, has set to his seal that God is true. The truth of humanity answers unto and fits into the truth of God, and the unity of both is proof of the truth of each. He who denies God in Christ, by the lie in himself makes

God a liar to him. For this is the witness of God: "that He hath given unto us eternal life, and this life is in His Son. He that hath the Son hath the life; he that hath not the Son of God hath not the life."

8. CHRISTIANITY AS A WITNESS

The last words of our Lord to His Apostles before His final taking up from among them were these: "Ye shall receive power, when the Holy Ghost is come upon you; and ye shall be my witnesses . . . unto the uttermost part of the earth." When the Holy Ghost was come upon them, the first testimony of the Apostles before the people was to this effect: "This Jesus hath God raised up, whereof—or, of Whom—we all are witnesses." And again, before the rulers: "Ye killed the Prince—or, Author—of life; whom God raised again from the dead, whereof—or, of Whom—we are witnesses." They everywhere emphasize their witness; and the ambiguity in the form of the pronoun only calls attention to the fact that Jesus and the resurrection are convertible, and to a certain extent identical terms: that testimony to the one is testimony to the other. Let us consider, first, the persons of the witnesses, and, secondly, the matter of the witness.

We might limit the persons of the witnesses to the number of the Apostles. Unquestionably, they were the primary witnesses, chosen with special reference to that end. When there was a vacancy in their number, they felt it necessary that "Of the men who had companied with them all the time that the Lord Jesus went in and out among them, beginning from the baptism of John, unto the day that He was received up from them, of these must one become a witness with them of the resurrection." Perhaps the claim is not unreasonable, that the Apostolate as a permanent institution is a standing monument and witness of Jesus and the resurrection to the end of time, as well as to the ends of the earth. There can be no question that the Episcopate, whatever be the details of its origin, was from the beginning intended and looked upon as the instrument and expression of the unity and universality—the catholicity—of Christianity, or of the Church, in both space and time. And what is either Christianity or the Church but the extension or universal inclusiveness of Jesus and the Resurrection?

But witness to Jesus and the Resurrection was not limited to the

Apostles, and certainly in no exclusive way has been transmitted through the Episcopate. There is a much deeper and truer sense in which all real Christians are witnesses, and Christianity itself is essentially the witness to Jesus and the resurrection. This will become apparent as we examine the witnesses more in connection with their witness. A large part of that witness was without doubt that of literal eyewitnesses to external and physical facts, historical incidents or events. Such, on one side of them, were certainly both Jesus and the resurrection. But if that were all, why—what possible reason or meaning could there be for—the promise, "Ye shall receive power, when the Holy Ghost is come upon you," as the condition of their becoming witnesses? Could anything more than sound senses, good memories, and common honesty be required for competent testimony to common facts? Is it not plain that these particular witnesses needed something more than physical or natural qualifications for testimony to something more than physical or natural facts? It was not enough, what they saw or heard with natural eyes and ears; the important point was, what they saw in what they saw, and heard through what they heard. When Jesus said, "He that heareth my words—" He by no means meant every one who had heard them with outward ears. "Take heed how ye hear"—were very solemn words in His mouth. "He that hath seen me hath seen the Father"— was very far from true of every one who had seen Him: there are very different kinds of seeing. The function of the promised Holy Ghost was to be that He should "take of the things of Jesus, and show them unto us." He was to give us eyes to see, and ears to hear, and hearts to understand, and minds to know. The Holy Ghost in us is our subjective qualification to receive the things that be of God, and that are addressed, not to our flesh, but to our spirit, to our sense for divine things.

Let us illustrate by the actual witness of one of the chief witnesses. Why was St. John so chief a witness to Jesus and the resurrection? Not because he could better see or hear or report with outer senses or understanding; but because he had the deeper inner vision, and saw and heard what to others was invisible and inaudible. Hear his testimony: "What was from the beginning, what we have heard, what we have seen with our eyes, what we beheld, and our hands handled, concerning the word of life—what we have seen and heard declare we unto you." Every term is used, every qualification enumerated, of the purest external testimony, and yet it is evident that the thing testified to is accessible only to the most inner and spiritual senses or perception. All that our Lord had said or done on earth, all the wonderful things that had happened, including even the resurrection, are passed by, and only that is testified to which is the, to most eyes, invisible import and significance of the whole matter.

The term *logos* or "word" ("word of life") is used here in a different way, but not in a discordant sense, from that in which it appears at the beginning of St. John's Gospel. In that it is used personally, in this impersonally; in that it is used to designate the Subject of the Incarnation, to express Who Jesus Christ is; in this it designates the subject matter of the incarnation, it tells what Christ is—not only in Himself, but also in us. God's eternal and essential Word, the principle and agent of all revelation, manifestation, or expression of Himself—that is, of all that is—is defined here, not as the divine Expresser, but simply as the divine expression, revelation, or manifestation of Life. He is here to be studied, not as Who is our life, but as what is our life; the question is to be, not how God is in us for our life, but what our life is as God's.

Our immediate subject then is as to the expression of life, how life manifests or evidences itself—and that especially in humanity, whether in Jesus Christ as its type or original, or in us as participants in it in Him. Christianity as a permanent witness is witness of a permanent thing: it is not transmitted testimony of a Jesus who lived or of a resurrection that once took place; it is direct evidence of a Jesus who lives and of a resurrection that is continuously taking place. It is Jesus as Life that we are witnesses of; it is the resurrection as the divine victory of human life that we are here to bear testimony to.

The truth of Adam is altogether independent of the historicity of such an individual man. Adam is only the root and type of our common or universal humanity. He stands for our common nature and our common condition by or in nature. We express simply a common or universal fact of nature when we say: In Adam we all sin, and in Adam we all die. That may be an inadequate account of the historical origin or cause, but it adequately describes the fact of sin and death. Now Jesus Christ stands for an equally generic and universal fact and principle in humanity, the principle of God in it, and of eternal life. If there were not in man an original principle and potentiality of all that Christ means, Christ could not become in us all that He does. "Whom God foreknew He predestinated to be conformed to the image of His Son." That means that God, in His eternal foreknowledge and fore-purpose of humanity, implanted in it the potency and promise of becoming, through unity with Himself, all that humanity has actually become in Christ, through His love, grace, and fellowship in and with it. This is involved in the truth of our sonship to God by nature. We are not all products of nature; we are, in highest part, children of God; and His "seed" in us, our natural derivation from and kinship with Him, is in itself potency and promise of our becoming of one life with Him.

In the first place then, Jesus Christ means the inner man potential in every man. But in the second place, He means that inner and merely potential man quickened and regenerate by the—not merely immanent, but transcendent—action of Himself upon it, and become the "new man." By transcendent action is meant action not naturally transmitted, but personally communicated. The media of personal communication are invariably Word and Spirit—the Word, by expression to the understanding, and the Spirit, by appeal to and influence on the sensibilities, affections, and will. The function of the Word is the conveyance of truth or reality to us; of the Spirit, the quickening of apprehension, reception, and life in us. The evidences of life are, the passing or death of the "old man" or "old Adam," of subjection to sin and death, and the birth and life in us of the Christ or "new man," of the likeness and life of God in us. Jesus Christ is described by St. Peter as having "brought us to God"—how? By being "put to death in the flesh, but quickened or made alive in the spirit." Flesh and Spirit had become—probably chiefly through the thought of St. Paul—synonyms for all that was respectively to be "put off" and "put on" by the supreme double act of the Death and the Resurrection of our Lord. It is not to be supposed that our Lord had not that which was to be put off in the flesh, as well as needed or was in want of that which was to be put on in the spirit. If it were not so with Him, then would He not be constituted and qualified to accomplish in our humanity that in which its salvation consists and upon which it depends: that is, the putting off the flesh and putting on the spirit; putting off nature and self in their deficiency and insufficiency, and putting on God as alone all sufficient for holiness, righteousness, and life. Jesus Christ did not put off sin and death, as having been Himself, personally, involved in them. He put them off by the act and fact of not having been involved in them: that is, by the act and fact of having overcome and abolished them. But He overcame them only in the human way of denying, mortifying, and crucifying the nature and self which, even in Him, were subject to sin and death, because incapable of holiness and life, and putting on God, who alone in us is sufficient, and is our sufficiency, for these.

The symbolical language—in so far as it is so—of the inner and the outer man, the old and the new man, Adam and Christ, the flesh and the spirit, death and resurrection, can never be improved upon or dispensed with in Christianity. Not only because they are the best possible symbols of facts and realities in human nature and experience, but because they are themselves more and truer than mere symbols. They are a language that is translatable, and must be translated, into all languages, because they are the exact expression of all higher human life.

Witness, then, to Jesus and the resurrection is nothing if it is not witness to a present Person and a present and actual experience. As to the present Person: the tendency emphasized in these days is to divorce the historical Jesus from the symbolical Christ; the next step to which would be to dispense with the symbol, and thus to reduce God, and Truth, and Life from Persons to abstract ideas and principles. Then will be the end of religion; for religion is only between persons; the relation with ideas and principles may be for us science or art or philosophy; it may give us ethics, but it cannot be religion. When God has become the mere personification of our own conception of perfect truth, order, and goodness; when Jesus Christ has become the mere symbol of our own ideal of truth, beauty, and goodness, or God, incarnate in us, then these objects of our worship will be simply reduced to ourselves and the creatures of our own minds. And when we have really discovered that, we shall cease to worship them. Just because truth, beauty, and goodness are personal, and only in persons, or not at all—not to know them eternal in God, or incarnate in Christ, is to know them nowhere except in ourselves. We cannot speak of them as present or operative in the universe as a whole, or anywhere in it outside ourselves; for we know none, and nothing, outside ourselves in whom or in which they can be. To speak of Goodness as an ultimate principle, or a principle at all, in the Universe, is to assume an objective or ultimate Personality in the universe.

I am perfectly aware of the ignorance and inadequacy of our ascription of personality to the Ultimate Principle of the universe; but the reality in that Principle, as is freely admitted by the truest agnostics, must infinitely transcend, and in nothing fall short of, the personality we ascribe, and must also include it. There can be nothing in us that is not in It. The ablest and devoutest Ethical Culturist I know—agnostic as to anything beyond that—worships, more devoutly than I, precisely What I do—but not Whom I do. If, as he believes, What he worships is more and higher than Whom I worship—he would not lower nor limit It to my conception or designation of It—then I believe that we worship, not only the same Thing, but the same Person. And I think that I lose nothing, and he would lose nothing in going as far as our limitations will permit, and ascribing to the supreme Object of our worship at least personality and personal relation with ourselves—whatever more we may be failing to ascribe. If he were not, implicitly, worshipping a Person, he would not be worshipping at all, and I believe that he is, quite as certainly as that I am.

Seeing, then, in Jesus Christ all that I do—the divine predestination and potentiality of my Self, as of all human selfhood; myself, not only thus purposed and promised, but in Him realized and fulfilled; the outer man in me displaced by the inner, the old by the new, the flesh by the spirit, the Adam by the Christ, nature and self in me by God—Jesus Christ is to me, not a name, nor a memory or tradition, nor an idea or sentiment, nor a personification, but a living and personal reality, presence, and power. He is God for me, to me, in me, and myself in God. Wherein else do we see God, know God, possess God than as we are in Him, and He in us? And wherein else are we so in Him and He in us, as in Jesus Christ? If God is unknowable in Himself, whether as immanent in, beneath and behind, or transcendent above all nature and all else, where does He become knowable but in His Word to us and His Spirit in us: and that is what we mean by Jesus Christ, and what He is to and in us. If God is not a Presence, a Reality, and a Power in Him, He is so nowhere. And if we are not to worship Him there, we worship Him not at all. "There is none other Name under heaven, given among men, wherein we must be saved." And "in His name" means "in Him," and "in Him" means "in His death and resurrection."

Our relation to, our interest and actual participation in the death and resurrection of Jesus Christ, is no mystery or magic. Assume that Christ is in fact the Power of God unto salvation, God in us unto and in our actual salvation, our holiness, our righteousness, our life, and so our redemption from sin and our resurrection from death; assume that through faith we experience enough to know this: we have the earnest and proof of it in ourselves; that in hope we appropriate and possess in anticipation all that we see and know in Christ;—if both the objective and subjective facts be actually so, is it either magic or, from the highest point of view, even miracle, that in Jesus we should see God and ourselves at one, and that His death should be our redemption, and His resurrection our eternal life?

It will of course be asked: "Yes, but is it not enough that the Christ shall be the ideal or spiritual Symbol of all that, as Adam is of all that goes before?" I admit that He is the symbol of it all, but not the mere symbol. By mere symbol I mean just that which is actually meant by those who contend for it: a sign that is not the thing, that represents only, and is not what it represents. The question is, Whose, and what kind of, symbol is it? If it is man's, and expresses his immanent conception or idea or ideal of God and himself, and the relation between, then it is only a sign, and by no means necessarily the thing signified. If, on the contrary, it is God's, and the direct manifestation and expression from Him of Himself and man, and the relation between, then faith is justified in taking it for no mere sign, but the Thing signified, and hope, in appropriating to itself the whole presence and power and reality of it. So, Jesus Christ is to us no mere idea, or sentiment, or aspiration, desire, or hope of our own, but God's truth and reality of our at-one-ment with Him, our redemption from sin, our resurrection from death. It is only so in faith and hope, and very imperfectly so in fact, from the nature of the thing, and of us the subjects of it. The thing is, our personal and spiritual oneness with God, redemption from sin, perfection in holiness, righteousness, and life. This is something which we have, not simply to receive, but to accomplish and attain of ourselves. It can be done only under the conditions and through the experiences of our life as it is: the conditions have to be met and overcome, and the experiences, not only to be endured and survived, but recognized and used as divine means and instruments of our making and raising to the full stature of ourselves. Nature is only the raw material of ourselves, and is incomplete without our own action and part in it. Ourselves are deficient and insufficient, and can accomplish our part in fulfilling our nature and realizing ourselves, only in union and communion, both immanent and transcendent, both physical and personal, both natural and spiritual, with the All Who is God, and in the fulness of that realized relationship with Him which is Jesus Christ. This can be only gradual and progressive, but the condition of it, the only possibility, means, or assurance of it, is the certain knowledge of God's part in it, upon which faith and hope may depend as absolutely as our actual and natural dependence is upon it. It is easy enough to say now, that the Christ is enough as an ideal symbol of our own creation, but as a matter of fact the Christ was manifested, not in thought only, or in word only, but in very deed and truth, in the personal, historical, human life, and essentially in the death and resurrection, of Jesus of Nazareth.

Jesus Christ is to us, now and always, all that He means; and what He means to us is Life: The Life was manifested, and we have seen it and bear witness to it. We speak that we do know, and testify that we have seen. The Life is the life of God; but it is the life of God as ours, and in us. The whole description of it, in Jesus or in us, is the description of a genuinely and essentially human life. It is no less, of course, a divine life, a life of divine love and grace and fellowship with us, of God Himself in us. But it is equally a genuinely human life, a life of human faith and hope and love. As Jesus means and is the life of God in man, so the resurrection means and is the victory of human life in God—the indestructibility and invincibility of faith, hope, and love, of God and the life of God in us through these.

Let us take the very earliest description of this: "Whom God raised up, having loosed the pangs of death: because it was not possible that He should be holden of it." Why was it impossible that Jesus should be holden of death? Is it because He was God? It is absurd to speak of the possibility or impossibility of God's being holden of death. The ground and cause of the impossibility must be sought in something in Jesus as man. There is neither point nor pertinence in the saying, if it does not mean the invincibility and indestructibleness of the divine life in the man Jesus—and, through Him, in humanity. The life that comes down from God as Love, Grace, and Fellowship, and lives in man as faith, hope, and love, is stronger than sin, stronger than death, is more than conqueror, overcomes the world, and puts all enemies under its feet. In Jesus the Woman's Seed bruises the serpent's head; the Seed of Abraham, the inheritor and perfector of his faith, accomplishes and gives to the world the blessedness of a divine righteousness; the Son of David sits upon the throne of a, in Him realized, and in us realizable, kingdom of God upon earth.

To see that the story of the resurrection is that of the predestined victory of human faith over all adverse conditions, influences, or powers; the putting all enemies under the feet of redeemed and risen humanity;—we have only to go on to St. Peter's account of why Jesus could not be holden of death. "For—," says he, and then proceeds to put into the mouth of Jesus the typical and prophetic experience of David. What was only figuratively, hyperbolically or poetically, true of David, has become actual truth or fact in Jesus. All true faith is in part a conquest of death: David, *in extremis,* had gone down into the grave, and by the grace of God had come up again—just as St. Paul describes himself as having done—and describes the experience as follows:

I beheld the Lord always before my face;
For he is on my right hand, that I should not be moved:
Therefore my heart was glad, and my tongue rejoiced;
Moreover my flesh too shall dwell in hope;
Because thou shalt not leave my soul in Hades,
Neither wilt thou give thy holy one to see corruption.
Thou madest known to me the ways of life;
Thou shalt make me full of gladness with thy countenance.

What could more truly or exactly describe the accomplished triumph of the resurrection, with which every deepest spiritual experience has at least the principle in common, and is therefore in its measure a type and prophecy of it?

What was put into the mouth of David as prophecy, as assurance of the ultimate working out of a principle, the anticipative operation of which he experienced in himself, we hear from the mouth of Jesus in fulfilment of the prophecy. And we now can utter it in Him, no longer in mere human aspiration, or prophetic anticipation, but in full assurance of divine manifestation and demonstration, that all that the Prince and Author of our life, and Finisher of our faith, has accomplished for us in Himself, He will accomplish in us through ourselves.

9. WHOM ELSE BUT GOD?

The vital truths of Christianity the most open to speculative question and doubt are the personality of God and the deity of Jesus Christ. The practical response of the human soul to those questions and doubts may be expressed in two utterances taken respectively from the Old and New Testaments. I do not profess to give the immediate or exact interpretation of the passages taken in their connection, but only to apply the words to the expression of the complete truths under consideration.

In reply to all questionings as to the God of Abraham's faith, or the God and Father of our Lord Jesus Christ, the God and Father whom He professed to know and to reveal, the general answer of the soul of religion is: If not Him, then Whom have we—or What? "Whom have I in heaven but Thee, O Lord? And there is none upon earth that I desire beside Thee."

Giving our own widest interpretation to the word "heaven," we may mean by it, primarily, all that is outside of our world of sensible or natural experience, all that is matter of faith and not of sight or science. There is no one who denies the existence of such "another" world; denial cannot go beyond the impossibility of any knowledge or experience of it, any communication or intercourse with it. All beginning or end, all substance or cause, all ultimate or essential reality belong to it—none of which we may know, but all which we must in some way admit. Religion, the religion of history and of civilization, has written upon that other world, which is the postulate and correlative of this one, its substance, cause, and meaning, the primal ground of all reality, the name of God.

Religion has gone further and transcended the notion that the world of the beyond, or of God, is one of mere speculative inference and of agnostic admission. It claims that, not merely has God not left Himself without witness within and through the world of sense, but that He has not left us without means and capacity for more direct and personal relation and intercourse with Himself in the world of spirit.

Heaven then is not a region, a world, without and beyond the reach of human experience, a sphere of being unseen and unseeable in itself, known only as inference from, as cause and condition of the things that are seen. It is indeed without and above all purely sensible experience: the search for it which we call natural and, at its best, scientific will rightly discover itself agnostic with regard to it. The question, of which the very fact of religion assumes the affirmative, is whether there is not an experience of God and heaven that transcends mere nature and pure science. If we are to admit God at all as the possible or probable postulate of the things we know— *some* postulate being a necessity of thought, and none other more probable or credible—then it is out of the question to assume that God shall have produced finite spirits capable and desirous of personally knowing Him, and then have remained personally unknowable by or to them. We assume then, with religion, that there are divine as well as human means and possibilities of knowing God. So far from knowledge meaning necessarily adequate or complete, or even at all developed, knowledge, it may begin in absolutely the most elementary way, as a bare potentiality. The infant knows its mother from the moment of birth, by feeling if not by cognition— but by a feeling which is already the beginning of cognition. That human knowledge of God, human experience of and association with God, should have begun in a thoroughly childlike way; that when humanity was a child, it should have spoken as a child, felt as a child, and thought as a child, is just what our evolutional science or philosophy should teach us to expect.

By heaven then, let us, for the time, mean this much more: not merely the world that, in itself, transcends sense and science; but the world that also to us is knowable, however little it may be known, by faith—meaning by faith all sense or faculty of the divine, of God and the things of God, all potential citizenship in the kingdom of heaven, that may be proper to humanity. Whatever of defect, error, irrationality, or even immorality, might by any stretch of conception or assertion be alleged against the God of the Old Testament, it would be easy to demonstrate that the God of religious history as a whole, of the Old and New Testaments and of the Christian Church is one and the same God. We have only to remember that the God of the Old Testament is only the Old Testament's conception of God, just as the God of the Church today is only the Church's present realization and understanding of God. No one would claim that we know God unto perfection, or that we ought not to be knowing Him more and more perfectly as humanity and the Church grow older and more experienced in spiritual or divine things. However perfectly God was in Jesus Christ, no more was or is actually communicated through Christ to the Church than was or is actually received and possessed by the Church. No one claims that we know either God or Jesus Christ, or the full power and life of the Holy Ghost, unto perfection. All that we do claim is, that the more of the Eternal Spirit of God we have in ourselves, the more we know God in Jesus Christ, and the more we know God in Christ, the more we know of God in Himself.

Who then, or What, is the God of our religious history, or of our historical experience? I take the Bible now for no more than Religion's own Record or History of Itself, its Autobiography. In tracing the spiritual evolution of the conception or knowledge of God we are to remember that it is not the making or shaping of objective truth or reality that we are engaged or concerned with, but only the story of our own apprehension and understanding of the truth. We need make no further claim for that than that it is based upon a right principle, has on the whole advanced along a right line, and moves toward the right end. The God of Christianity may be a truer God than that of Hebraism, as the true God is truer than as we know and worship Him; but the more or less truth, the relativity, is in us not in the reality. It is the same God all the way through, imperfectly and progressively conceived and known.

Let us glance briefly at the history of the idea or knowledge of God from the beginning of that Record of it to which we attach the name of Scripture and the sacredness of Revelation. Its first essential feature is found in the fact, that in the very terms ''Creation'' and ''Creator'' is involved and expressed the truth of a rational, spiritual, we may say personal, origin, meaning, and destination of the world. From the beginning the first word of religion has been that which is still the first article of every Christian creed. The world begins and ends with, is upheld and governed by, is the expression of Reason and Purpose. God is neither identified nor confounded with the world, nor on the other hand separated or excluded from it. His Mind, Will, or Word is the immanent and causative principle of it, while in Himself He as actually transcends it as we do our acts or expressions. We are not saying too much but too little when we ascribe to God, in terms of ourselves, intelligence, affection, will, purpose, character—in a word, personality.

Religious history has from the beginning had most to do with the more distinctively spiritual side or aspect of the divine nature. Its primal quality is Holiness. Holiness may be defined simply as "what God is"; as its correlative and contradictory, sin, is "what is contrary to God." Holiness is not simply a law; it is a spirit, a disposition, a nature; and sin is not merely transgression of a divine law, it is violation of the divine Spirit, a break with the divine nature and disposition.

The Old Testament had fully attained to and worked out the truth that Virtue, Morality, Righteousness is at once the law of God and the law of life. Righteousness, an obedience to God's will growing out of oneness with God's nature and participation in God's spirit, is that which alone truly makes or exalts either the individual or the nation. The world means God, means Holiness, means Righteousness—and is predestined to end in the New Heavens and the New Earth wherein shall dwell Righteousness.

The Old Testament had already pierced to the heart of the matter and recognized, not only the fact, that God is holy, but the truth of what holiness is. To say that God is holy, is simply to say that God is "what He is." It may mean, in addition, that God wills and requires in us what He is in Himself; that He conditions the blessings and blessedness of life upon our sharing His spirit and keeping His law: "The righteous Lord loveth righteousness." But to say so much is not to say what holiness or righteousness—and, in the true sense, life and blessedness—are. The Old Testament, if it did not attain the full and final manifestation and expression, yet implicitly included the substance of the truth, that God is Love: that holiness, righteousness, life, blessedness, are all rooted and grounded in that Love which is the one perfect bond, and one bond of perfectness, which, as God Himself, is the All in all.

But what most distinctively the history of the Old Testament had to contribute to the growth of religion was the development of the principle of *faith* as the human medium or means of participating in the divine spirit and nature and so sharing the divine activity and life. A function supposes an organ, as also an organ assumes a function. As a matter of creative evolution, or evolutional creation, it makes no difference which was prior and produced the other. The point is the present fact or actuality of personal relationship and intercommunion with God. If religion is or exists at all, and is an integral factor in human life, and if it is a matter between us and God—"God and the soul, the soul and its God"—then God is no mere conjectural inference from known facts, no mere conclusion of speculative reason, but an object of actual experience and direct knowledge. In some way the Eternal Spirit bears witness with our finite spirits of the relationship between them, and the mind and affections, the will and purpose, the actions and character, the nature and life of God have entrance into and influence and shape those of men.

The organ or function of the divine within the human, our faculty or capacity for God, however defined, we call in general faith. It is a matter of secondary importance in what sense an Abraham walked with God, or talked with God, or was the friend of God. It is enough that he was a developed instance, the type, of an actual spiritual or personal association with and knowledge of God, potential in all men but most highly evolved in him. The claim is simply this; that human experience, human influence, direction, and end, is not only through sense and self, but comes also from without and above and leads and lifts us beyond ourselves and all our mere sensible conditions. That faith in its origins and earliest forms should have been simple and elementary, that its historical traditions and records should have been expressed in terms of the ideas and general knowledge of the time, is too patent a necessity to insist upon. The wonder is not in its childlike expression or in its manifest incompletenesses and imperfections. It is rather that underneath these it was in principle and in essence so infallibly and demonstratively, and therefore so persistently and permanently true.

The faith of Abraham—as much the father of those who believe as Aristotle is still master of all who think—is essentially the faith of Jesus Christ, as that is forever the faith of all who truly know God. The story of Abraham, no matter how we criticise, explain, or interpret it, contains in germ the perfect principle of salvation by faith in Jesus Christ. To the developed Christian experience and consciousness, it is absurd to think of human salvation—which means spiritual and moral, or personal, redemption, completion, and destination—by either mere process of nature or mere act of man himself. We are so manifestly in no sense either all ourselves, or capable of becoming so of ourselves; we are so transcendently *of* God, and

God is so transcendent a part of ourselves, that salvation in any sense, of redemption, completion, or perfection, is unthinkable without or apart from Him. When we say that to know God is eternal life, we mean that, in the very deepest sense of knowing, we only know ourselves as we know God: God is so much of ourselves, so much ourselves, that we do not know ourselves at all out of or apart from Him.

More than this, and consequent upon this—the faith of Abraham teaches us that, apart from the knowledge and love and grace and obedience, the holiness and righteousness and life of God, we are as inevitably sinners against Him and ourselves; that is, that without faith, which brings us into relation with all these and makes us the living subjects of them, we are as incapable of being what God is and so becoming our true selves—as, without the exercise of right reason and free will, we could rise above mere animals and become truly men.

What historical religion owes to Abraham, or to the type of faith represented by him, is the defining of the proper personal attitude of man toward God. This attitude has been expressed by the term *dependence,* by which must be understood nothing less than, not only the entire respect in which, but no less the complete extent to which God constitutes actual part of our nature and must enter personally into our lives, in order that we may become all ourselves and attain all our ends. To say that "in Him we live and move and have our being," as the expression of a mere immanent or natural fact, as a declaration of the speculative truth or belief that God is the underlying and containing cause or condition of all that is, is a presupposition of religion. But it is not religion merely as such; it only becomes religion as, through spiritual and moral consciousness, acceptance, and experience, the mere natural fact passes on up and transmutes itself into personal act—that is, as we ourselves in our nature, and not only our nature in us, are personally living and moving, finding, possessing, and exercising our whole being, in God. There is no religion in the mere immanent relation between us and God, nor in any merely speculative or even moral attitude toward that relation. All personal relation whatever is transcendent, not immanent; and only in such personal relation between us and God does religion really consist or exist.

In the story of faith from Abraham to Jesus Christ we may trace the historical evolution of the attitude or relation of man to God through faith. Abraham simply lives in the consciousness of God, believes, trusts, follows, and obeys God, finds all his good in Him, is the recipient of all blessings from Him. It is an implicit and child-like faith; and in such an integral, undeveloped faith there is the germ and promise of all life and blessedness. But the faith of Abraham and that of Jesus Christ are far apart in the evolutional development and completeness of an identical principle. In both there is the necessary and inseparable element of the trial, proving, and perfecting of faith; but while the faith of Abraham moves on elementary and temporal lines, the faith of Jesus Christ compasses and accomplishes the entire eternal and divine destiny of man.

What is the common principle of all true faith, but is realized and accomplished fact only in Jesus Christ, is that truth of the proper relation between God and man of which we are in search. Whether from the standpoint of ethics or of religion, no human being—but One—stands even to himself, to the accomplishment of his law and the perfection of his spirit, in the relation or attitude of actual fulfil-ment. If we are to be judged by any standard that humanity has ever set, or can set itself, there is no man that can be justified by his works—that is to say, by actual obedience to his own law and by actual conformity to the spirit which he enjoins upon himself. If he requires of himself only a perfect manhood or virtue, personal and social—courage, temperance, justice, generosity—there is none that can justify himself by actual standing in these qualities, otherwise than by either unjustifiably lowering them to a very relative, average or comparative, standard, or else by frankly confessing that these virtues, as virtue in general, are only maxims or ideals to him, expressions of what he would be and very far beyond what he is. Kant is scientifically exact in the assertion that man is the natural subject of an infinite or perfect law. Before such a law he can stand justified even to himself only by an illicit lowering his conception of the law to the obedience he is willing to render it.

What does this mean but that to himself, to the law of his own being and the spirit of his own life, man can stand in no relation and can set up no claim of fulfilment or actuality? Himself is ever, at the best, only a matter of faith and hope to him. He has ever to be just-ified, not by what he is, but only by what he would be, by the un-attained maxim and ideal of his life, by what he believes in, and hopes for, and loves. Justification by faith, properly and scientifically understood, is the principle of all human life, progress, or destiny. We are forever only potentially and prophetically, never actually, ourselves: we shall be that only in the complete possession of our spirits and in the full realization of our law.

It is here that religion comes in as the only solution and completion of ethics. The trouble is that no natural, human, merely moral or ethical law is discoverable that will fit man only as he is. And the reason is that man never *is* only as he is: he never is as brave, or as temperate, or as just, or as generous, or as *anything,* as he ought to be. His true being and self is always something beyond what he is. That "always beyond" has to be taken into account in the definition of his law and in the measure and estimate of himself. And there is no limit here, or in present human experience, to the "beyond"; no man on earth ever is as wise or true or right or good or great as he ought to be, and the nearer he is to any of these, the further off he knows himself to be. How then shall we go about constructing an ethics or a law which shall just express what we ought to be and therefore can be *here?*

The universal natural law of evolution seems to give us a clue to at least the right statement of the facts of the case. Man passes from any previous lower stage into that of reason and freedom, or of personality, by not merely the acquired potentiality, but the actual exercise of his right reason and his free will. In the necessary, and necessarily long, process of progressive reason and freedom, man must become and be a law to himself, must be autonomous. His reason, his freedom, his personality can exist at all, only as his own. Reason and freedom are the only proper subjects of law, and the obedience of these is its only proper correlative. There could be no true law if there were no rational and free obedience, but neither could there be reason or freedom without a law of obedience and without obedience to the law. The function of reason and freedom is obedience to absolute truth and infinite right.

As reason and freedom progress, men more and more discover at once the absolute obligation and the infinite transcendence of law. There is no end to either truth or righteousness, and there is no compromise with either. Does nature, and our own nature—does God subject us to an "ought" to which there is no corresponding "can"?

Thus it is that the true ethics of humanity drives us to religion.

The only law for man is one impossible for him either in or of himself. And the explanation is that there is no such thing as man in or of himself: as a natural fact he lives and moves and has his being only in God. And no less, as a spiritual act or actor, as a rational, free, and moral personality, as son of God, as part and parcel of God Himself, he cannot obey his law, he cannot fulfil his nature, he cannot be himself apart from God. The greatness and the littleness of man are equally incontestable facts. No matter what we are, we have no origin and no destiny but God. Man can propose no other end or purpose to himself than that perfection of truth, of righteousness, of love and goodness, that fulness and completeness of divine life which is God Himself. We cannot think of God but as the Infinite of all that we ourselves ought to be; nor of our own true and right selves otherwise than in terms of what God is. As children of God we can have no other end or destiny than to share His nature and live His life; and we can fix no other limit to that aim and intention than "to be perfect as our Father in heaven is perfect."

This is, of course, assigning to man an infinite law and an impossible obedience; but it is based upon the fact that he is partaker of an infinite nature and the subject of an immortal life. What else or less can be meant by the now largely professed faith in the natural divinity of man? Once admit for man the fact of an infinite or endless law, and express obedience to or fulfilment of that law by the term "righteousness"—and in what possible relation can a man stand to his own righteousness but that of faith, hope, and love? What man can feel himself "justified," or lay claim to a righteousness satisfactory and acceptable to either God or himself? "Abraham believed God, and it was accounted to him for righteousness:" the germ of the whole truth of justification by faith was as truly contained in the attitude of Abraham, as the whole truth itself was perfectly fulfilled and expressed by the act and in the person of Jesus Christ. There is no way of actual righteousness but through identification of ourselves by faith with the righteousness of God in Jesus Christ: which means simply, that there is no way of obeying our law, fulfilling our nature, being ourselves, otherwise than by faith identifying ourselves with God Himself in Christ.

"Whom have we in heaven but Thee, O Lord?" The Psalmist is right in asserting that we have, and can have, none other. The common sense and traditional faith of historical religion has made many mistakes about God, but underneath and through all the God of its faith has been the One only true God, to know Whom is life, and to serve Whom is freedom. And not only have we none other, but the Psalmist is right too in asserting that we *have* Him. The God whom Abraham believed is the God whom Jesus Christ so perfectly knew as to personally manifest and reveal; it is the God whom, through the Word without us and the Spirit within us, we so know, that He is no longer merely God—but *our* God, substance of our life and matter of ourselves.

V.

"THE TRINITY" (1911)*

*The Gospel in the Gospels is divided into three sections which corre-
spond to the three levels characteristic of DuBose's thought: the natural, the
moral, and the spiritual. The last chapter of the third section is "The Trinity." In contemplating the Trinity DuBose unites the speculative and experiential dimensions of theology through his ecumenical process
perspective in a theological tour de force that serves as a summary of
DuBose's life and thought. Shortly before his death DuBose told his family
that the Eternal Father, the Risen Christ, and the Blessed Holy Ghost had
been his companions. Because this chapter illustrates the interconnected-
ness of DuBose's life and thought, his spiritual odyssey, and his spiritual
theology, it seemed an appropriate conclusion to this volume.*

THE TRINITY

The truth takes its own forms and expresses itself in its own
ways. Our efforts at defining, proving, or establishing it are all acts
after the event. It is what it is, and not what we make it. Christianity
prevails in the world in a fact which we have called Trinity, and
which *is* Trinity, however inadequate and unsatisfactory our explanations of the term or our analyses of the thing may be. I would describe Christianity in its largest sense to be the fulfilment of God in
the world through the fulfilment of the world in God. This assumes

---

* The original text that follows is from *The Gospel in the Gospels* (New York:
Longmans, Green, and Co., 1911), pp. 274–289.

291

that the world is completed in man, in whom also God is completed in the world. And so, God, the world, and man are at once completed in Jesus Christ—who, as He was the *logos* or thought of all in the divine foreknowledge of the past, so also is He the *telos* or end of all in the predestination of the future. That is to say, the perfect psychical, moral, and spiritual manhood of which Jesus Christ is to us the realization and the expression is the end of God in creation, or in evolution. I hold that neither science, philosophy, nor religion can come to any higher or other, either conjecture or conclusion, than that. But now, when we come to the actual terms or elements of God's self-realization in us and ours in Him, we cannot think or express the process otherwise than in the threefold form of the divine love, the divine grace, and the divine fellowship, in operation or action. Putting it into scriptural phrase, we speak as exactly as popularly in defining the matter of the Gospel to be, The love of the Father, the grace of the Son, and the fellowship of the Spirit. As our spiritual life is dependent upon each and all of these three constituents, so we can know God at all only as we know Him in the actual threefold relation to us of Father, Son, and Spirit.

The first element in the essential constitution of the Gospel is the fact in itself that God is love. That God is love means that He is so not only in Himself but in every activity that proceeds from Him. The very phrase The love of the Father expresses the whole principle of the universe. That God is Father means that it is His nature, or His essential activity, to reproduce Himself, to produce in all other that which He Himself is. That God in Himself is love carries with it the truth that from the beginning all things else mean, and are destined to come to, love in the end. The mystery on the way that somehow light must come out of darkness, that love must needs conquer hate, and that in everything good seems to be only the final and far off goal of ill, may puzzle us but it does not disturb the principle itself. When we come to enter fairly upon the evolution of the future, the higher not merely psychical or social or moral but spiritual life and destiny of man, all the truth gradually dawns upon us in the following discoveries, which are already established facts of spiritual experience: The truth of all spirit is love; the matter of all law is goodness; God is not creator or cause only, nor lord or lawgiver only, but Father of all things, since all things through man are destined to share His spirit, to be partakers of His nature, and to reproduce Himself as

Father in themselves as children. In order to be sons of God through actual participation in the divine nature there stands in the way indeed the need of a mighty redemption from sin and an as yet far off completion in holiness; but no matter how unredeemed or incomplete, we know beyond further question that all our salvation lies in redemption and completion, and that we shall be ourselves and the world will come to its meaning only when the self-realization of God as Father shall have accomplished itself in our self-realization as His children. If we knew the fact only that God in Himself is love, it would be to us a gospel indeed of great joy, because it would carry in it the assurance of the highest good, whatever that might be. But it would be but a partial gospel, and in fact only a gospel at all through its certainty of proceeding further.

The phrase Grace of the Son expresses that which perfectly complements and completes all that is meant by the Love of the Father. What is Fatherhood without a correlative Sonship? And what is all love even in God as its subject apart from its actuality and activity as grace in man as its object? The divine propriety of the terms Father and Son as applied to God cannot be too much magnified. The distinction between God as He is in Himself and God as He is in all possible expressions of Himself is one that we cannot think Him at all without making. The most perfect expression of love is contained in the statement, that Love loves love. Its nature is to produce, to reproduce, to multiply itself. Itself is forever the true object of itself, at the same time that it is ever a going forth from itself into that which is not itself. This essential principle of love or self-reproduction is what makes God eternally Father. But the eternal Fatherhood is actualized only in an eternal Sonship. Nothing proceeds from the Father which is not reproduction of the Father, and is not therefore Son. Man sees himself now in nature and destinature son of God. He feels his call and obligation to fulfil God in him as Father by realizing himself in God as son. His spiritual end and impulse is to know as also he is known, to love in return as he is first loved, to apprehend that for which he is apprehended of God in Christ. In proportion as he finds the meaning and truth of his own being in the reproduction of God, in being son of God, he finds the meaning and truth of the whole creation realized and expressed in his own sonship as heir of all and end of all. And in proportion again as he thus finds all things meaning and ending in sonship, he comes at last to see God Himself as realized in the universal sonship—Himself therein realized as Eternal Father. So it is that in Jesus Christ we see everything expressed, because everything realized or fulfilled. He is all truth, because He is the truth of all things—God, Creation, Man. And because He is thus truth and expression of all, He is *Logos* of all. What else could the *Logos* of all be but Son, or the Son but *Logos?* What could perfectly express God but that which is the perfect reproduction of Himself, or what is perfect sonship but perfect likeness?

The Grace of the Son is the divine gift of sonship. How could we have known God only in Himself? How could God have been actually our Father without the actuality of our sonship to Him? And could we have known, could we have wanted, could we have willed, could we have accomplished or attained our sonship without the gift or grace of sonship in Jesus Christ? God, we are told, predestinated us unto sonship through Jesus Christ unto himself. He predestinated us to be conformed to the image of His Son, that He might be the first born among many brethren. In bringing many sons to glory, He gave to us a Captain of our salvation, an Author and Finisher of the faith of sonship and so of the sonship of faith, who was Himself perfected as Son through the sufferings that are necessary to the perfecting of sonship in us. We see in Jesus Christ all that is meant, involved, or implied, in the fact that He is the divine Fatherhood realized and expressed in human sonship.

If that fact, viewed in its totality, signifies not only a human act, nor only a divine act, but a divine-human act, an act of God in man which is equally an act of man in God,—then we say that Jesus Christ is not only as well the humanity as the divinity in that act, but He is the divinity as well as the humanity. He is not only the *gratia gratiata* in it but the *gratia gratians*—not only the manhood infinitely graced but the Godhead infinitely gracing.

Jesus Christ is therefore to us no mere sample or example of divine sonship. He is no mere one man who more successfully than others has grasped and expressed the ideal of a divine sonship. Neither is He a single individual of our race whom God has elected from among equally possible others, in whom as mere revelation or example to all others to manifest the truth of God in man and man in God. On the contrary, Jesus Christ is Himself the reality of all that is manifested or expressed in Him. He is as God the grace communicating and as man the grace communicated. He is both Generator and generated with reference to the life incarnate in Him—both the sonship eternally in God to be begotten and the sonship actually begotten in man. As He was in the beginning with God and was God, so is He universally with man and is universal man.

When we have thus adequately conceived Christ as the universal truth and reality of ourselves, and in ourselves of all creation, and in creation and ourselves of God, then we are prepared for the conclusion that we know God at all, or are sons to Him as our Father, or are capable in that relation of partaking of His nature or entering into His Spirit or living His life, only in and through Jesus Christ; because Jesus Christ is the incarnation or human expression to us of the whole *Logos* of God—that is to say, of God Himself as in any way whatever knowable or communicable. We cannot get at God to know or possess Him otherwise than as He reveals and imparts Himself; and He reveals Himself through His own Word and imparts Himself in His own Son. There and there alone is He to be known, and there He is all our own. The *Logos* who is the eternal Self-revelation of God manifests Himself as ideal principle, first and final cause, meaning and end, of creation; and the end of the whole creation which manifests God is realized through spiritual humanity in the imparted sonship of the Everlasting Son of the Father.

There is yet one other condition of truly knowing or really possessing God as wholly our God. As God is unknowable and incommunicable but through Christ, so is Christ, however perfectly He is in Himself the self-revelation and self-communication of God, not so to us but through the coequal action of the Holy Ghost. There is no knowledge of God in Himself only, there is no knowledge of God in creation only, or in others, or even in Christ only, without the answering knowledge of God in ourselves also. It is only like that answers to like. The deep that answers to deep must be the same deep. Jesus Christ expected in every son of man not only the answer of the man in him to Himself as eternal and universal Son of man, but the answer of the God in him to the perfect Godhead in Himself. Ye cannot see God in me, He says, because ye have not God in you. No man cometh unto me except the Father draw Him. I do not wish to urge the mere conventional language of Christianity, true as I believe it and helpful as I may find it to myself. I would if possible speak in the common language of common experience. When we speak of knowing God, and having God, it must mean knowing Him where He is to be known and having Him as He is to be had. Now, whatever God is in Himself, He is knowable to us only in Jesus Christ, and He can be *our* God only as He is conceived in us by the operation of the Spirit of God and born of the want which He implants and the faith which He generates.

The doctrine of the Trinity is ordinarily thought of as the very extreme of speculative reasoning upon the nature of God. But let us remember that practical faith in the Trinity antedated any speculative thought or doctrine of the Trinity. And behind that faith the fact itself of the Trinity is all that makes God knowable by us or us capable of knowing God. Before there was the word Trinity, the new world of Christianity had come to know God in Christ, and to know Christ in itself. The entire doctrine developed out of that actual experience was nothing but a positive affirmation and a determined defence of the fulness of the truth of God in Christ and Christ in us. We can do no better than conclude this entire exposition of the Gospel with an interpretation of it in the only terms in which it is expressible, viz.: in terms of the Trinity.

We have to do now with the Trinity, not as matter of doctrine nor as object of faith, but as fact in itself. But at the same time we neither forget nor minimize the essential Christian conviction that the fact of the Trinity through the actual operation of God's Word and Spirit has been so made matter of spiritual observation and experience as to be legitimate object of faith and material for doctrine. Our object at present, however, is not to define God but to define the Gospel, and our contention is that the Gospel is definable in facts that taken together make up the truth of the Trinity.

The first condition and constituent of the Gospel is the fact that God in Himself is love. How do we know that God is love? I believe that actually or historically we know it in Christ in whom the fact of the divine love is consummated and manifested. But in the light now of Christianity I believe that it is also philosophically demonstrable that goodness or love is the essential principle and the ultimate end of the universe. *How* God is love, not only in antecedent nature but in the actuality of self-fulfilment in the world, may be readable too in nature,—after the light thrown upon it by Christianity,—but in fact it is known in its reality only in Christ. Love is no more in God than in us an abstract disposition or affection. All the love we know is in concrete relations and the forms of affection determined by the character of those relations. Human love is marital, parental, filial, etc.—out to the wider and widest forms of national, racial, and human affinity and affection. The concrete form in which alone we can know God as love is expressed by our designation of Him as eternal Father. That gives shape and definiteness to not only our conception, but the reality itself of His relation to us and ours to Him, and no less of how that relation is to be fulfilled. The full reality of fatherhood comes about in actuality only in the full realization of sonship, and that therefore must be God's meaning and end for all that is in the universe of His self-expression. We begin so to anticipate the truth that is to be expressed in such statements as that God has foreordained or predestined us to sonship through Jesus Christ unto Himself, that God has foreordained us to be conformed to the image of His Son, and many others to the same effect. But before we come to these unfoldings of the divine nature and purpose, let us reflect upon the following antecedent truth.

The beginning of all distinction between a pantheistic and a theistic conception of the world lies in recognizing the world as the expression, not of God Himself—or, as we say, "of His substance,"—but of His *Logos,* His Thought, Will, Word. The *Logos* of God, then, is not God (ὁ θεόξ); we distinguish Him. And yet certainly the *Logos* is God (θεόξ); we identify Him. Moreover, when once we have conceived and accepted God as eternal Father, we are in position to assume that the *Logos,* not merely as the principle of the divine self-expression but as God Himself self-expressed, must manifest Himself universally as Son or in sonship; since universal and everlasting Sonship is the only self-expression of eternal and essential Fatherhood.

The first constituent, therefore, of the Gospel is the fact in itself of the divine Love in Fatherhood. The second is, the equal fact in itself of the actualization of the divine Fatherhood in creature—or, definitely, in human—Sonship. The love of the Father fulfils and manifests itself in the grace of the Son. Love is grace *potentiâ;* Grace is love *actu,*—just as Fatherhood itself is Sonship potential, and Sonship is Fatherhood actualized. When we have once seen all humanity perfected as son in Jesus Christ, it is not hard to see in Him the whole creation so perfected in man as its head and as heir of its destiny. And then still less hard is it to see how we could never have known

God as Father if He had not so fulfilled and manifested Himself as Son.

The hesitation and reluctance to see all God, and highest God, not only in the humanity but in the deepest human humiliation of Jesus Christ, is part of the disposition to measure exaltation by outward circumstance and condition instead of by inward quality and character. We find it impossible to recognize or acknowledge God in the highest act of His highest attribute. We cannot listen to the thought that it is with God as it is with us, that it only is with us because it is with God, that self-humiliation is self-exaltation. Not only in this way do we refuse to know God Himself as love, but we refuse to understand the universe as love. If we would but surrender our reason as well as our heart and will to God in Christ, we should cease to prate as we do of the mystery and the incomprehensibility of things. We could see how our Lord could say of the cross itself, Father, the hour is come. Glorify thy Son, that the Son may glorify thee. We lose thus the supreme lesson of human experience: Not merely to conjecture that *somehow* good is the final goal of ill; but to know by actual trial just how the supremest ills are the necessary steps to the highest goods. As St. Paul says, the cross of Christ is foolishness and a stumbling-block only to the earthly wise and the self-righteous. To them that are saved, or are ever so little being saved, it is the wisdom of God and the power of God. To know God in Jesus Christ is to know the divine *Logos,* through whom alone God is knowable. It is to know him, not in His inferior activities of physical creation, nor yet in His higher capacity of lawgiver and law in a world of intelligent reason and free will. Rather is it to know Him in the act and process of that self-communication of love, grace, and fellowship, which is the basis and condition of the only real knowledge.

The third constituent of the Gospel is the fact in itself of the fellowship of the Spirit. Truly, our fellowship is with the Father and with His Son Jesus Christ. The possibility or potentiality of such a real unity and community with God must exist somehow beforehand in our nature as spirit, or in the natural relation of our finite spirits to the Father of spirits. But the actuality of spiritual relation or intercommunication which we call fellowship is no fact of nature but an act or interaction of spirits. It is not for us to say how, theoretically, spirit can act upon spirit; all that we can do is to understand how, practically and actually, spirit does act upon spirit. The most perfect expression of the actual action of the divine upon the human spirit is contained in the words, The Spirit beareth witness with our spirit, that we are the sons of God. Let us assume the objectivity or truth in itself of the eternal Fatherhood—that is to say, not only Father-relation but Father-spirit, love, will, purpose or predestination, etc.—of God in Himself. Let us also assume the objective reality as matter of fact of all that we have claimed to have happened in Jesus Christ: viz., that in Him as Logos God revealed Himself in the universe, and that in Him as Son God fulfilled Himself in humanity. In other words, let us assume that all that God is in Himself as Father has evolved itself through nature and man in the universal and everlasting Sonship realized in Jesus Christ; God in Christ as Son is *actu* all that He is *potentiâ* in Himself as Father. When we have assumed all that body of objective truth—the truth in itself of the Father and the Son—what remains still to make it the Gospel to ourselves? Undoubtedly something remains. All the reality in the universe can be no Gospel to us so long as it remains objective, or until it enters into living relation with ourselves. Of course, it can never so enter unless there is in us the natural potentiality of entering into relation with it. But equally certainly that potentiality can only be actualized by ourselves. What is necessary within ourselves to give effect to all that is true without us is a corresponding response, or a response of correspondence, on our part. That correspondence is, I repeat, not a fact of natural relationship, but an act of spiritual communication or self-impartation. When the Spirit bears witness with our spirit, that we are sons of God, it is not only God who communicates the gracious fact, but it is God who awakens the humble and grateful response, and puts it into our heart to say, Abba, Father. If we cannot thus know God subjectively in ourselves, we cannot know God objectively in Jesus Christ. And if we cannot know Him in His Word and by His Spirit, we cannot know Him at all.

As we can know the eternal and universal Sonship incarnate in Jesus Christ only in the perfection of the human sonship realized in Him—in other words, as we can know the Word or Son of God only in the man Christ Jesus, so we can know the Spirit of God only in ourselves or in our own spirit. We cannot know any spirit other than our own otherwise than through a certain oneness or identity of it with our own. There must be both an inter-penetration of the two as distinct and the identification of them as one. Hence the common demand upon men to be of one spirit. What a subject of reflection then, and of realization or actualization, is there for us in the fact of our fellowship, our participation, with the Father and the Son in the unity and identity of a common Spirit. It is in this eternal Spirit that God Himself is God and is Love. It was in this eternal Spirit that the whole creation in humanity offered itself without spot to God in the person of Jesus Christ; and in that consummate act fulfilled His relation to it through realizing its own relation with Him. It is through this eternal Spirit, which is God's and Christ's and ours, that we pass from ourselves into Christ and through Christ into God.

We have seen that there could have been no Gospel of God to us except one of objective Word and subjective Spirit. All life is defined as internal correspondence with external environment. We saw, I think, long ago that as it is the function of the divine Word *aptare Deum homini,* so is it that of the divine Spirit *aptare hominem Deo.* On the same line we may say, that as eternal life is given to us in Jesus Christ to be received, so is it given to us by the Holy Ghost to receive the life. Our Lord said of the promised Spirit, that its function should be to bring us to Him. There would be nothing to which to come if there were no objective fact and gift of life, there would be no coming to the life if there were no subjective preparing for and drawing to the life. How then finally does the Spirit fit us for Christ and fit us to Christ? It is the act and operation of the Spirit, first, that from the beginning, though yet a very far off, we can already know Christ as our own. That is the power of faith, which lives by God's Word and takes what that says as though it were. To faith Jesus Christ is the divine, not only revelation but reality of itself from the beginning of the foreknowledge of God in the eternity of the past to the end of the predestination of God in the eternity of the future. To faith Jesus Christ is all the eternal love, the all-sufficient grace, the perfect fellowship or oneness-with-it of God, which is salvation *ex parte Dei*— or *salvatio salvans;* and no less in Jesus Christ the perfection of our own faith, hope, and love, our own holiness, righteousness, and life, our own death to sin, and our own life to God, which is salvation *ex parte hominis*— or *salvatio salvata.* The Spirit thus brings us first to a perfect correspondence of faith with the fact of our life of God in Christ. But just because faith *means* life, that is, knows, desires, wills, and intends it—therefore it *is* it. God already imputes, as He will impart, and faith already appropriates, as it will possess, the life which is so believed in. So believing in it we have it already in faith, and as surely shall have it at last in fact. Attuned to Christ by the anticipatory spell of faith, hope, and love, we shall be by a natural process of spiritual assimilation transformed into His likeness in act, character, and life, until coming to see Him perfectly as He is we shall be wholly what He is.

It has not been my object to add to the solution of the speculative problem of the Trinity. I have only aimed to show practically and spiritually that if at all we are to know and worship God in reality as our God, we must do so as Christianity has always done—in Trinity. We must worship God in the Father, and the Son, and the Holy Ghost. Because God is, and is operative for us, not alone in one but in all these. We cannot but distinguish the Three; it is only in the completeness of their threefold operation that we can perfectly know the One.

SELECT BIBLIOGRAPHY

(For a complete bibliography see *A DuBose Reader,* pp. 209–214.)

I. THE WRITINGS OF DUBOSE

The Christian Ministry: A Sermon Preached at the Ordination of the Rev. O. T. Porcher, Abbeville, S.C., May 15th, 1870. Charleston, Walker, Evans and Cogswell, 1870.
"The Interpretation of the Bible in Relation to the Present Condition of Learning and Science," In *The Fifth Annual Church Congress.* New York: M. H. Mallory & Co., 1878.
The Soteriology of the New Testament, New York: Macmillan Company, 1892. (New edition, with a new preface, 1899.)
The Ecumenical Councils. Vol. III of *Ten Epochs of Church History.* Edited by John Fulton, New York: The Christian Literature Company, 1896.
"Wade Hampton," *Sewanee Review,* 10, 3 (July, 1902): 364–368.
The Gospel in the Gospels. New York: Longmans, Green, and Co., 1906. (Many reprintings until 1923.)
The Gospel According to Saint Paul. New York: Longmans, Green, and Co., 1907.
High Priesthood and Sacrifice: An Exposition of the Epistle to the Hebrews. New York: Longmans, Green, and Co., 1908. (The Bishop Paddock Lectures at the General Theological Seminary, New York, 1907–1908.)

The Reason of Life. New York: Longmans, Green, and Co., 1911.
Turning Points in My Life. New York: Longmans, Green, and Co., 1912.
Unity in the Faith. Edited by W. Norman Pittenger. Greenwich, Connecticut: The Seabury Press, 1957. This book consists of eleven essays published in *The Constructive Quarterly* and one article, "Christian Defense," originally published in *The Sunday School Teacher's Manual.*
"Preparedness: Some Essential Preliminaries to Christian Unity." *The Churchman,* 145 (February 13, 1932): 10–12; "Part II," *ibid.* (February 20, 1932: 13–15).
"Reminiscences," compiled by William Haskell DuBose. Xeroxed paper, 1946. Archives, the University of the South, Sewanee.
"From Aristotle to Christ," edited by Alberry Charles Cannon, Jr. Typewritten paper, 1963. (DuBose wrote this work 1913–1918.) Archives, the University of the South, Sewanee.

II. WRITINGS ABOUT DUBOSE

Bratton, Theodore DuBose. *An Apostle of Reality: The Life and Thought of the Reverend William Porcher DuBose.* New York: Longmans, Green, and Co., 1936.
Kezar, Dennis Dean. "Many Sons to the Father's Glory," Ph.D. dissertation, New College, Oxford University, 1974.
Luker, Ralph E. *A Southern Tradition in Theology and Social Criticism 1830–1930: The Religious Liberalism and Social Conservatism of James Warley Miles, William Porcher DuBose and Edgar Gardner Murphy.* New York: The Edwin Mellen Press, 1984.
_____. "Liberal Theology and Social Conservatism: A Southern Tradition, 1840–1920," *Church History,* 50 (June, 1981): 193–204.
_____. "The Crucible of Civil War and Reconstruction in the Experiences of William Porcher DuBose," *South Carolina Historical Magazine,* 83, (January, 1982): 50–71.
Marshall, John S. *The Word Was Made Flesh: The Theology of William Porcher DuBose.* Sewanee: University Press, 1949.
Murray, J. O. F. *DuBose as a Prophet of Unity.* London: SPCK,

1924. "A Series of Lectures on the DuBose Foundation Delivered at the University of the South."
Sanday, William. *The Life of Christ in Recent Research*. New York: Oxford University Press, 1907, pp. 152, 157, 257–312.

III. ANTHOLOGIES

A DuBose Reader: Selections from the Writings of William Porcher DuBose, comp. Donald S. Armentrout. Sewanee: The University of the South, 1984.

INDEX TO INTRODUCTION

INDEX TO TEXTS

Other Volumes in This Series